CRITICAL ISSUES IN EDUCATIONAL LEADERSHIP SERIES

Joseph Murphy, Series Editor

Cognitive Perspectives
on
Educational Leadership

EDITED BY
PHILIP HALLINGER
KENNETH LEITHWOOD
JOSEPH MURPHY

Foreword by Larry Cuban

Teachers College, Columbia University
New York and London

This project was conducted under the auspices of the National Center for Educational Leadership, a consortium of Harvard University, Vanderbilt University, and the University of Chicago. This center is supported by U.S. Department of Education Grant No. R117C8005. The views expressed in this paper are those of the authors and do not necessarily represent those of the sponsoring institutions. The authors would like to acknowledge the contributions of Elizabeth Bon, Melinda Hall, and Rischelle Jenkins in the preparation of the manuscripts for this volume. A singular acknowledgment for assistance in the preparation and management of the book goes to Charles Hausman.

Published by Teachers College Press, 1234 Amsterdam Avenue, New York, NY 10027

Library of Congress Cataloging-in-Publication Data

Cognitive perspectives on educational leadership / edited by Philip Hallinger, Kenneth Leithwood, Joseph Murphy.
    p.   cm.—(Critical issues in educational leadership series)
   Papers originally presented at a conference held at Peabody College, Vanderbilt University, in September, 1991.
   Includes bibliographical references and index.
   ISBN 0–8077–3278–8.—ISBN 0–8077–3277–X (pbk.)
   1. School administrators—Training of—United States—Congresses. 2. Educational leadership—United States—Congresses. 3. School management and organization—United States—Congresses. I. Hallinger, Philip, 1952–   . II. Leithwood, Kenneth A. III. Murphy, Joseph, 1949–
IV. Series.
LB1738.5.C62   1993
378.1'11—dc20   93-22705

ISBN 0–8077–3278–8
ISBN 0–8077–3277–X (pbk.)

Printed on acid-free paper
Manufactured in the United States of America

99 98 97 96 95 94 93 7 6 5 4 3 2 1

Contents

Part III
Applying Cognitive Perspectives
to the Preparation of Administrators

to
Brother Blue
Jackie
Schoolgirl

Foreword

These articles that Philip Hallinger, Kenneth Leithwood, and Joseph Murphy have brought together and edited were presented as papers at a conference held at Peabody College, Vanderbilt University, in September, 1991. I had wanted to be there but other commitments prevented me from attending. For me, the next best thing happened. The editors asked me to write this Foreword, giving me a second chance to read the papers after they had been rewritten and edited. In reading these articles, most of which apply research findings of cognitive psychologists to educational administration, I was reminded of the intellectual history of the field itself, particularly its character as a craft and applied science.

Briefly, the preparation and professional development of principals and superintendents went through at least two phases. From the early decades of the twentieth century to World War II, university preparation drew on the experiences of administrators extracting rules and prescriptions for newcomers to pursue while adding to the formal curriculum specialized subjects (e.g., finance, plant maintenance, etc.). It was a "how-to" approach common to the early stages of other professions as they became institutionalized within the university. The second phase began after World War II, particularly in the 1950s and 1960s, when many educational administration professors borrowed heavily from the social sciences, especially psychology, sociology, and political science, to create theories of administration, leadership, and organizational behavior in schools and districts. These theories were used to guide the preparation of newcomers to the occupation and programs for practicing administrators.

Not until the late 1970s and early 1980s, after findings from researchers who investigated nonrational features of organizational behavior began to seep into the thinking of opinion-molders within educational administration, were serious questions raised about the value of theory-driven preparation of principals and superintendents. The growing debates within the field about the obvious limits to research findings in shaping practice, and the noticeable lack of investigations of what administrators actually do, diminished hope for the future of the occupation. The sudden frenetic interest in the principal as an instructional leader in the early to mid-1980s was an instance of a field being driven by policy pressures for concrete results from research and the lack of usable theory to help practitioners grow effective schools. Researchers and policymakers produced lists of behaviors that "effective" principals were observed to be using in schools labeled "effective." These lists of behaviors were converted by researchers and policymakers into prescriptions, regardless of the setting, for new and veteran principals to use in their schools if they desired to become instructional leaders. By the late 1980s, the ambiguous and even negative evidence of such efforts yielding desired outcomes were obvious to informed scholars.

If anything, by the late 1980s, deep skepticism, often slipping into cynicism about the quality of existing research and university preparation, permeated the thinking of professors, practitioners, and policymakers committed to educational administration.

Within this climate of professional opinion, this volume of articles appears. The book summarizes and applies the last two decades of findings from cognitive psychology on learning, the creation of knowledge and its daily use, and the importance of context. The volume's theoretical anchor in cognitive psychology should give strength to those who see virtue in social science research guiding the field. The volume's concentration on the mind of the individual administrator offers renewed hope to both professors and practitioners that a particular administrator can make a difference in the lives of teachers and pupils. Finally, the volume's stress on the social construction of understanding and the critical importance of the setting in shaping practice should give comfort to those who have persisted in believing that a deep understanding of context is an essential prior condition for leadership.

The strengths of this volume are considerable. First, the research findings of cognitive psychologists about how individuals learn are applied in a serious manner to those preparing to become practitioners, those who are new to the field, and those who have been engaged in practice. While occasional articles have been written aimed at using cognitive perspectives to understand further why principals and superintendents do what they do, this collection of articles nicely covers a range of topics that would appeal to those who teach aspiring administrators, work with practitioners, and study their actions.

Second, the volume is rich in its reach across several domains within educational administration. Professors report results of their using cognitive perspectives to reshape courses they have taught in educational administration. Researchers report on studies of principals' and superintendents' thinking about practical problems and how they solve them. Investigators summarize findings on how expertise is developed and how novices and experts display their knowledge in both school and nonschool settings.

Third, the sharp focus on the intentions, values, and beliefs of individual administrators coping with complex situations in unique settings produces insights that have radical implications for preparing administrators, should these insights be put into practice within universities.

Finally, the volume asserts clearly the importance of theories that combine wise practice, reflection, and context as critical elements in revising mainstream assumptions about what educational administration can and cannot do. By clearly focusing on the individual's intentions, knowledge, beliefs, and actions within a unique setting, this book adds a missing piece to the crucial question of "why" administrators act as they do; of more importance, however, the writers ask different questions that derive from the context. They ask "when" and "where" and suggest that these are necessary queries for researchers, practitioners, and policymakers to ask.

While there are considerable strengths, there are some limitations to the volume, most of which derive from publishing diverse conference papers on the broad topic of "cognitive perspectives." For example, by concentrating on individuals' problem-solving and creation and use of knowledge there is a mild tilt toward reductionism: What administrators do depends on what they think. While such a position is a worthy corrective to behavioral theories and prescriptions that denied even the merit of an administrator's intentions, values, and beliefs, it nonetheless ignores the impact of political, organizational, and cultural factors in shaping administrative behavior. Fortunately, the editors included at least two papers in the volume that attended to these other factors in discussing principals and superintendents. Striking a balance between these varied factors remains a dilemma in the field itself and, in all fairness, is beyond the scope of this book. But the tilt is there and readers need to watch for it.

Another limitation is the deeply embedded ambiguity of most writers in this book over making distinctions between managing and leading. Although the title of the collection states that it is about leadership, readers should know that these authors (except for two) and editors do what their colleagues historically have done and currently do, which is to treat managing and leading as equivalent terms. They are not. In fact, as I read the articles, particularly research findings on problem-solving, I could easily make a case for managers and leaders' framing problems differently. This persistent ambiguity over what, if any, distinctions can be drawn (or are even worthwhile to draw) between managers and leaders is evident in this volume.

These limitations aside, for they derive in large part from the nature of collecting conference papers on a broad topic into one volume, Hallinger, Leithwood, and Murphy have done a signal service to the community of researchers, practitioners, and policymakers interested in improving the theory and practice of educational administration by organizing the conference and editing the papers for this volume.

Larry Cuban
Stanford University

Introduction

This volume contains papers written for the Cognition and School Leadership conference held at Peabody College of Vanderbilt University in September, 1991. The conference was co-sponsored by the National Center for Educational Leadership (NCEL), a consortium of research universities supported by the U.S. Department of Education, and the Centre for Leadership Development at the Ontario Institute for Studies in Education (OISE). Our goal in designing the conference was to stimulate interest in "cognitive perspectives" on the practice, study, and development of school leadership.

Our interest in this venture grew from several sources. There was a desire to extend work that we had been conducting during the 1980s—Hallinger and Murphy at Vanderbilt and Leithwood at OISE—on principal effectiveness and instructional leadership. In addition, we felt a need to expand the predominant theoretical and methodological perspectives that were driving research in educational administration. For example, one question—what do effective principals do?—had led to a set of widely disseminated descriptions of on-the-job practices. While these descriptions were an incremental improvement over the earlier knowledge base in school administration, they were also severely limited both theoretically and practically. Simply stated, studies of principal behaviors and practices would never provide the type of information needed to understand how leaders adapted to the complex contexts in which they worked. Such understanding would result only from investigations that incorporated explorations of the thinking that accompanied such practices or behaviors.

This recognition began to lead students of school administration to seek other perspectives that would better illuminate how principals enact their roles. In addition, increased interest among policymakers in the development of school leaders stimulated a concurrent search for educational approaches that held greater promise for generating usable knowledge for those engaged in the preparation of school administrators. This led us, as well as others represented in this volume, to study how people develop the capacity to think and act, to the field of cognitive psychology.

Cognitive psychologists had already begun to apply their theoretical lenses to the analysis of teaching and to a lesser extent to the study of managerial roles in the private sector. As we worked with this literature, its salience for the practice, study, and development of school leadership became apparent. Somewhat independently, research and development projects at OISE, Vanderbilt University, and Stanford University were exploring issues concerned with principal problem-solving and thinking, the nature and development of administrative expertise, and problem-based learning. Moreover, researchers in other education domains (e.g., student problem-solving, teacher education) had already made considerable progress on similar issues.

Thus, we felt that the timing was right to bring scholars in school administration together with colleagues who have applied cognitive perspectives in related fields. We invited a diverse group of scholars to prepare papers that would address key issues involved in the application of cognitive frameworks to school leadership and its development.

The volume is organized into three sections. The first section explores how cognitive perspectives illuminate the conceptualization of problems—specifically the types of problems that school administrators face. While it has been accepted for some time that problem-finding represents an important task of leaders, these chapters seek to extend our understanding of the ways that administrators—both inside and outside of education—think about and act on the problems that arise in their organizations and environments.

The second section of the book explores the nature of administrative expertise. Given the paucity of empirical investigations of administrative problem-solving in education, important work is included here from studies of managerial problem-solving in other organizations. Together with selected studies of problem-solving in school administration, these chapters will provide the reader with a sense of how cognitive perspectives shed new light on recurring issues in our field.

In the final section, the authors examine how cognitive perspectives might inform our understanding of the processes that can be used to assist school leaders in learning their craft. Here again, the contributors draw on findings from studies inside and outside the field of school administration in an attempt to bring fresh ideas to how we think about the education of school administrators. As suggested above, these chapters focus explicitly on what has been learned about our ability to develop the capacity, as learners, to think about and apply knowledge.

In the final chapter of the book we attempt to clarify a set of salient research and development issues for those interested in pursuing this avenue further. As noted at the outset, our goal for the conference and this book has been to stimulate dialogue in our field, not to sell others on the merits of this perspective. We hope that the ideas presented in this volume are sufficiently interesting to accomplish this aim. The test will be the extent to which we begin to see additional commentary as well as empirical research in this area in the future.

Philip Hallinger and Joseph Murphy
Peabody College, Nashville, TN
Kenneth Leithwood
Ontario Institute for Studies in Education, Toronto

PART I

Classifying, Framing, and Defining Administrative Problems

In this first section, we begin to address how a "cognitive perspective" can inform our understanding of educational leadership. The initial steps in this venture involve a series of examinations of how leaders view and interpret the "problems" they confront in the workplace. The notion that core functions of educational leadership involve problem-finding and problem-solving is fundamental to a cognitive perspective.

This perspective on leadership finds theoretical and empirical support from literatures in educational administration, general management, and social and cognitive psychology. Each of these literatures is amply represented in this volume. Despite the interdisciplinary nature of this book, we would note at the outset that cognitive approaches tend by nature to focus explicitly on the thinking processes of individuals. In the application of this perspective to the study of leaders and managers, there is an inherent bias toward a "micro-view" of leadership in organizations. While this results in inevitable conceptual limitations, such a perspective can also illuminate important issues concerning the motivations and actions of leaders.

As studies conducted in diverse organizations have found, leaders tend to operate in fast-paced, changing environments. Their work is often characterized by brief encounters with many different people, numerous interruptions, partial information, and conflicting expectations from multiple constituencies. In such environments, it has become popular to acknowledge the importance of a "vision" to leaders, in other words, where they choose to focus their attention. We believe that a cognitive perspective offers the opportunity to better understand the means and processes by which leaders exercise vision. This is where the book begins.

Many writers have sought to operationalize the concept of vision in the context of organizational leadership. From a cognitive perspective, it is natural to examine how leaders "find the problems" to which they attend, how they develop an understanding of these problems, and how their interpretations affect subsequent action. Thus, chapters in this section of the book explore the processes that characterize and shape the thinking of leaders about their work.

Lee Bolman and Terry Deal contend that most discussions of leadership and leadership development give higher priority to problem-solving and decision-making than to "problem-finding and making sense of complex and shifting human dynamics." Consequently, their chapter focuses "on the cognitive maps that leaders need to make sense out of their complex worlds." Simply stated, they explore how leaders frame the problems they encounter or seek out in the workplace. This chapter extends earlier conceptual work on "problem-framing" conducted by Bolman and Deal and presents preliminary empirical findings from studies with leaders in different organizational settings.

Over the past several decades, it has become increasingly clear that our understanding of leadership must incorporate what Bolman and Deal term the "meta-rational" side of organizations. A hallmark of cognitive approaches is their concern with the processes of human thought and action as enacted in real or simulated settings. The tools of inquiry used in cognitive science are well designed for exploring the meta-rational behavior of life in organizations.

Charles Kerchner's chapter addresses the perspectives that leaders bring to everyday problem-solving. He further notes that "modern organizational theory rests on recognizing limits to cognitive rationality. . . . We probably overeducate for the unusual and fail to teach students to recognize the strategic potential in their everyday activities." He subsequently explores the range of strategic potential that lies within the grasp of managers in the conduct of their normal organizational routines. Here the focus is on problem-framing and problem-interpretation in the daily work of educational administrators and on the implications for developing expertise as leaders.

As Richard Wagner notes later in this volume, "managers have difficulty conceptualizing problems in ways that transcend their own prior knowledge and experience"; in most cases, they tend to "discover what they expect to discover." Wagner's assertion calls attention to the important role of prior experience in shaping a leader's perceptions. This observation makes instances in which prior beliefs change an interesting opportunity for understanding the dynamics of leaders' thinking.

John Glidewell addresses this issue as he explores the nature of the cognitive processes that lead chief executives to change their minds about previously held beliefs or decisions. Drawing on empirical data from interviews with sixty-nine chief executive officers (CEOs), he develops and tests a conceptual model for explaining how and why organizational and personal factors cause leaders to change their minds. In the context of a cognitive perspective on leadership, understanding the processes that cause a change in one's belief system is fundamental to the design of programs aimed at leadership development. This topic is addressed more explicitly and fully in the final section of the book, but important issues are foreshadowed here.

A common belief espoused in these chapters is that richer descriptions of how leaders classify the often ambiguous and increasingly massive amounts of information they receive is essential to our understanding of leadership. Given the previously noted concern with the meta-rational side of life in organizations, there is an explicit emphasis in the emerging cognitive literature in management on how leaders view and subsequently act on what Tiiu Raun and Ken Leithwood refer to as "swampy problems." These are the messy problems that leaders typically confront in their work—problems that are characterized by ambiguity, partial information, unclear goals, value judgments, and conflicting expectations.

In the final chapter of this section, Raun and Leithwood pay particular attention to the issue of how the values held by leaders shape their conception of administrative problems, as well as their actions. According to Raun and Leithwood, the leader's values influence which problems are addressed, how those problems are interpreted, and the solution processes formulated, intentionally or unconsciously, in response. This chapter adds to our understanding of how the values of leaders give meaning to their vision. The findings from their study of the values of education chiefs, in combination with findings from the broader cognitive literatures, suggest that the domain of values in administration and leadership deserves more explicit attention in preparation and training programs.

1 The Strategy of Teaching Strategy

Charles T. Kerchner

The relationship between practice and the academy requires that the university have the means for understanding how practice works, how individuals involved in practice come to decisions, and how they attack problems. The practice–academy relationship also presupposes that it is possible to teach decision-making to people who will or have entered practice. The teaching mission of the university requires insight into how decisions are made and where the points of strategic leverage lie.

Most of the literature on strategic decision-making involves big bureaucratic choices. As Hickson, Butler, Cray, Mallory, and Wilson (1986, p. 27) say of their studies, "The decisions which are the subject of this book are those made at the top about bigger matters." As a result, the focus on decision processes is almost always on protracted deliberative processes that yield distinct decisions. These decision-making processes reflect the cognitive and organizational framework of organizational problem-solving. To exclusively characterize organizational strategy and strategic decision-making in this way, however, misses much of its richness and much of its reality. Decision-making in educational organizations is better characterized along three dimensions:

- External and internal decisions
- Discrete and incremental decisions
- Individual and group decisions

First, historical examination reveals that the most powerful educational decisions of the last half century have been made outside of school districts. Since World War II, schools have been transformed not so much by internal strategic decisions but by decisions to desegregate, to introduce categorical funding, and to allow collective bargaining. Unlike corporations, schools grew in enrollment and then contracted not because of strategic plans about marketing or production but in reaction to family decisions to migrate and to procreate.

Second, discrete and incremental decisions differ. The conventional literature essentially defines a strategic decision as one at the center of things. Other decisions may follow from it, but the big decision sets the precedent for the smaller decisions that follow. "Precursiveness" and "rarity" are the terms used by Hickson et al. (1986, p. 41). Strategic direction is not always determined in this way. Often, strategic direction is the result of either a series of decisions linked by time and feedback or a cluster of decisions made relatively independently. The strategic importance may be recognized only in retrospect (March & Olsen, 1976). For example, the cumulative effect of categorical funding programs, each enacted to advance and protect a class of students, may be to formalize the organization, making timely student service delivery difficult.

Internal decisions are further divided into group and individual questions. The literature frequently considers decisions made by groups, sometimes groups established specifically to make big decisions (Allison, 1971; Keller, 1983). Some of the groups operate under government or corporate secrecy, such as John F. Kennedy's crisis council during the Cuban Missile Crisis. Some operate in the open. In both cases the organization and the participants recognize the locus of the decision, the legitimacy of the decision-makers, and the fact that a decision will emerge.

Other strategic decisions are made much more privately, centering around single individuals, who may or may not lead organizations. Autocrats, entrepreneurs, and treaty negotiators make decisions with organizations in mind, but the process of making decisions differs markedly from that used in group decision-making.

These three dimensions produce the six-celled grid shown in Table 1.1. External decisions can be of the conventional interest-group variety; they can be revolutionary "systems shock" decisions deliberately made to force change; or they can result from many individual or family decisions. Discrete group decisions are typified by conventional big decisions. Incremental group decisions are typified as "muddling through," a series of immediate connections between problems and solutions. Individual strategic decisions take the form of discrete acts of entrepreneurship or other authoritarian decision, or they represent the gradual result of adopting new teaching or managerial practices.

What is the value of these distinctions? First, different decision processes typify each of the six cells. The descriptive theory of strategic decision is altered depending on the type of decision process elected. Second, teaching about strategic decision-making is as much a matter of knowing how to move decisions from one cell to another as it is of acquiring craft knowledge of techniques within a cell. The job of a chief executive, or a teacher of chief executives, is to guide decisions to the setting in which better decisions are likely to be made. The qualitative dimension that underlies strategic decision making is what to decide and where to decide it. Thus, the argument in this chapter rests partly

Table 1.1 A Typology of Strategic Decisions

	External	Internal	
		Group	Individual
Discrete	• Interest Groups • Revolutions • Unitary Politics	• Conventional big organizational decisions	• Entrepreneurial decisions • Treaty decisions among elites
Incremental	• Erosive trends	• A series of incremental decisions	• A series of individual role taking decisions

on the work on problem-framing (Allison, 1971; Bolman & Deal, this volume). Individual decisions connote biases, worldviews, and cognitive frames. Group decisions involve the problem of combination or synthesis. External decisions involve more explicit political calculation and maneuvering. It is the combination of these approaches that gives us a full view of strategy (Schwenk, 1988). That is, part of that which makes decision-making strategic is the capacity of a given process to find strategic content, a process aided by taking multiple perspectives to problem-framing.

In the following sections of this chapter, I explore each of the dimensions shown in Table 1.1. First, I consider discrete versus incremental decisions, then individual versus group decisions and external versus internal decisions. The final section returns to a discussion of the relationship of these dimensions to teaching strategy.

DISCRETE VERSUS INCREMENTAL STRATEGIC DECISIONS

Modern organizational theory rests on recognizing limits to cognitive rationality. The inability to optimize separates Simon's (1957) "administrative man" from economic rationality. Even as computers were increasing the capacity for calculative decisions, the developers of new fields, such as operations research, warned of their limitation:

> The sort of simple explicit model which operations researchers are so proficient in using can certainly reflect most of the significant factors influencing traffic control on the George Washington Bridge, but the proportion of the relevant reality which we can represent by any such model or models in studying, say, a major foreign-policy decision, appears to be almost trivial (Hitch, 1957, p. 718).

If one cannot be calculatingly rational, then one can, in Lindblom's (1959) words, "muddle through." Lindblom recognized the inherent value of small, measured steps in solving immediate problems. Small steps lead to an intertwining of values and empirical analysis. "The idea that values should be clarified, and in advance of examination of alternative policies, is appealing," but often there "are no preferences in the absence of public discussion sufficient to bring an issue to the attention of the electorate" (p. 81). (For a description of the role of values in public schooling, see Chapter 4 by Raun and Leithwood.)

The primacy of action informing consciousness and values is common to both radical theory and contemporary educational reform strategy. Reformers in Jefferson County, Kentucky, have adopted Schlechty's phrase "little tries" (1990). Individually, changes need not be particularly heroic or radical for the combined effect to be significant (Kerchner, 1991b). The "little tries" philosophy is consistent with Gage's (1985) findings about progress in the soft sciences: Few reforms will yield huge outcome effects, but many will yield a 2–3 percent difference. Weick (1984) invokes the same concept in noting that successful football teams distinguish themselves by not making mistakes when they play weaker opponents rather than by always knocking off powerful rivals. Programs that aim at easy targets can quickly become part of a school's repertoire. Making many changes insulates schools from the accusation that any single change has failed.

The risk of little tries is twofold. In some cases the sum of the parts is insignificant. Change sometimes requires discontinuity. Second, a series of small decisions may become disjointed and circular in their logic, the dog chasing the tail of whirling preferences (Arrow, 1974). As the decision topic moves from person to person and meeting to meeting, the "trajectory" is seldom straight (Hage, 1980). It pauses while further information is sought or disputes are resolved, and it may recycle time after time (Hickson et al., 1986; Mintzberg, 1973).

The Boundary Between Incremental and Discrete Decisions

Though their power is by no means absolute, managers can strongly influence a decision's discreteness or incrementalism through structuring the decision process. Routine periodic decisions, such as setting the annual budget, are unlikely to produce novel ideas or bold departures from the past. While the decisions may involve serious issues, such as budget cutbacks, they are unlikely to produce new direction or leadership. Preplanned organizational routines take over (Allison, 1971; Hickson et al., 1986). However, a manager can transform the decision into a discrete one in at least three ways: Declare a crisis, create a mandate, and define a large decision.

Declare a Crisis. A declared crisis changes the rules for decision-making. Crisis legitimates a chief executive's personal involvement in matters that would normally be subordinated. Crisis allows lower-level subordinates to deliberate with top managers, and it creates an expectation of path-breaking change (Kerchner & Schuster, 1982). Some organizational crises, such as a fire in a school or a riot at a football game, are recognized spontaneously, but others are declared. For example, *A Nation at Risk* was worded and presented to deliberately create a crisis in public education. It clearly succeeded. In a matter of months, public education moved from obscurity to the center of public debate. The educational reform movement of the 1980s and 1990s sustained public attention of greater intensity and duration than the 18 months usual for a public issue.

Create a Mandate. Managers can bind themselves and their organizations to making large, discrete decisions by creating an external mandate for change. Virtually all of the school districts that have taken on large-scale restructuring or revitalization in the past decade used prestigious external boards or commissions to declare that change was necessary (Hill, Wise, & Shapiro, 1989; Kerchner, Koppich, King, & Weeres, 1990).

Define a Large Decision. Less dramatic and more internal, chief executives can create ad hoc committees specifically to take on large decisions. In higher education this device has been used to address problems that proved intractable through faculty senates, administrative councils, or other conventional means (Keller, 1983).

Managerial inaction allows organizational routines—standard operating procedures—to take hold and govern decision patterns. Managers who seek stability create and intensify these routines. Each of the same school districts that created external mandates to initiate their reform efforts created internal restructuring councils to *routinize* the changes. Pittsburgh, Miami, and San Diego schools have created such entities. These reforms illustrate the importance of movement between discrete and incremental decisions in the same reform process. As Starbuck and Nystrom note, "A well designed organization is not a stable solution to achieve, but a developmental process to be kept active" (1981, p. CQ).

INDIVIDUAL VERSUS GROUP DECISIONS

Cognition bounds individual strategy. The central idea of humans as administrators is that of bounded rationality. Our inability to hold and operate on more than a few facts or concepts at a time limits the ways in which we attack problems. We break problems into smaller parts, work sequentially, and seek satisfactory rather than optimal answers. Sophisticated strategy rests on schemata, cognitive representations of relationships that constitute common-sense social theories (Schwenk, 1989).

Cognitive theorists argue that powerful general models exist to expand the capacity of individuals to solve problems and that research into the work of expert problem-solvers, such as chess masters and experienced professionals, provides examples. The primary limitation on individual problem-solving ability is thought to reside in the inherent limitation of working memory to store and operate on information, a limitation thought to be on the order of six or seven items (Fredericksen, 1984). It is argued that training can assist in increasing the number of problems to which an individual can respond automatically. "Once a process becomes automatic, it can be carried out rapidly, with a minimum of attention, and with minimal demands on the limited capacity of working memory, making it possible to use that capacity to deal with more complex or novel aspects of a problem" (Frederiksen, 1984, p. 391).

In an entrepreneurial setting, or in other organizational settings subject to close personal control, a leader's schema or worldview becomes the organization's strategy-making mechanism. Mintzberg and Waters (1982) tracked strategy-making at Steinbergs, a Canadian retailer led for more than a half-century by one person, Sam Steinberg, who guided the business from a mom-and-kids enterprise to a multidivisional corporation with sales of more than $1 billion. Over the course of 57 years there were only six strategic shifts, three major ones. After concluding their studies, Mintzberg and Waters argued, "The conception of a novel strategy is an exercise in synthesis, which typically is best carried out in a single, informed brain" (p. 496).

The literature on organizational transformations characterizes leaders as bold decision-makers. From Drucker's (1976) case examples to Peters and Waterman's (1982) heroic managers, we are presented with pictures of individuals who so deeply "knew" their organization that they could walk confidently into an uncertain future even when things looked bleak. As Mintzberg and Waters (1982) said of Sam Steinberg, "This is what gave the organization its spirit, its drive. . . . Mood cannot be discounted as a factor in strategic behavior" (p. 495).

Mintzberg concludes:

> This study shows how effective such knowledge can be when it is concentrated in one individual who (a) is fully in charge (having no need to convince others with different views and different levels of knowledge, neither subordinates below nor superiors at some distant headquarters); (b) retains a strong, long term commitment to his organization (knowing that, barring a natural disaster, it is he who will be here in the long run); and (c) possesses the vision

and ability to switch from narrow focus to broad perspective. . . . No other mode of strategy making can provide the degree of deliberateness and of integration of strategies with each other and with the environment. None can provide so clear and complete a vision of direction, yet also allow the flexibility to elaborate and rework that vision. (Mintzberg, 1973, pp. 495–496).

The weakness of a single unified mind approaching a decision is that it has no limits other than its own. When entrepreneurial decisions are wrong, they are often gloriously and dramatically wrong. Schwenk (1988) writes of the decisional schema acquired by John DeLorean at General Motors and carried into the ill-fated vehicle that bore his name. High production and exciting cars made DeLorean successful at General Motors. It also led him to scale production of his own cars at a rate six times that which marketing firms estimated initial sales potential to be.

Increasing the Capacity for Individual Decisions

Decisions do not easily debureaucratize. As one executive put it, "Asking a large company to engage in entrepreneurship is like trying to get an elephant to ice-skate" (Barmash, 1971, p. 9). Moving decision-making from groups to an individual requires managerial intervention. Individual discrete decisions are associated with treaties between powerful elites and entrepreneurial behavior of individual leaders, such as a Steinberg or a DeLorean. In either case, they represent a concentration of decision-making capacity in a single individual. In proprietorships ownership concentrates decisional capacity, but in large corporations and public bureaucracies, with thick manuals of organizational policy and routines, the ability of individuals to make decisions must be created and guarded.

Secure internal authority enhances a manager's capacity for treaty-making. Boundary spanning—working between one organization or subunit and another—is risky work. Labor negotiators and others who routinely perform such tasks are frequently subject to harsh criticism *within* their own organizations. The ability to create treaties requires the ability to withstand, ignore, or delegitimate internal criticism. Consider, for example, the recent history of labor relations in the Pittsburgh public schools.

In the mid-1980s both superintendent Richard C. Wallace, Jr., and union president Albert Fondy held secure positions (Kerchner, 1991a). Wallace had been brought to Pittsburgh in 1981 by a reform-minded board and had established a reputation for tough-minded, data-driven change. Fondy, who had led the Pittsburgh Federation of Teachers for more than 20 years, had no conspicuous electoral rivals. Labor negotiations had been tough and there had been four strikes, but the new reforms created an incentive for peaceful settlement. In

1985, Fondy, Wallace, and school board president Jake Milliones settled a labor contract a year before the prior contract expired without going through the conventional bargaining process. The contract was a symbol of "labor peace" destined, in the words of the *Pittsburgh Post-Gazette* (1985), to give the schools "even more national visibility." The settlement itself was reached "very privately," according to a union settlement announcement (Pittsburgh Federation of Teachers, 1985). The school board and the union negotiating team knew that talks were under way, but they were not party to the discussion. The 2,100 teachers at the ratification meeting overwhelmingly approved the contract, as did the school board.

The capacity for individual decisions is increased by creating organizational safety zones for change and development. Two techniques are being used by school districts engaged in reform and restructuring: the creation of experimental organizations within the larger public bureaucracy and the deliberate devolution of decisions to school sites. The Dade County (Florida) Public Schools Saturn Schools projects exemplify setting up experimental organizations. Each Saturn school follows a unique design. In the case of South Pointe Elementary School in Miami Beach, opened in 1991, a joint venture was created between the school district and Minneapolis-based Education Alternatives, Inc., which runs two private schools. The same school system has also experimented with site-based decision-making, allowing budgetary decisions to be made at schools and allowing schools to seek waivers of union contract provisions, school board regulations, and even state laws.

Group Decisions and Their Limits

Individual decision-making has natural limits. For Steinberg, the need for public financing, which occurred in 1953, brought his organization both outside lenders and a set of new stores with which the leader had no personal experience. At the individual–group juncture, strategizing becomes more complex in two ways. First, individual cognitions change as people come to recognize the effects of organizational and political factors that had been unimportant before. Second, the decision process changes radically. The process is driven by multiple individual strategic decisions, with each individual possessing a different cognitive scheme. The juxtaposition of individuals with different cognitive schemes is recognized in such classics as Allison's (1971) description of the Cuban Missile Crisis. Some participants, such as Robert Kennedy, viewed the events as primarily political, while others, such as Robert McNamara, saw them as needing an economically rational solution. Sometimes the participants are unaware that others are thinking of the problem differently, as Benjaman (1980) found when she traced the cognition of participants on a governor's task force on early childhood education. Sometimes decision participants are literally playing different games. They seek different objectives, and count different outcomes as winning (Long, 1958).

Individual cognitions are interspersed with organizational processes that extend over time and have uncertain participation patterns. March and Olsen (1976) describe an incomplete cycle of choice in which individual preferences do not necessarily lead to actions to achieve those preferences. In studies of university, corporate, and government decisions, they found individual participation highly fluid. In very lengthy decisions, the people who began the decision process were seldom those present at the end.

The complexity of organizational decisions makes matters of structure and process difficult to unravel. Hickson and his colleagues (Hickson et al., 1986) attempted to create an ordering of what counts by studying more than 150 major managerial decisions in 30 organizations in England ranging from 100 to more than 57,000 employees.

They describe three different group decision processes: 1. *Sporadic:* often multiyear processes beset with disrupting delays, interruptions, more sources of expertise with greater differences of confidence placed on information and views, more informal interaction, and final authority at a higher level than the decision participants. 2. *Fluid:* relatively speedy processes handled in relatively formal settings with much discussion channelled through prearranged subgroups, fewer disruptions. 3. *Constructed:* allowing less scope for negotiation, made at a level below highest management, generally relying on internal rather than external experts. Generally less complex and with less activity.

The complexity and politicality of decisions statistically mapped on the three decision types produce three classifications:

Vortex–Sporadic Decisions. Vortex decisions are infrequent, weighty, and controversial matters from which "eddies run throughout the higher echelons to suck everyone and everything into swirls of activity" (Hickson et al., 1986, p. 174). These decisions tend to be complex, although not necessarily precursive or determinant of future decisions. They also involve contentious political interests influenced externally.

Tractable–Fluid Decisions. Tractable decisions are less complex and serious than vortex–sporadic ones, but they often have diffuse consequences. These decisions are rare, but appear to have consequences for the future. Politically, they are noncontentious. Fewer specialists from the organization are involved and fewer are called in from outside.

Familiar–Constructed Decisions. Familiar decisions concern recognizable and limited questions. They are the least complex or unusual, and their consequences are limited. These decisions follow standard operating procedures.

"Management can guide this sort of decision along constructed pathways which have been traveled by its predecessors" (Hickson et al., 1986, p. 185).

The Boundaries of Big Group Decisions

Groups tend to rationalize the decision process and moderate the outcome—the more familiar the decision, the more moderate the process. Thus, they create an organizational paradox. Organizational learning takes place through practice, including practice among groups or teams of workers. This is how organizations learn (Hedberg, 1981). Responses that match stimuli will become increasingly likely to be evoked by similar stimuli in the future. Problems that are novel to beginners become routine to experts. Process criteria are frequently substituted for outcome criteria. The question becomes "Did the group use a good decision process?" rather than "Was the decision successful?" Public bureaucracies, in particular, show a marked tendency toward judgments of decision participants based on procedural propriety. Organizations adopt or accept criteria that are independent of the efficient coordination and control of production activities. This universal process has been defined as "the iron law of ossification" (Peterson, 1981, p. 72).

EXTERNAL VERSUS INTERNAL DECISIONS

As decisions become rarer and more critical, they edge toward consideration of the external environment. Two characteristics of the public schools' extraorganizational environment strongly affect their capacity to engage in strategic planning and decision-making. First, many strategic decisions are made within state and federal governments and other places external to school organizations. Schools cannot make many of the decisions that corporations think of as strategic. Second, the environment of the most troubled public school districts is extremely turbulent. Environmental turbulence undermines the validity of organizational knowledge built up over years of forecasting and planning.

The Political Environment

In the last 50 years, education's major strategic decisions have been made in settings external to school organizations. Desegregation was brought to the schools by the hand of the Supreme Court, not the deliberation of school boards. Congress created categorical funding, which externally directed programs and finances. State legislatures adopted collective-bargaining statutes, which reordered school authority structures and resource allocations.

When one looks at the set of decisions that typify corporate strategic planning, one is struck by the extent to which relatively few of these decisions are available to educational organizations. School districts are highly constricted in decisions about entering or leaving different markets and in the ability to flee from adverse situations. There are many schools but few shopping centers on the South Side of Chicago and in South Central Los Angeles. School districts, like corporations, frequently decide to combine. Consolidation has reduced the number of school districts from 130,000 in 1920 to fewer than 17,000 now (Tyack, 1989), but school districts have much more difficulty entering or leaving areas of service. Their core businesses and much of their operating requirements are externally determined. There are no school district analogies to W. R. Grace's abandonment of the shipping business or R. J. Reynolds' transmutation beyond tobacco. In many ways, individual school districts are much more like franchises than they are like corporations. While school districts explore coordinated childrens' services and the addition of specialty magnet schools, they are not generally free to decide that "special ed looks like a loser, let's close down the programs." Although there is great variation by state, school districts are generally fiscally constrained. Most lack independent taxing authority. Most are highly limited in charges they can make for services. Unlike corporations, they do not issue stock and their ability to take on debt is limited.

All these factors increase the importance of external strategic decision-making. External decision-making requires a political logic that varies according to the type of politics involved:

Issue Politics. Conventional, issue-oriented politics are not very different outside the organization than they are inside, just more explicit. The routines and the internal hierarchy of organizations dampen explicit displays of individual or departmental interest. In external settings, the strategy of decision-making quickly recognizes the presence and legitimacy of competing interests and those stakeholders attached to particular interests. The first strategic decision is the choice of an issue and its presentation. Whatever the decision-making system—Congress, legislature, agency—the initial task is to seize a place on the agenda (Cobb & Elder, 1972). The next decision involves aggregating support around the issue.

Revolutionary Politics. The object is not to reach agreement among the participants and find mutually acceptable solutions, but to overthrow the existing order. Much of educational politics in the 1980s and 1990s is revolutionary in character, an effort to deliver a set of "system shocks" to the existing institution. Voucher, tax credit, and privatization schemes are explicit attempts to decrease the internal control of existing schools and districts.

High Politics. Within the last few years, authors from different disciplines have rediscovered that aspect of public life which goes beyond self-interest (Mansbridge, 1990). Psychologists have become interested in "prosocial behavior" and political scientists fascinated by situations in which public officials cast votes against the apparent self-interest of their constituents. This variant of politics follows a logic different from the other two. Prominent, powerful, and public sponsorship is required. In the case of ESEA (Koppich, 1990), the president and high-ranking congressional leaders, as well as civil rights groups and religious and labor organizations, sponsored the measure.

Environmental Turbulence

For organizations like schools, which work in turbulent environments and which are dependent on them, strategic decision-making often equates to reading the environment and trying to outguess its direction.

Almost all theories of organizational learning build on the idea of stimulus response. The detection and correction of errors and the construction of knowledge are highly moderated by past learning. Over time, cognitive schemes translate into organizational routines. Organizational routines amplify and connect with one another to the point that a drop of environmental stimulus produces a river of organizational response. Consider the simple act of enrollment forecasting.

All school districts forecast student enrollments. Changes in the number of students or the composition of the student body affects the district budget, school-site boundaries, space allocation, special program requirements such as English as a Second Language, and staff assignment. But if the assumptions on which enrollment forecasts are made are inaccurate, then the river of organizational response is misdirected.

Many school districts failed to recognize the end of the post–World War II baby boom. Particularly for those school districts that engaged in long-range planning and built schools using early 1960s fertility assumptions, the 1970s produced a shocking undersupply of students. Localized environments change even more rapidly. In South Florida and Southern California, the new ports of entry for immigration, neighborhoods can change from one ethnic and language group to another in just a few years. Neighborhoods such as Watts, which symbolized black America to a generation, are rapidly becoming Hispanic. Road signs in Westminster, the archetype of white suburbia, point to Little Saigon, the settling place for a half-million Vietnamese.

Individual ability to integrate the environment, to make sense of one's surroundings, declines when environments become overly complex (Hedberg, 1981). Attempting to listen to the environment produces such mixed messages that any sense of overall direction becomes difficult. Under these conditions, the clear message of the last decade is that decentralization produces the ability of individuals in schools—teachers, classified workers, and administrators—to respond quickly. Rules about response need to be swept away, and workers need to be encouraged, even required, to solve problems at the grass roots (Peters, 1987; Peters & Waterman, 1982).

CONCLUSION: THINKING BIG BY THINKING SMALL

How does one teach about strategic thinking when major strategic decisions occur rarely—in the Steinberg case, once every 15 years or so? Students in university classes on organizations analyze cases every week. When we teach rational planning, we introduce devices such as rolling five-year plans, periodic reviews of direction by state education agencies, or accreditation team visits.

Mintzberg and Waters (1982) argue that these exercises, "like 'crying wolf too often' may actually *desensitize* managers to strategic issues, so that the need for substantive change may not be recognized when it does arise. Conversely, it may encourage change when it is unnecessary—a kind of *oversensitivity* to strategic issues" (p. 494). Miller and Friesen (1978) write about the impulsive firm as a type of strategic behavior.

We probably overeducate for the unusual and fail to teach students to recognize the strategic potential in their everyday activities. In a Far West Laboratory study, successful principals were distinguished by their attention to detail and their ability to connect the routine activities and decisions made within the school to the grand strategy of instructional leadership (Dwyer, Lee, Rowan, & Bossert, 1983). Most administrative time is spent in routine, not extraordinary, decisions and many of those decisions are considered trivial (Leithwood, 1987; Mintzberg, Raisinghani, & Theoret, 1976). To the extent that strategic decision-making is both individual and incremental, much of what the strategy of a school becomes is contained within the ordinary and the everyday.

Education for strategic decision-making is thus as much a matter of recognizing the strategic import of daily decisions as it is a matter of establishing and operating "big" strategic-decision operations. Finding the strategic potential in ordinary actions provides the opportunity to interconnect daily life and the enactment of a vision or direction. Problem-finding is as important as problem-solving (Peterson, 1986).

Educational strategy is also about making connections. Schools have always faced a turbulent environment and very permeable boundaries between the external social and political environments and school programs and policies. Well-educated administrators need to understand the connections between schools and their environments, need to know how to scan beyond the school walls and how, like a good sailor, to take advantage of the prevailing winds while avoiding the squalls.

Interdependence also implies bridges between organizations and environments, between individuals and organizations. Managers control access to bridges, gateways, networks, and other organizational structures. They make up agendas. They influence where things are going to be decided. The decision about where a thing is to be decided often determines its strategic import.

Administrators—novice and veteran—need to understand the strategic import of daily life, the connection between the smallest individual activity and the grandest external mandate, and the importance of moving decisions between one domain and another.

NOTE

I wish to thank David Quinn for his assistance in locating books and articles, a task that saved many valuable hours.

REFERENCES

Allison, G. T. (1971). *Essence of decision.* Boston: Little, Brown.

Arrow, K. (1974). *The limits of organizations.* New York: Norton.

Barmash, I. (1971). *Welcome to our conglomerate—You're fired!* New York: Delacorte.

Benjaman, B. (1980). *Perceptions of decision-makers: A Q-study of organizational choice using four models of decision.* Unpublished dissertation, The Claremont Graduate School, Claremont, CA.

Cobb, R. W., & Elder, C. D. (1972). *Participation in American politics.* New York: Holt, Rinehart & Winston.

Drucker, P. (1976). *Management.* New York: Harper & Row.

Dwyer, D., Lee, G., Rowan, B., & Bossert, S. (1983). *Five principals in action: Perspectives on instructional management.* San Francisco: Far West Laboratory for Educational Research and Development.

Frederiksen, N. (1984). Implications of cognitive theory for instruction in problem solving. *Review of Educational Research, 54* (3), 363–407.

Gage, N. L. (1985). *Hard gains in the soft sciences: The case of pedagogy.* Bloomington, IN: Phi Delta Kappa.

Hage, J. (1980). *Theories of organizations: Form, process and transformation.* New York: Wiley.

Hedberg, B. (1981). How organizations learn and unlearn. In W. H. Starbuck & P. C. Nystrom (Eds.), *Handbook of organizational design, Vol. 1* (pp. 3–27). New York: Oxford University Press.

Hickson, D. J., Butler, R. J., Cray, D., Mallory, G. O., & Wilson, D. C. (1986). *Top decisions: Strategic decision-making in organizations*. San Francisco: Jossey-Bass.

Hill, P. T., Wise, A. E., & Shapiro, L. (1989). *Educational progress: Cities mobilize to improve their schools*. Santa Monica: RAND Center for the Study of the Teaching Profession.

Hitch, C. (1957). Operations research and national planning—a dissent. *Operations Research, 5,* 718–723.

Keller, G. (1983). *Academic strategy: The management revolution in American higher education*. Baltimore: Johns Hopkins University Press.

Kerchner, C. T. (1991a). *Pittsburgh: Reform in a well-managed public bureaucracy*. Claremont, CA: The Claremont Graduate School, Claremont Project VISION.

Kerchner, C. T. (1991b). *Louisville: Staff development drives a decade of reform*. Claremont, CA: The Claremont Graduate School, Claremont Project VISION.

Kerchner, C. T., Koppich, J., King, B., & Weeres, J. (1990, October 29). *This could be the start of something big: Labor relations reforms in the 1990s*. Paper presented at the annual meeting of the University Council for Educational Administration, Pittsburgh.

Kerchner, C.T., & Schuster, J. (1985). The uses of crisis: Taking the tide at the flood. *The Review of Higher Education, 5*(3), 121–142.

Koppich, J. (1990). *Educational reform as high politics: Toward a political theory of school reform movements*. Unpublished doctoral dissertation, University of California, Berkeley.

Leithwood, K. (1987). Using the principal profile to assess performance. *Educational Leadership, 45* (1), 63–68.

Lindblom, C. E. (1959). The science of muddling through. *Public Administration Review, 19*(1), 79–88.

Long, N. (1958). The local community as an ecology of games. *American Journal of Sociology, 64*(2), 249–261.

Mansbridge, J. (Ed.). (1990). *Beyond self-interest*. Chicago: University of Chicago Press.

March, J. G., & Olsen, J. P. (1976). *Ambiguity and choice in organizations*. Bergen: Universitesforlgaet.

Miller, D., and Friesen, P. (1978). Archetypes of strategic formation. *Management Science, 24* (9), 921–933.

Mintzberg, H. (1973). *The nature of managerial work*. New York: Harper & Row.

Mintzberg, H., Raisinghani, D., & Theoret, A. (1976). The structure of "unstructured" decision processes. *Administrative Science Quarterly, 21,* 246–275.

Mintzberg, H., & Waters, J. A. (1982). Tracking strategy in an entrepreneurial firm. *Academy of Management Journal, 25*(3), 465–499.

Peters, T. (1987). *Thriving on chaos*. New York: Knopf.

Peters, T. J., & Waterman, R. H. (1982). *In search of excellence*. New York: Harper & Row.

Peterson, K. (1986). Vision and problem finding in principals' work: Values and cognition in administration. *Peabody Journal of Education, 63*(1), 88–106.

Peterson, R. (1981). Entrepreneurship and organization. In W. H. Starbuck and P. C. Nystrom (Eds.), *Handbook of organizational design, Vol. 1* (pp. 65–83). New York: Oxford University Press.

Pittsburgh Federation of Teachers. (1985). *A unique and national significant education/ negotiations achievement in Pittsburgh.* Pittsburgh: Author.

Editorial. (1985, September 5). *Pittsburgh Post-Gazette,* p. 6.

Schwenk, C. R. (1988). *The essence of strategic decision making.* Lexington, MA: Lexington Books.

Schwenk, C. R. (1989). Linking cognitive, organizational and political factors in explaining strategic change. *Journal of Management Studies, 26*(2), 177–187.

Schlechty, P. (1990). *Schools for the 21st century.* San Francisco: Jossey-Bass.

Simon, H. (1957). *Administrative behavior* (2nd ed.). New York: Macmillan.

Starbuck, W. H., & Nystrom, P. C. (1981). Designing and understanding organizations. In W. H. Nystrom and P. C. Starbuck, *Handbook of organizational design, Vol 1.* New York: Oxford University Press.

Tyack, D. (1989). Long-term structural trends in public schools. *Teachers College Record, 92*(2), 183–195.

Weick, K. E. (1984, January). Small wins: Redefining the scale of social problems. *American Psychologist, 39*(1), 40–49.

2   Everyday Epistemology in School Leadership: Patterns and Prospects

Lee G. Bolman and Terrence E. Deal

A good leader does three things well. First, he [or she] knows what's going on. Second he [or she] knows the right thing to do. And, third, he [or she] makes the right thing happen, working through subordinates well organized and motivated to get things done.

Carlyle A. H. Trost, Chief of Naval Operations, U.S. Navy

In three succinct sentences, Admiral Trost gets closer to the heart of leadership than do most discussions of the topic. Scholars write in abundance about leaders' traits, styles, and deeds, but pay little attention to how leaders think. This is one reason that our billion-dollar investment in leadership-development programs has produced so much disappointment. We teach aspiring leaders how to look and act, but give much less attention to how they "size up" situations. Problem-solving and decision-making get higher priority than problem-finding and making sense of complex and shifting human dynamics.

Trost's down-to-earth observation offers an important precondition to the effective exercise of leadership. Above all else, a leader needs to know what is going on. That is no easy task in modern organizations. Leaders, like physicians, are ethically obliged to think before they act. They need to organize vague symptoms into a meaningful diagnosis before they choose a course of intervention. Leaders' thinking defines and frames reality for themselves and often for their constituents. How they frame problems or dilemmas has a decisive impact on what their organization notices, what it does, and what it eventually becomes. A French word for leadership, *encadrement,* also means framing, a sign that they may understand the process better than we do. Leaders' cognition is a poorly charted but critical area, ripe for further research and development.

In this chapter we argue that an adequate theory of leaders' thinking must have at least two fundamental characteristics:

1. Its view of cognition must incorporate both the rational and meta-rational features of complex social environments.
2. It must focus directly on the cognitive maps that leaders need to make sense out of their complex worlds.

We will first develop this argument conceptually, and illustrate the implications of our view for school principals. We then present data that profiles the leadership frames of school principals in the United States and Singapore. Finally, we describe and discuss our program of action-research to expand cognitive repertoires of principals, enabling them to think more flexibly about the issues they face every day.

LEADERSHIP FRAMES

New developments in understanding cognition have rekindled interest in how people think and organize their thoughts. Rather than placing heavy emphasis on how people feel or respond emotionally, cognitive psychologists delve into how "they think about their experiences and act in conjunction with their thoughts" (Gioia, 1986, p. 341). Underneath this conceptual canopy, researchers employ a variety of labels to capture basic elements in cognitive structures and processes. These include schema theory (Lord & Foti, 1986), schemata (Fiedler, 1982; Fiske & Dyer, 1985), representations (Frensch & Sternberg, 1991; Lesgold & Lajoie, 1991; Voss, Wolfe, Lawrence, & Engle, 1991), cognitive maps (Weick & Bougon, 1986), paradigms (Gregory, 1983; Kuhn, 1970), social categorizations (Cronshaw, 1987), attributions, implicit organizing theories (Brief & Downey, 1983), and others.

The underlying assumption is that humans classify people, objects, and experiences in terms of categories or prototypes derived from previous experiences (Pitre & Sims, 1987). These schemata allow us to "process an overwhelming amount of incomplete, inaccurate, or ambiguous information, quickly, efficiently, with relatively little effort" (Sims & Gioia, 1987, p. 12). Even when they are inaccurate, cognitive schemata permit a quick response rather than paralysis or inaction. They protect people from being overwhelmed by uncertain, non-routine experiences. They also contain scripts for how to deal with particular categories of objects, people, roles, or events (Argyris & Schön, 1982, Pitre & Sims, 1987).

Cognitive structures often capture only the rational dimensions of complex organizations, neglecting the powerful political and symbolic issues that are deeply rooted in every human group. To capture these subterranean forces, conceptions of cognitive processes must be enlarged to encompass symbols (Gioia, 1986), metaphors (Gentner, 1988; Saudar, 1986; Schön, 1983), and images

(Mitchell, Rediker, & Beach, 1986; Morgan, 1986). These expressive devices serve as prisms through which people interpret and respond to presenting circumstances. Cognitive psychologists often offer a largely rational view of human thinking, but anyone who has worked in complex organizations knows that competing interests and unconscious drives produce powerful meta-rational dynamics. Cognitive theory needs to embrace "hot cognition" (Bransford & Stein, 1984) in order to encompass these symbolic and political forces.

Our research incorporates both rational and meta-rational elements in a view of leaders' thinking (Bolman & Deal, 1991). Borrowing from pioneering work in sociology and other disciplines (Bateson, 1972; Berger & Luckmann, 1966; Gardner, 1983; Goffman, 1974; James, 1950), we use the notion of "frames" to capture the idea that people are simultaneously sensible, selfish, scheming, and symbolic. As they enter and exit from hundreds of different situations every day, people define circumstances so that they know what to do and how to understand what others are doing. In the course of asking "What is going on here?" people frame each situation that they enter. This process of framing

> allows its user to locate, perceive, identify, and label a seemingly infinite number of concrete occurrences defined in its terms. He [or she] is likely to be unaware of such organized features as the framework has, and unable to describe the framework with any completeness if asked, yet these handicaps are no bar to his [or her] easily and fully applying it. (Goffman, 1974, p. 21)

Without our giving it a second thought, the frame we choose determines the reality we experience and the script that guides our actions.

> What people understand to be the organization of their experience, they buttress, and perform self-fulfillingly. They develop a corpus of cautionary tales, games, riddles, experiments, newsy stories, and other scenarios which elegantly confirm a frame relevant view of the workings of the world. (Goffman, 1974, p. 563)

Leaders in particular are required to make sense of ambiguous, complex, and puzzling events. When they frame accurately and respond appropriately, puzzles and problems become promising opportunities. When frames distort or overlook essential elements of a situation, leaders "lose the bubble," feel out of control, and fall back on familiar scripts even if their actions only make things worse. This is especially likely in nonroutine, crisis situations:

> Since there is good evidence that decision makers in crises consider less information, focus on shorter term consequences, and stereotype more, it seems likely that cause maps [frames] would not be shielded from these effects. Specifically, as stress increases, dominant links should exert relatively stronger

effects over what is perceived. Concepts that are more complex and more recently learned would be likely to disappear from maps sooner than older, simpler concepts. Cause maps [frames] which are hard enough to understand in times of quiescence would likely seem especially baffling in crises and to be ignored. (Weick & Bougon, 1986, p. 121)

Complex organizations are full of deceptive, ambiguous, confusing, and nonroutine situations (Bolman & Deal, 1991). Such environments create dilemmas for humans, who confront biological limits in memory and information processing (Simon, 1957, 1969). Frames that are too simple distort and mislead. Frames that are too complex overwhelm our capacity to think clearly, thus compounding the problem of confusion and ambiguity.

A manageable number of frames, each offering a window on different spheres of social complexity, provides a way out of the dilemma. The ability to use multiple frames has three advantages:

1. Each frame can be coherent, parsimonious, and powerful
2. The collection can be more comprehensive than any single frame
3. Multiple frames enable leaders to reframe.

Reframing is a conscious effort to size up a situation using multiple lenses. Leaders who cannot reframe in times of crisis and overload feel confused and overwhelmed. Sometimes they are immobilized; other times, they plunge mindlessly into reckless and misguided action.

THE FOUR FRAMES

Some years ago, we were assigned to teach together in an introductory course, "Organizations: Theory and Behavior." We immediately found ourselves nose-to-nose in a struggle over what to teach and how to teach it. Working through our own disagreements, as well as those of the field, led us to conceptualize four distinct frames, each representing a different facet of human organizations that requires attention.

The Structural Frame. The structural frame emphasizes productivity and assumes that organizations work best when goals and roles are clear, and the efforts of individuals and groups are well coordinated through both vertical (command, rule) and lateral (face-to-face, informal) strategies.

The Human Resource Frame. The human resource frame highlights the importance of needs and motives. It posits that organizations work best when individual needs are met and the organization provides a caring, trusting work environment. Showing concern for others and providing ample opportunities for participation and shared decision-making are two of the ways that organizations enlist people's commitment and involvement at all levels.

The Political Frame. The political frame points out the limits of authority and the inevitability that resources will be too scarce to fulfill all demands. Organizations are arenas in which groups jockey for power, and goals emerge from bargaining and compromise among different interests rather than from rational analysis at the top. Conflict becomes an inescapable, even welcomed byproduct of everyday life. Handled properly, it is a source of constant energy and renewal.

The Symbolic Frame. The symbolic frame centers attention on symbols, meaning, and faith. Every human organization creates symbols to cultivate commitment, hope, and loyalty. Symbols govern behavior through informal, implicit, and shared rules, agreements, and understandings. Stories, metaphors, heroes and heroines, ritual, ceremony, and play add zest and existential buoyancy. The organization becomes a way of life rather than merely a place of work.

Organizations are simultaneously rational, emotional, ideological, and fictional enterprises. They can be fully understood only by a combination of frames that encompass both the cognitive notion of schema and the metaphoric idea of imagery.

In working with graduate students and leaders across a variety of organizations, we came to see the frames as more than intellectual constructs. People typically prefer one frame over others. Faced with contradictory feedback, they often fall back on a familiar logic—even when it is clear (at least to others) that their script is not working. Helping people reframe a situation almost always generates feelings of freedom, empowerment, and self-confidence. They find new, more effective ways to deal with highly perplexing situations.

The frames came initially from existing literature and our own experience in organizations. To give them a more systematic, empirical foundation, we conducted a series of studies to measure the frame orientations of leaders. To determine whether our concepts were observable in the thinking and action of practicing managers, we have used both qualitative analysis of critical incidents and a survey instrument that measures leadership orientations.

Several reports of this work (Bolman & Deal, 1992a, 1992b, in press) present results from studies of leaders in business, higher education, and health care. Here we summarize results from research on school principals in the United States and in Singapore. (More extensive discussion of our research methods appears in Bolman & Deal, 1992a, in press.)

PATTERNS IN SCHOOL PRINCIPALS' THINKING

There are distinct patterns in the ways that principals think, and interesting links between those patterns and principals' effectiveness as managers and leaders: 1. Principals in both the United States and Singapore rely mainly on one or two frames—usually human resource and structural (in that order); 2. how principals think about their work is related to how well they perform. In both countries, the structural frame dominates ratings of effectiveness as a manager, while the symbolic frame dominates rating of leadership effectiveness. Equally important, all frames are significant predictors of effectiveness as both manager and leader, which supports our belief in the importance of multiframe thinking.

These findings help to focus a critical leadership issue in our schools. School principals, particularly in the United States, show a strong preference for the human resource and structural frames. They focus primarily on shaping their school to meet individual needs, and secondarily on designing a formal structure for achieving educational goals. They are less apt to emphasize the political issues in their schools, or to encourage a culture that promotes meaning and faith. Schools today are arenas for power struggles and value conflicts. Internal conflicts among administrators, teachers, and students are surpassed in intensity only by those between school and community. Ethnic, racial, and other community tensions regularly wend their way into the principal's office. Each day is filled with frustration and stress for principals who cannot think and act in political terms.

Schools today also wrestle with complex issues of public and professional confidence. Typically, local schools still receive high marks from parents and local residents. But education with a capital *E* is held in much lower regard. Even though evidence of a decline in school effectiveness is equivocal, the nation as a whole is clearly experiencing a crisis of confidence in its schools. Political leaders from the White House to town hall decry the inadequacies of public education and call for massive reforms. Meanwhile, the professional confidence of educators themselves is in major decline. What once was a meaningful profession has become a dispiriting and unrewarding job for many teachers. The crisis of education is largely a symbolic problem—a loss of confidence in the schools. Instead of helping, constant reform efforts have weakened the moral and spiritual understandings that give meaning to the educational enterprise. At a time when many business leaders have taken a renewed interest in strengthening their organization's culture, principals and other educational leaders have devoted more attention to restructuring and retraining (Deal, 1984, 1985, 1990). This is not surprising for leaders who frame their world primarily in structural and human resource terms.

The future will almost certainly bring more pressures for change, which in turn will generate new issues of conflict and loss. If principals are to understand such issues, their cognitive repertoires will need to expand, encompassing the assumptions and imagery of the political and symbolic frames.

REFRAMING: EXPANDING PRINCIPALS' THINKING

We have begun to explore how school principals can learn to think more flexibly. In joint ventures with two U.S. school districts and the Ministry of Education in the Republic of Singapore, we have designed a process with three main assumptions or beliefs: individual reflection, group reflection, and activating inert knowledge.

Individual Reflection

We believe that principals can step back and reflect on how they typically define and respond to situations that arise in their schools. As Weick and Bougon (1986) note: "A decision-maker can become a more sophisticated thinker by externalizing and studying a previously implicit map. Particularly attractive is the fact that this externalization does not require an outside expert and can be done in private" (p. 130).

One way to promote individual reflection is to generate data about principals' frame orientations, particularly data that enable them to compare how they see themselves with how they are seen by others.

Group Reflection

Individual reflection can be enhanced by shared language and concepts that enable groups of principals to give each other feedback, define problems of practice, and generate strategies for dealing with school and district issues.

> When we move from private to public use of cause maps [frames], there is agreement that maps allow groups to diagnose disagreements and manage those disagreements . . . a result of negotiations over individual maps among team members is that there is a careful and gradual change of mutual understanding which is evidenced as each individual map absorbs more concepts from the team maps and, conversely, the team map absorbs more individuality. (Weick & Bougon, 1986, p. 130).

A powerful stimulus for such public discussions is written cases that the principals prepare. We ask them to write a brief account (ranging from a couple of paragraphs to several pages) of a critical incident that presented a significant leadership challenge. In large- or small-group discussions, principals practice reframing by looking at the critical incidents from different perspectives. They apply different frames to the same case to expand understanding of what is really going on and to generate options for what might be done. For example, a Broward County principal wrote a case describing a disastrous experiment in teacher empowerment. A local bank sent consultants to increase teachers' influence on schoolwide decisions. After two meetings, the teachers voted to have the consultants leave and followed through by developing their own program. The principal actually interpreted this as a failure. However, as the situation was reframed, she came to see that in dismissing the consultants the teachers exercised their power.

Activating Inert Knowledge

We believe that principals often know more than they think they know. Cognitive schemata and images are formed largely from experience. Through trial and error, people sort out ideas about what works and what does not. Experience can mislead, but it can also create a stock of highly effective seat-of-the-pants knowledge that principals rarely use. Cognitive psychologists (Bransford & Stein, 1984) call this "inert" knowledge. Exposure to "contrasting sets" can evoke knowledge that might otherwise be dismissed as irrelevant. The frames provide contrasting views of leadership that help principals access and label what they already know.

PILOT PROJECTS: REFRAMING IN ACTION

The National Center for Educational Leadership (NCEL) has joined with two school districts and the education ministry in Singapore in ventures intended to train principals to think more flexibly. Each party contributes resources to ensure that both research and training objectives can be met. In Broward County, Florida, the project included 50 volunteer principals. In Beaverton, Oregon, district administrators as well as principals from all the district's schools were part of the project. More than 300 principals from Singapore were included in the effort there. The duration of the process varied across the projects. Broward County principals spent four full days in workshops. The dialogue in those workshops led to a variety of initiatives, including a cadre of principals who have taught the reframing process to other colleagues. Beaverton's project began with a two and one-half day workshop, with a follow-up scheduled for nine months later. For the Singapore principals, the reframing workshop lasted two days. We jointly facilitated the process in Broward. Deal facilitated the effort in Beaverton, while Bolman worked with the principals in Singapore. The details varied from situation to situation, but the general approach was the same.

AN ACTION-RESEARCH APPROACH TO REFRAMING

The steps in our reframing process are similar to survey-feedback or action-research designs. After an initial introduction, participating administrators rate themselves on the leadership-orientations survey instrument and ask at least four other people to rate them. Principals often choose to sample parents, staff, and students, and they are able to get separate results from each group that they identify. One principal color-coded his questionnaire—the new teachers received yellow instruments; those of the veterans were blue. It turned out that the yellows and the blues had noticeably different perceptions, confirming something that the principal had suspected for some time.

The instruments are sent to NCEL offices at Harvard or Vanderbilt for analysis. In a subsequent workshop, participating principals receive personal profiles showing how their frame preferences correspond to the perceptions of their colleagues. We also display data for the entire group, and provide comparative portraits from other educational or business organizations—either here or abroad. (We now have data from more than 20 nations in Europe, Latin America, Asia, Australia, and the Middle East.)

We begin the feedback session by introducing the idea of frames and their relationship to leaders' understanding and action. We then discuss and elaborate the four frames, showing the contrasting language, metaphors, and assumptions of each. To link the frames to everyday experience we use a variety of short film clips and videotapes. These allow the principals to see a frame in action and to appreciate its cognitive, emotional, and symbolic content firsthand. Short lectures, followed by discussion and selected cases from other situations, reinforce the ideas. Principals begin to develop insights into their own situations as they move through the frames. Phrases such as "Aha," "I knew that but didn't know I did," or, "Ohmigosh! What was I thinking about when I did that!" are common reactions. We think such responses confirm some of the assumptions underlying the reframing process.

Once the principals have mastered the frames, we introduce the feedback process. We begin by explaining the eight subscales—two for each frame (see Table 2.1). Next, we ask the group to predict what its group portrait will look like. In all three cases, the predictions were surprisingly accurate. Each of the three groups generated provocative hypotheses to account for their own array and why it differs from those of other groups.

In the next stage, voluntary feedback groups form, composed of people principals trust and with whom they feel comfortable. Each member of the

Table 2.1 Eight Dimensions of Leadership

Structural Dimensions	Human Resource Dimensions
I. Analytic: • Thinks clearly and logically • Approaches problems through careful analysis • Approaches problems with facts and logic • Pays strict attention to detail	I. Supportive: • Shows support and concern for others • Shows concern for others' feelings • Is consistently responsive to others • Gives Recognition for work well done
II. Organized: • Very well organized • Develops and implements clear policies • Provides clear, consistent goals and direction • Strongly believes in clear structures and systems	II. Participative: • Fosters involvement in decisions • Listens well • Is open to new ideas • Highly participative manager
Political Dimensions	**Symbolic Dimensions**
I. Powerful: • Able to mobilize people and resources • Highly persuasive and influential • Effective in getting support and cooperation • Develops alliances for a strong base of support	I. Inspirational: • Inspires others to do their best • Communicates a strong vision • Generates loyalty • Raises enthusiasm
II. Adroit: • Very skillful negotiator • Responds well to organizational conflict • Politically sensitive and skillful • Knows how to win when against opposition	II. Charismatic: • Leads with an emphasis on culture • Highly imaginative and creative • Generates new, exciting possibilities • Highly charismatic

feedback group makes predictions about others' preferred orientations. After the predictions are discussed, each principal receives his or her individual profile. The room typically becomes very quiet as principals privately reflect on how their self-perceptions compare with ratings from those with whom they work. Some principals are surprised by the amount of agreement, others by the size of the discrepancy. After studying and distilling their results, the administrators return to the feedback group. There they are at liberty to divulge as much information as they wish. The group is used to confirm, modify, or expand on whatever a principal chooses to share. These sessions last for nearly an hour and complete the first day's activities.

The second day usually begins with a brief recapitulation of the frames. As a warmup activity, we often show a videotape and ask the participants to interpret it through each frame. Then, the entire group does the same thing with one or two of the short cases that the participants prepared describing situations through which they are currently working. After the large-group discussion, participants return to their feedback groups. Individuals present their own critical incidents for discussion and reframing, and groups regularly identify new issues and possibilities, enabling the case writer to gain a deeper understanding of the case and to develop new strategies for action.

The second day ends with another recapitulation of the frames—usually through short films or film clips. Principals then engage in future-oriented conversations around their own personal-developmental goals, and identify ways that they can work together on issues of mutual importance.

CONCLUSION

We are still assessing the impact of the reframing process, but the early returns are encouraging. In the short term, participants have provided very positive comments about the value of the survey feedback and the reframing workshops. We have received reports of new initiatives that were triggered by their participation. Anecdotal evidence also suggests that reframing seeps into everyday language and action. In districtwide meetings, for example, people will say "Let's look at that another way," or "I see the assumptions behind your proposal, but what happens if we reframe the situation?" We will be revisiting these districts to see whether reframing becomes an integral part of an individual's leadership repertoire—as well as an integral part of a district's culture.

The well-documented problems of American education present school principals with formidable challenges. Wise and effective leadership is more important than ever, but it requires a complex array of lenses to distinguish traps and dead-ends from promising opportunities. Multiframe thinking reduces administrators' stress and enhances their effectiveness. In the long term, the measure of our success will be how well principals can reframe the problems they face so as to discover and invent new solutions that significantly enhance the performance of their schools.

NOTE

This research was funded in part by a grant from the Office of Educational Research and Improvement of the U.S. Department of Education to the National Center for Educational Leadership. We thank the many school administrators in the United States and Singapore whose investment of time, energy, and caring made the research possible.

REFERENCES

Argyris, C., & Schön, D. A. (1982). *Theory in practice: Improving professional effectiveness.* San Francisco: Jossey-Bass.
Bateson, G. (1972). *Steps to an ecology of mind.* New York: Ballantine.
Berger, P. L., & Luckmann, T. (1966). *The social construction of reality.* Garden City, NY: Doubleday.

Bolman, L. G., & Deal, T. E. (1991). *Reframing organizations: Artistry, choice and leadership.* San Francisco: Jossey-Bass.

Bolman, L. G., & Deal, T. E. (1992a). Leading and managing: Effects of context, culture and gender. *Educational Administration Quarterly, 28*(3), 314–329.

Bolman, L. G., & Deal, T. E. (1992b). Reframing leadership: The effects of leaders' images of leadership. In K. E. Clark & M. B. Clark (Eds.), *The impact of leadership* (pp. 269–280). Greensboro, NC: Center for Creative Leadership.

Bolman, L. G., & Deal, T. E. (in press). Leadership and management effectiveness: A multi-frame, multi-sector analysis. *Human Resource Management Journal.*

Bransford, J. D., & Stein, B. S. (1984). *The ideal problem-solver.* New York: Freeman.

Brief, A. P., & Downey, H. K. (1983). Cognitive and organizational structure: A conceptual analysis of implicit organizing theories. *Human Relations, 36*(12), 1065–1090.

Cronshaw, S. F. (1987). Effects of categorization, attribution, and encoding processes on leadership perceptions. *Journal of Applied Psychology, 72*(1), 91–106.

Deal, T. E. (1990). Healing our schools: Restoring the heart. In A. Lieberman (Ed.), *Schools as collaborative cultures: Creating the future now* (pp. 127–149). London: Falmer.

Deal, T. E. (1984, Summer). Searching for the wizard: The quest for excellence in education. *Issues in Education, II*(1), 56–67.

Deal, T. E. (1985). The symbolism of effective schools. *Elementary School Journal, 85*(5), 602–620.

Fiedler, K. (1982). Causal schemata: Review and criticism of research on a popular construct. *Journal of Personality and Social Psychology, 42,* 1001–1013.

Fiske, S. T., & Dyer, L. M. (1985). Structure and development of social schemata: Evidence from positive and negative transfer effects. *Journal of Personality and Social Psychology, 48*(4), 839–852.

Frensch, P. A., & Sternberg, R. J. (1991). Skill-related differences in chess playing. In R. J. Sternberg & P. A. Frensch (Eds.), *Complex problem-solving.* Hillsdale, NJ: Lawrence Erlbaum Associates.

Gardner, H. (1983). *Frames of mind: The theory of multiple intelligences.* New York: Basic Books.

Gentner, D. (1988). Metaphor as structure mapping. *Child Development, 59,* 47–59.

Gioia, D. A. (1986). Symbols, scripts, and sensemaking. In H. P. Sims, Jr., D. A. Gioia, & Associates (Eds.), *The thinking organization.* San Francisco: Jossey-Bass.

Goffman, E. (1974). *Frame analysis: An essay on the organization of experience.* Cambridge: Harvard University Press.

Gregory, K. L. (1983). Native view paradigms: Multiple cultures and cultural conflict in organizations. *Administrative Science Quarterly, 28,* 359–376.

James, W. (1950). *Principles of psychology.* New York: Dover.

Kuhn, T. S. (1970). *The structure of scientific revolutions.* Chicago: University of Chicago Press.

Lesgold, A., & Lajoie, S. (1991). Complex problem-solving in electronics. In R. J. Sternberg & P. A. Frensch (Eds.), *Complex problem-solving.* Hillsdale, NJ: Lawrence Erlbaum Associates.

Lord, R. G., & Foti, R. J. (1986). Schema theories, information processing, and organizational behavior. In H. P. Sims, Jr., D. A. Gioia, & Associates (Eds.), *The thinking organization*. San Francisco: Jossey-Bass.

Mitchell, T. R., Rediker, K. J., & Beach, L. R. (1986). Image theory and organizational decision making. In H. P. Sims, Jr., D. A. Gioia, & Associates (Eds.), *The thinking organization*. San Francisco: Jossey-Bass.

Morgan, G. (1986). *Images of organization*. Beverly Hills: Sage.

Pitre, E., & Sims, H. P., Jr. (1987, Autumn). The thinking organization: How patterns of thought determine organizational culture. *National Productivity Review*.

Saudar, A. (1986, Summer). Metaphor and belief. *Journal of Anthropological Research, 42*, 101–122.

Schön, D. A. (1983). *The reflective practitioner*. New York: Basic Books.

Simon, H. A. (1957). *Administrative behavior* (2nd. ed.). New York: Free Press.

Simon, H. A. (1969). *The sciences of the artificial*. Cambridge: M.I.T. Press.

Trost, A. H. (1989). Leadership is flesh and blood. In L. Atwater and R. Penn (Eds.), *Military leadership: Traditions and future trends*. Annapolis, MD: Action Printing and Graphics.

Voss, J. F., Wolfe, C. R., Lawrence, J. A., & Engle, R. A. (1991). From representation to decision: An analysis of problem-solving in international relations. In R. J. Sternberg & P. A. Frensch (Eds.), *Complex problem-solving*. Hillsdale, NJ: Lawrence Erlbaum Associates.

Weick, K. E., & Bougon, M. G. (1986). "Organization as cognitive maps." In H. P. Sims, Jr., D. A. Gioia, & Associates (Eds.), *The thinking organization*. San Francisco: Jossey-Bass.

3   How CEOs Change Their Minds

John C. Glidewell

This chapter is about how 69 chief executive officers (CEOs) of profit-making corporations changed their minds about the business utility of four resources: foreign markets, computers, women, and public images. Although profit-making corporations are quite different from educational organizations, executives in both settings may change their minds in similar ways. Some CEOs did not change their minds about some issues, but this chapter addresses those matters about which all of them changed their minds to some extent. I will begin with some abstract assertions and follow with concrete examples referred to the abstract statements.

OVERVIEW

I propose to explain the following general process:

1. Humans put faith in *cognitive models,* developed over years of confirming experiences. Some such models concern the efficacy of the resources available to the humans. (E.g., IBM makes top quality products.)
2. On occasion, the resources are more or less efficacious than the model predicts they will be. I will call these *discrepant experiences.* Cognitively, the discrepant experiences are first compartmentalized as "special cases" or "exceptions that prove the rule (model)." No change occurs. (IBM is having some quality problems, but they will recover soon.)
3. A *pressure for explanation* of the discrepant experiences, if any, leads to awareness that the model *may* have flaws. (My computer breaks down daily. Why? Could I be wrong about IBM?)
4. With repeated discrepant experiences and continuing pressure to explain them, the explanation integral to the model is *modified* to explain both the confirming and the discrepant experiences. (IBM was once dependable; now it is not.)

For CEOs, each step in the cognitive-change process is accelerated or impeded by these factors:

1. Value conflicts involved in the change (impeding).
2. Changing opinions of the most respected members of the CEO's social network (accelerating).
3. The extent to which the discrepant experiences are seen as a challenge (accelerating) or a burden (impeding).
4. The CEO's perception of the business efficacy of changing his or her model (accelerating).
5. The CEO's general propensity to shift her or his perspective so as to see alternate explanations of experiences, both congruent and discrepant with his or her model (accelerating).

In order to explain this general process of cognitive change, I shall begin with a specific illustration of the general process in the experiences of a typical CEO, then turn to a theoretical explanation of the conceptual framework and the factors accelerating or impeding the process. Having explained the theory, I will describe the methods of the research and present its findings for each of the four resources: foreign markets, computers, women, and public images.

AN INTRODUCTORY ILLUSTRATION

I observed 69 CEOs of for-profit corporations in a number of industries in the United States and abroad. During those observations, the CEOs made important policy changes. The decision-making leading to the policy changes lasted 4 to 8 weeks; policy implementation lasted 8 to 15 months. Immediately after the observations, I interviewed the CEOs about the process of making the decisions to change policy, and about the influences on them during the process. All were faced with pressures to change their minds about some established policies. One policy issue faced by all the CEOs was the issue of increased investment in international markets. The following vignette is typical. All names are fictitious. All quotations are from my notes.

In the late seventies I was studying a very successful American electronics company, then about twelve years old, its market 96 percent in the United States. Will Springer, the CEO, had a reputation for innovation, foresight, and risk-taking, and the company had a reputation for inventive and dependable electronic circuits. This is an account of his thinking, feeling, and actions concerning entering the international market of the nations of the Pacific Rim, as I discerned them from what he did and said.

The Cognitive Model

On one occasion, Will was preparing for a meeting with all the officers of the corporation. "This is an important meeting," he said. "We have to decide if we are going to invest in the Pacific Rim. Oriental businessmen have private rules of loyalty . . . tied to the deepest part of their cultural beliefs, [rules] that they keep closely to themselves. They screw outsiders as a matter of principle. I'm scared of them."

In the meeting, Will made such statements as the following: "Let's take Japan first. That's closed as tight as a submarine." A little later: "All right, the Rim is a lot more than Japan, but, man, those are strange cultures. Centuries old. Very, very polite. Their ways may not be genetic, I don't know, but they are hard-wired in them. They give kick-backs to their brothers and screw all foreigners. It's all tied together."

In Will's mind the components, such as family favoritism, excess courtesy, deceit, secret rules, and sabotage of foreigners, were tightly linked partly because he regularly had found them together in his contacts with or in accounts of the markets, but more so because of what he saw as an underlying force generated by the deepest beliefs of the cultures: "Hard wired in them." The activation of one component in Will's mind activated all the others.

Discrepant Experiences and Compartmentalization

A fellow CEO expressed confidence that, if IBM could make money in Japan, so could other high-tech companies. Will, however, responded, "Japan is a closed market to me. . . . We are one-tenth the size of IBM and have none of their cross-cultural experience. *IBM is a special case. Doesn't apply to us.*" When Will's marketing vice-president excitedly forecast a ballooning of the Pacific Rim market, he again resisted: "What I hear is trouble. We just don't buy into bribery. OK, it will be a really big market, but *it just doesn't fit our management style.*" During the following year, Will often said, "I'm tired of hearing about the Pacific Rim. It's an alien world." He was burdened by the discrepant cases and by his view that the prospects of growth violated values of honesty, fairness, and freedom, values he held deeply.

Pressure for Explanation

Will placed great value on rationality. All events had causes. Will explained the disutility of this foreign market by attributing the practices and values he saw in the Pacific Rim to deep, driving cultural forces. That explanation held the components of his model tightly together. Yet the very pressure for rationality that generated his explanation (however valid) of the alien world he perceived was also the pressure that demanded that he explain his "special cases." In addition, some members of his social network challenged him to explain the accumulating collection of special cases. Will began to accept the challenge. "It's a fact," he said to one fellow CEO. "Our profits [from the Rim] are increasing without much effort from us. I sure didn't expect that. There's a reason, I just don't know what it is—yet . . . *I could be wrong, you know.* There's a good reason why good American companies are doing good business in Singapore."

The next month Will sent a group of his subordinates to Thailand to estimate the company's market potential there and in Singapore. "A toe in the water," he said to the group as they left. "I have to find out *if I have been wrong* about this whole thing," he said to me after they were gone.

In summary, the pressure to explain his own unexpected successes, and those of others, challenged Will and he began to question his model. He saw that the preference, deceit, graft, and exclusion did not, in fact, occur as he expected. All those accumulated special cases demanded explanation, at least for Will. Trying to find that explanation led Will to experiment with some new decisions and actions, as a "toe in the water."

A New Model

After another year, Will had invested heavily in the Pacific Rim, had at least broken even, and was saying very different things to his subordinates, to his peers, and to me. "Well, we won the respect of a few influential people there, real respect. We did what we said we would do and did it well. Our circuits work well. . . . Now we have our own buddies. OK, we're not relatives, but we are not foreigners either. We're respected trading partners."

Another time: "Koreans are as competitive and individualistic as we are. All we needed were a few rules and a few contracts and a few excellent products." Will was now attributing successes to common motives and values: "competitive and individualistic as we are."

Soon afterward, Will articulated a complex new model: "It's a new economic world. A very future-oriented world, a very change-oriented world, and a whole world economy, a whole world market. If we are to survive, let alone grow, we have to compete in that world market, and we are doing it. Think about that, Jack, a new, free, worldwide market. No matter what goes on inside a country, a free world market will regulate them. [I frowned.] O.K., it's a long way from free now, but look at the change in the last year. That's the way the world is moving. I finally got that through my head, and man that was tough for me, but the tough changes pay off, don't they, if you figure the risks and figure them right. The people in the Pacific Rim are . . . *driven to work in a free, competitive world just like we are.*"

Summary

This general process of changing one's mind was characteristic of all 69 CEOs. Leaving the illustrative vignette, I now propose to elaborate the conceptual framework and accelerating factors, then to report the methods of the research and the findings for the four resources at issue. First, the concepts.

CONCEPTUAL FRAMEWORK

Cognitive Model

Following Hayes-Roth's (1977) definition of a schema and the dissent from "schema theory" by Lakoff (1987), I maintain that a cognitive model is a set of psychosocial components, more or less tightly linked to each other, more or less unitized, and often named. The components include ideas, percepts, values, motives, and feelings. The linkages of the components can be relationships such as these: simple closeness in time and space (baseball and hot dogs are seen at the same times and places; although they have no common components, they "go together"), similarity along some dimension ("Competitiveness is much like ambition"), part-whole relationships ("Fair trade, quid pro quo, is an integral part of business"), covariance ("Deceit increases when oppression increases"), sequential order ("Polite overtures come first, entrapment comes next"), causation ("caused by deep cultural beliefs"), or some goal-directed joining of the components (such as "things needed to fly a kite," or "uses of computers in management decision-making"). I shall argue that, in these data, attributed causation by some underlying influence was a particularly powerful linkage.

Unitization is a function of the strength of the linkages. The more tightly components are linked, the more extensive the activation of other components by a single component; the more extensive the activation of the whole model by the activation of one component, the greater the unitization. For Will, any one of the components—closed social networks, exclusion, deceit, bribery—immediately activated the whole model "Pacific Rim."

A schematic illustration of the initial and the modified cognitive models of the utility of computers in business is shown in Figure 3.1. The size of the oval represents the importance of the component; the number of connecting lines represents the strength of the linkages; the distance between the ovals represents the speed with which they activate each other. The modified model includes a component called "Organize Intuition," a new component not included in the initial model. The initial component "Complex Software" has become "Heuristic Business Models" and given much more importance. The most tightly linked components of the initial model are quite different from the

Figure 3.1 Schematic Diagram of Cognitive Models

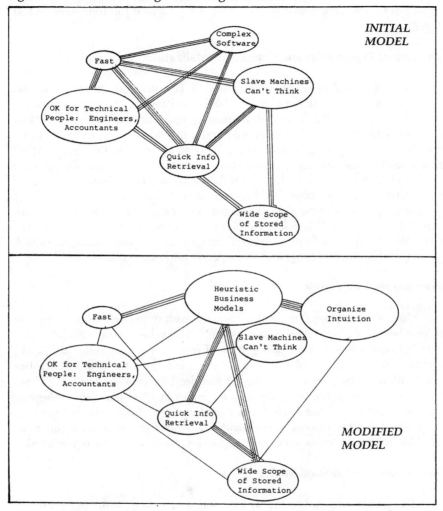

tightly linked components of the revised model. Unitization of the revised model is not complete but advanced.

The initial models of the business utility of the four resources at issue were well developed, quite tightly linked, moderately unitized, and referred to by these names: foreign markets, computers, women, and public images. I studied 69 quite different CEOs as they changed their models of the utility of four resources; thus, there were 276 such changes. I focused, however, on the common elements of the ideas of the 69 CEOs, and used the four models *common* to all the CEOs for my analysis, one model for each of the four resources at issue.

Discrepant Experiences and Compartmentalization

Following and combining the ideas of Higgins and Bargh (1987) on changes in social cognition and those of Medin (1989) on changes in cognitive models, I maintain that a new, discrepant component (experience) is at first excluded from the model and is considered a special case, not to be confused with the usual dependable case represented by the model. Remember Will's insistence that the strange overseas successes were special cases that did not apply to his situation. Often but certainly not always, the relegation to special circumstances can be considered stereotypical beliefs and/or case thinking: "Oh, that's a case of engineering management. You'd expect a lot of computer runs." The new and excluded components can be considered compartmental-ized ideas about disconfirming experiences, ideas kept separate from the model, as observed by Taylor (1981) and Weber and Crocker (1983).

Pressure for Explanation

Once a special case is recognized as discrepant from one's model, it usually demands explanation. "Why is this special?" The value set on rationality and explanation is one key to the integration of new components into old models, and to a change in the explanation of the main linkage of the components. Re-call Will's concern: "There's a reason; I just don't know what it is yet." These CEOs acted and talked as if the four resources at issue had some inherent, natural, inner forces that made them what they were, linked the components of the model of the resources, and made the resources useful for business or troublesome for business, very much as Medin (1989) would have predicted.

Movement to a Modified Model

The pressure to explain the surface phenomena (e.g., Will's perception of deceit, exclusion, graft, and exploitation in the Pacific Rim) by attribution to underlying, deeply rooted forces (centuries-old cultural beliefs) also, to some extent, drives one to explain special cases and, in the process, to modify one's model (e.g., Will's attribution of competitive urges and individualism in addition to alien cultural beliefs). Eventually, one finds old and new forces to be similar, fuses the old and new explanations, and develops a changed explanation that includes both special and familiar cases. A modified model emerges, a model that includes new components, new linkages (explanations), a model not yet tightly linked and unitized but becoming so. For example, Will's excited forecast and explanation: "Think about that, Jack, a new free, worldwide market. . . . The people in the Pacific Rim are . . . *driven to work in a free, competitive world just like we are.*"

How certain could I be that a modified model emerged, that a CEO had changed his or her mind? Said one, "I didn't change my mind; I just improved our policy."

Whether or not they admitted the change, what I saw and what they (and their subordinates) told me about their confidence in clear and explicit new policies made me certain that a cognitive change had taken place, that a modified model had emerged.

VARIABLES AFFECTING COGNITIVE CHANGE

Celerity Factors

Each of the five celerity factors accelerating or impeding cognitive change was specific to the combination of the CEO and the resource at issue, neither a stable personality characteristic of the CEO nor a stable property of the resource at issue. They had been identified as relevant in previous research. (1) *Value conflicts,* and especially conflicts between values and commonplace practices, have often been found to be factors in social change (e.g., by Lewin, 1943). (2) *Social networks,* studied both by Lewin and by Wellman (1988), showed that interactions in social networks have changed ideas as well as resisted such change. (3) With respect to *challenge,* Kobasa (1979) has confirmed that hardiness under stress was partly due to perceiving the stress to be a challenge rather than a burden. (4) The effect of *business efficacy* was a logical derivation from pragmatism of the economic institution. I have been asked, "Wasn't it business greed that changed their minds?" I answer, "No, but it speeded up the change." (5) Concerning *ease of shifting perspective,* Feffer (1970) successfully adapted Piaget's decentration (an ability to change one's focus of attention or change one's perspective) concept to apply to adults. One could also call the tendency "open mindedness" about the utility of a resource.

Background

Three sets of external forces may have accelerated or impeded the cognitive changes: (1) contextual: the nature of the organization and its industry; specifically, the size of the organization, the competitiveness of the industry, the age of the organization; (2) personal: the age, pragmatism, and characteristic mood of the CEO; (3) resources at issue: foreign markets, computers in management, women executives in business, and contrived images. I maintain that the celerity factors were independent of the background variables, because the strength of the discrepant experiences and the pressure for explanation of them was similar for all people in all contexts.

METHODS

This research on social cognition was part of a larger research project on the exercise of power by corporate chief executive officers. The research began because, in the process of training in organization development, some CEOs asked, "Jack, couldn't you and I find some time just to put our feet up on a rail and talk, just talk privately?" Those private talks led me to make systematic observations, take notes, and interview the CEO about my observations. The observations and interviews were often made in the context of consultation and training. With a limited number of exceptions, the CEOs and I became friends and confidants.

The research had no external financing. I was paid for consultation and training. Neither the CEOs nor the corporations made any financial contribution to the research. I was given permission to publish my findings on the condition of complete confidentiality.

Sample

Data were collected from the CEOs of 69 corporations. The corporations were a sample of convenience, determined by the interest of the CEO. Of those 69, 56 were in the United States and Canada, 6 in the United Kingdom and Europe, 6 in Mexico and South America, 1 in Australia. The corporations were from the major industries of the world. With respect to size, 13 had revenues over $1 billion, 30 had revenues over $100 million but less than $1 billion, and 26 had revenues less than $100 million. Of the 69 CEOs, 38 were appointed to the position, 22 founded the company and created the position, 9 inherited the position in a family-owned company. With respect to age, 12 were in their thirties, 27 in their forties, 22 in their fifties, and 8 in their sixties. Only two CEOs were women.

Data Collection

Data were collected from 1969 through 1983. I followed the CEOs in their daily work and after it, and I interviewed them almost immediately about their goals and the means of attaining them, their roles, their hopes, fears, and ideas about "what was going on" in their activities. The minimum contact was 10 hours a day for five consecutive days (13 cases); the maximum, 15 hours a day, one day every two months, for five years (11 cases); the typical, one 10-hour day, monthly for one year (45 cases).

Our commitment to confidentiality was very strong. The interaction was almost always relaxed, informal, and quite frank. The interviews were more introspective than is typical for these people, who tended to act rather than reflect. But the CEOs began and continued the daily sessions over the varying periods specified above because they had strong needs for very confidential— and atypical—reflection on their lives and roles.

Data Analysis

To analyze the data I read, reflected on, re-read the notes, and inferred the nature of the processes of the change of cognitive models. I found that all of the 69 CEOs confronted issues of the utility of the four resources previously specified. I found the background data and ages in public sources. Personal data, celerity factors, and confidence in new policy were my observations or taken from company records.

THE FINDINGS

Foreign Markets

This section is confined to 47 American CEOs who were not heads of multinational corporations at the time I began the study as well as the one Australian who was so like the Americans on this issue that I chose to include him with them. The nine North American multinational CEOs, like five of the six CEOs in the United Kingdom and Europe, and all six in Latin America had confronted the issues of the utility of foreign markets quite some years before. They still had some distrust of "foreign" cultures, but they had much more experience and confidence in markets that were foreign to them—for those in Europe and Latin America, especially the foreign U.S. market.

The Initial Model. The data were collected between 1969 and 1983, a time when CEOs were becoming more and more aware of both foreign competition and the lure of foreign markets. The opportunities and risks of entering foreign markets were salient in the conversations and in the minds of many business men and women.

As with Will, so it was for all the nationally focused CEOs. At first, value conflicts developed because foreign markets were seen as strange, unjust, oppressive, deceitful, and frightening—even if ripe for development. These officers had heard much about oppressive sweatshops with their neglected and belittled workers in Latin America and Asia, of government-supported cartels, and of the exclusive business circles of both Asia and Europe. To develop a foreign market meant, in their minds, to collude in deception and corruption, and in the deprivation of many very vulnerable people. A typical comment was "I understand holding down labor costs and how desperate people need jobs, but I also understand sucking blood from desperate people, and I will always oppose it."

Although it was not a time of intense patriotism, the offices and work areas of the U.S. corporations were infused with American symbols. Early in the studies, the Vietnam war was intense and the conflicts about it were equally intense among corporate officers. Nevertheless, posters, paintings, furniture, tools, sculpture, pin-ups, clothes, and automobiles were those that were in vogue and made in the United States.

Discrepant Experiences and Compartmentalization. The first pressures for change came from the social network. The other business men and women in that network often expressed their awe of the fact that IBM was drawing steadily increasing proportions of its profits from overseas. They talked of many food companies, such as the Heinz Company, that had been multinational in Western nations for 50 years. Now, however, more of the multinationals' corporate profits were from outside the United States; all had at least an outpost in Asia. The word was out. These CEOs were just beginning to say such things as "Malaysia may be unstable, but, God, what a potential, what a dynamic market it could be." All the countries in the Pacific Rim were seen as alien and unstable, but the network buzzed with talk of the challenging opportunities for those who could afford the risks. Almost all, however, saw the discrepant reports and experiences as "special cases." "Those are special and really risky markets; they just don't fit into our strategic plan."

Pressure for Explanation. Next, there was, as there was with Will, pressure for rational explanation of the unexpected experiences and reports, and attention to possible underlying causes. The needed explanation was easy for some, hard for others. Note these comments:

> The culture is alien but you have to say they are very future-oriented and out for change toward our way of business. You have to figure that out, if you're going to know what's going on there.

> They want more power in the world; well, so do we. That power drive explains our dedication and our greed. I guess it explains their dedication and their greed. What explains their ethnocentrism? What explains ours?

In their basic drives they are human, too, just treacherous, really treacherous. The basic drive is cultural, I know, but I want to know more about what makes them tick as business men.

The Modified Model. Then, later, I heard the fusion of the old and the new explanations, reflected in the following comments.

Economically, we are in a new world order now, right now. The world market is now regulated by market forces, even in communist countries. If they are in the world market, they are regulated by market forces.

The exclusiveness, corruption, and acquisitiveness of the old model is now fused with a vision of a world market, competitive and acquisitive, but regulated by forces of supply and demand that, sooner or later, can contain, they believed, even exclusive, corrupt, and acquisitive cultures.

By 1982, the U.S. offices and work areas were markedly more international. The amount of time spent outside the United States by the CEOs had increased from an average of 10 percent to an average of 30 percent. Only half of the posters, paintings, and ceramics were inspired by American symbols. Furniture, tools, telephones, and automobiles made overseas were everywhere in evidence. Audio and video equipment was almost all from foreign manufacturers.

Summary. I discerned a movement from a tightly linked, moderately unitized explanation of the inadvisability of entering foreign markets to a clear recognition of special cases. Next I saw an attempt to explain the special cases. The drive for explanation led to a shift of perspective: "They are individualistic, competitive, and ambitious. All they need is a little morality." "I doubt we have anything to be concerned [read 'frightened'] about." Finally, a new model emerged that incorporated foreign markets as a part of an explanation of all markets, including the changing United States: "We are in a new world order right now. The world market is now regulated by market forces, . . . even in the face of really dumb government interference."

Computers

The Initial Model. During these studies, business became more and more dependent on computers. The pressure to harness the new, super-fast kind of information processing was intense. At the beginning, in 1969, computer language was largely confined to the "computer whizzes." There were no computer graphics on office walls or on easels in conference rooms. Computers' lack of utility for management was explained by their basic automated nature—"mindless electrical circuits." With respect to value conflicts, computers were seen as paragons of restricted freedom, especially freedom of thought, and only as honest as those who fed them. "Computers are automatons. They can store and supply a library of information, and they are miraculously fast, but they solve mathematical problems, not management problems."

Discrepant Experiences and Compartmentalization. Apple's introduction of the PC kicked off the change. As PCs appeared in the homes of the senior corporate officers, they, and their families, began to acquire a little of the perspective of the "computer whizzes." Using computers became a challenge rather than a burden. Network members who owned PCs also began to use the language and concepts of computer models. One had to keep up with one's friends, sometimes with one's children.

PCs were at first compartmentalized special cases. "They're OK for engineers and accountants, sure, but [computers] can't think, can't create, can't manage. They're bound by their software." "Computer models of business are pretty simplistic." Furthermore, computer terminals had a keyboard attached. To get information from the computer, one must type. Typing was a symbol of low status. Focusing on the keyboard, CEOs said, "Put it on my secretary's desk. I'm no typist."

Pressure for Explanation. Computer models of management issues (running on PCs as well as main-frames) were indeed simple. Nevertheless, the software models of business planning sparked the pressure for development of what could be very useful business models and challenged the CEO's readiness. CEOs said such things as, "Why not construct my own models, the way *I* believe the management variables are related?" Selecting or making computer models of business phenomena forced the CEOs to think in ways unnatural to many of them. Often the CEOs did not accept the read-out from their models, but they had to defend their disagreement to themselves. As the CEOs found themselves challenged by arguing with their own computer models, the business utility of the computer was established.

The Modified Model. The explanation of special cases (PCs and main-frames in accounting and engineering) had merged with a broader and deeper explanation of the utility of the generic computer. It made one take account of more contingencies, more data, and organize them, qualitatively and quantitatively, more nearly completely into a model. Further, the output from the computer made one argue and think.

There were, of course, individual differences in the tightness of the linkages and the unitization of the modified model, but the variance was not as wide as that of the changes for the other resources at issue. The business utility of computers was no longer an issue by the end of the 1970s—but the new model had the old name, "Computers."

Women Executives

This section includes the two women CEOs. They had become CEOs during a period of time, the 1960s, when women CEOs were even more rare than they are now, and they were not typical of contemporary women CEOs. In fact, in 1970, these two shared the model of women that the men held. They believed themselves to be exceptions, and they believed that only radically exceptional women—"more like a man"—had any place in business.

The Initial Model. Ignoring for the moment the usual individual differences, these officers (men and women) started with a cognitive model that explained the uselessness of women to business on the basis of genetic and social heritage. By virtue of that heritage, women were driven by protective and nurturing motives that led them to be soft-hearted, deceitful, seductive, and demanding of commitments that restricted the freedom of others. A typical 1970 comment was, "Women are great facilitators of development of people, great HRD people, but really wimpy management people, the proverbial tits on a boar."

Discrepant Experiences and Compartmentalization. Soon the women's movement was going full steam and successful women entrepreneurs popped up in the social networks. A few gained membership in the networks. The history of the 1970s and 1980s is replete with accounts of these successful business women. Even so, in the minds of these CEOs, women fell in a rather tight cognitive compartment of their own, albeit a very complex one—for example:

> Look, any culture has to have some feminine roles—some life-giving, life-protecting, human value-upholding, nurturing roles. Men may be necessary to fertilization, but women are necessary to birth, and the physical closeness of birth makes them the life-givers, the protectors, the nurturers, people that any civilization has to have to sustain itself and improve the quality and meaning of its lot . . . [I say] mothers and children, but, man, let me tell you, adults must have some form of life-protection and teaching and healing. Take that function away and you undermine the civilization. Women develop people; men exploit them. Women protect the planet; men endanger it. Women cure diseases, men ration cures. Women ensure justice; men deceive it. Get women really, really into technological, financial efficiency and you destroy the civilization. Please, keep women out of the real business part of business.

Pressure for Explanation. Effectiveness demanded explanation. Women challenged such values as cold rationality and freedom from commitment, and invoked such familiar values as justice and truth. Respected friends began to change their policies about hiring and promoting women executives. Men CEOs found a shift of perspective quite difficult, but again the pressure in their own minds for explanation sparked changes.

Changes were initiated as soon as one tried to find explanations for the fast-growing number of exceptional women executives. "As destructive as business men? Maybe. Maybe not. Time will tell," said one CEO. These executives had to explain the new values, new perspectives, new opinions, new challenges of women. They saw the business efficacy of bargaining for *joint* returns. They sought equity as getting a return proportionate to one's contribution, rather than to one's advantages. Controversies over successful women executives engaged the CEOs and they argued the pros and cons in dining rooms as well as board rooms. In the engagement, they began to include new components and new explanations in changing cognitive models of women executives.

The Modified Model. At first, legal pressures for affirmative action challenged the CEOs to find and promote "rare" talented women. Later, they even negotiated creatively with a few talented women who were militant to the point of making quite excessive demands. For example, one recent graduate of a law school, applying for a job as a staff attorney, demanded that a new position be created for her, a position reporting directly to the CEO rather than through the general counsel. Another applicant with two years of executive experience demanded a senior vice-presidency of finance. In my view, these demands were opening positions to begin negotiation, but even as openers they shocked the CEO. "Did you hear what she asked for? Man, that's some chutzpah!" These applicants were often exceptional executives. Their initial demands were followed by remarkably creative and successful negotiations, in both my view and those of the CEOs involved. Most—certainly not all—of the men were challenged by the prospects of creative negotiation. It was a new kind of negotiation for mutual respect, and considering the pressing demand, legal and consensual, for talented business women, the negotiations could lead to important resources for the corporation.

Value conflicts about nurturance versus economic utility changed to congruencies about skillful negotiation, aimed at maximizing joint returns, very much as Pruitt (1981) might have recommended. Over the 14 years of these studies, the CEOs (including the two women) and their social networks saw that women were important business resources in ways impossible to ignore.

Many men decided that the recently perceived inherent forces driving women were also the forces driving business. "Women do sharp negotiation. That yields profits for us and everybody, growth of all the resources available to all the people. Free business is freedom to pursue profits and growth—all of us are after that." Individual variations in the change of explanations were great, but the change gradually reached *every* CEO in this sample. The name of the model remained "Women," but it was spoken with a tone of challenge rather than a tone of burden.

Image Building

The Initial Model. For most of these executives, to construct a deliberately contrived, guilefully altruistic image of the corporation violated even their pragmatic view of the value of truth. If their spoiling of the rivers or the air injured the corporate reputation, they wanted to recapture respect without shading the truth or touting aspirations devoid of accomplishments.

But this initial model was unstable. Guile was attractive. Their aspirations were more encouraging than their accomplishments. The value conflicts were there for all of the CEOs, but they varied from somewhat uncomfortable to quite painful. "A public image of a corporation—or a CEO—that is not true, well, it just leads to bad business judgments." The initial model was built on the attribution of honesty as the underlying force, but the force was not as strong as in models of the other three resources. The model was not as tightly linked, as unitized, but it was named "Image Building."

Discrepant Experiences and Compartmentalization. While "reasonably" honest public relations had been a routine function in the corporations, the seventies brought a sharp increase in discrepant experiences: contrived image building. Corporations were severely criticized during the sixties and seventies for a callous indifference to the well-being of both employees and customers and to the rape of the physical environment. The pressure to counteract these allegations, just and unjust, was very strong.

Moreover, the leaders of the networks of the CEOs were often master image builders. They succeeded in developing and keeping corporate reputations for both rare business talent and rare dedication to public interest, whether accurate or not. Those exemplars were ever-present, attractive role models. Their guileful but clear successes demanded explanation. The successes were at first considered to be the usual special cases, "all right for a dishonest corporation, but not for an honest one, such as ours."

Pressure for Explanation. The honesty issue was raised in locker rooms, at dinner tables, and in business conferences. Was honest image building good for the business? Did not customers look for the best buys no matter how callous the corporation? Would overstatements be exposed as deceit and discredit the corporation in the long run? Not as far as these CEOs could see. (*Exxon Valdez* had yet not gone aground.) They had to admit that inspiring, enticing images seemed to be quickly accepted by investment communities and by customers. The data available to the CEOs led to a clear, new, and different explanation: People desperately wanted to believe that the corporations they so much depended on were, indeed, dependable.

Sooner or later logos and mottoes rang with high purposes and with commitments to quality. "Quality is our first priority!" "People are our most important asset!" "We protect our planet." These dubious slogans were shouted by both actors and workers from television sets, were spread across *New York Times* and *Fortune* ads, were repeated by articles in trade journals and popular business magazines. I asked, did they work? "Well, they certainly seemed to." I asked, "Why?" "People wanted to hear them."

The Modified Model. In this psychosocial climate of opinion, the CEOs were much rewarded for focusing on aspirations while leaving actual practices, accomplishments, and failures under clouds of haze. The explanations for those rewards for deceit were more cynical than many CEOs could tolerate, and therefore they held, quite precariously, that their own companies' image constructions were the honest exceptions to the general cognitive model, exceptions explained by the CEO's integrity. Others shifted to the cynical explanation: "Tell the folks what they want to hear and they'll buy your products and your stock." In this imagery, the fusion of old and new forces was an exceedingly difficult fusion of deceit and honesty. Most adopted the cynical explanation of the utility of image building.

The change of cognitive model was a change from clear values, however deep or shallow their roots, to a cynical manipulation of part truths and outright distortions. Often the publicity to counter an allegation of callousness was an ad campaign of denial that showed actors playing the roles of workers and customers attesting to the warm and caring actions of the company. A quite recent example of denial is General Motors' announcing the closing of *some* plants without specifying which. Newspapers quoted Stempel, the CEO, thus: "We are not in the process of 'whipsawing' [putting one local labor union in conflict with the others to offer concession to keep their plant open]. I want to be very clear about that right up front." Most denials were more guileful than GM's, but denial was the norm. Every CEO changed at least a little toward the cynical model of image building; most changed enough to change policies; a few changed to an extremely cynical model. "People need to believe you are noble. Publicize your lofty goals, forget your selfish schemes. It's just good business; you can't get away from it." But the explanation was not an integration of old and new; it was an all new, cynical explanation. Business efficacy was the major accelerating force.

Table 3.1 The Process of Cognitive Change

	The Resources at Issue			
	Foreign Markets	Computers in Business	Women in Business	Image Building

Phases of the Cognitive Change Process				
Initial Model	Treacherous Exclusive	Mindless Technology	Useless Motherly	Honest Informative
Discrepant Exper/ Others Compart'ization	Profitable for Others	Fast, Handy Rigid	Successful when Man-like	Some Dishonest
Pressure for Explanation	Why Profit for Others	Explain Own Business Model	Why so many Successful	Why Deceit Rewarded
Modified Model	Free World Market	Useful Tools for Analysis	Astute Executives	Enhanced Image Demanded

Accelerating and Impeding Factors				
Value Conflict	Oppression vs Freedom	Technology vs Heuristic	Nurturance vs Competition	Honesty vs Dishonesty
Social Network	Endorse Feasibility Profitability	Endorse Heuristic Models	Endorse Negotiation Talent	Endorse Pragmatic Enhancement
Challenge/ Burden	Opportunity Challenging	Model Bldg Challenging	Negotiation Challenging	Honest Images Challenging
Business Efficacy	Profitability Attractive	Model Bldg Efficacious	Woman's Perspective	Enhancement Works
Propensity for Shifting Perspective	Not ready for Shift	Open to New Perspective	Resistant to Shift	Beguiled into Enhancement

SUMMARY

Table 3.1 provides a condensed summary of the findings. CEOs began to change their minds when discrepant cases were experienced but kept separate from the tightly linked, unified, and named cognitive models that were challenged by the special cases. The CEOs sought explanations for the special cases, attributing, as causes, both familiar and newly inferred inner forces underlying the phenomena. As the special cases became more frequent, the CEOs found similarities between the old and new inner forces, and eventually fused the old and new into a changed explanation that included both special and familiar cases. The speed of the movement toward new explanations and the development of new policies were influenced by these factors: value conflicts; discrepant social network opinions; whether the discrepancies were seen as a challenge or a burden; the perceived business efficacy of a possible new policy; and the facility for changing perspective on the resource at issue. In these 69 cases, the outcome was a new cognitive model, including new components and new linkages (explanations), a model not yet tightly linked and unitized, but becoming so, and identified by the old name.

These findings do not lend themselves to "how-to" prescriptions for changing one's mind and one's policies, or for facilitating the change of mind in others. The research was intended to enhance understanding of "how some humans did change their minds," rather than "how humans should change their minds." The findings do provide some new understandings of how executives, and perhaps many of us as we consider policy changes, are influenced by value conflicts, economic efficacy, opinions of respected others in our social networks, the sense of challenge or burden of social pressures, and our own facility for changing our perspective about the utility of new resources. I doubt that this understanding alone will enable us simply to resist or accept the influences identified by these data. However, a fuller awareness may enable us to avoid misinterpretations of why we or our colleagues did or did not change our minds about the utility of some new, and perhaps strange, resource.

REFERENCES

Feffer, M. (1970). Developmental analysis of interpersonal behavior. *Psychological Review, 77*, 197–214.

Hayes-Roth, B. (1977). Evolution of cognitive structure and process. *Psychological Review, 84*, 260–278.

Higgins, E. T., & Bargh, J. A. (1987). Social cognition and social perception. *Annual Review of Psychology, 38*, 369–425.

Kobasa, S. (1979). Stressful life events, personality, and health: An inquiry into hardiness. *Journal of Personality and Social Psychology, 37*, 1–11.

Lakoff, G. (1987). *Women, fire, and dangerous things*. Chicago: University of Chicago Press.

Lewin, K. (1943). *Personality and social change*. New York: Dryden.

Medin, D. L. (1989). Concepts and conceptual structure. *American Psychologist, 44*, 1469–1481.

Pruitt, D. G. (1981). *Negotiation behavior.* New York: Academic Press.

Taylor, S. E. (1981). A categorization approach to stereotyping. In D. L. Hamilton (Ed.), *Cognitive processes in stereotyping and intergroup behavior.* Hillsdale, NJ: Lawrence Erlbaum Associates.

Weber, R., & Crocker, J. (1983). Cognitive processes in the revision of stereotypic beliefs. *Journal of Personality and Social Psychology, 45,* 961–977.

Wellman, B. (1988). Structural analysis: From method and metaphor to theory and substance. In B. Wellman & S. D. Berkowitz (Eds.), *Social structures: A network approach* (pp. 19–61). Cambridge: Cambridge University Press.

4 Pragmatism, Participation, and Duty: Value Themes in Superintendents' Problem-Solving

Tiiu Raun and Kenneth Leithwood

There is an extensive literature in the fields of management and administration concerned with decision-making and problem-solving processes (e.g., DeBono, 1985; Fox, 1987; Kepner & Tregoe, 1981). By far the bulk of this literature, as described by Wagner (this volume), is prescriptive in nature and assumes that such processes ought to be almost entirely rational—for example, Kepner and Tregoe (1981) entitle their book *The New Rational Manager.* In contrast, a smaller but impressive body of literature has devoted theoretical attention to the role of values in administration (e.g., Barnard, 1938; Simon, 1976; Weber, 1949). This literature acknowledges for administrators what is considered common sense for people more generally: that values are a critical aspect of thinking and problem-solving (Frankena, 1973; Rokeach, 1973). In spite of this seemingly common sense proposition, the empirical study of administration has traditionally "ignore[d] value and sentiments as springs of human action" (Greenfield, 1985, p. 59). The study reported in this chapter is a response to this neglect.

While research about the values of educational administrators is in its infancy, the values of business executives have been explored more extensively. Both theoretical and empirical insights from such research are helpful in the study of educational administrators' values and similarities with results of the limited research in education are already apparent. Hambrick and Brandon (1988), for example, propose a conception of the links between values and actions (or problem-solving, for our purposes) that begins to explain, with some precision, *why* values are critical in problem-solving. Of the two links they propose, one is direct: Values influence executives' actions directly when such actions or solutions are selected strictly because of their preference. Begley and Leithwood (1989) reported instances of such influence in principals' decisions about adopting computer technology in their schools. Leithwood and Stager

(1989) also reported a form of direct influence of values on problem-solving in their comparison of differences in how expert and typical principals solved ill-structured (knowledge-lean) problems. Experts were much clearer about their values, and, as a consequence, could and did use them as substitutes for the more problem-specific knowledge, which would have helped them but which they lacked. The direct influence of values on problem-solving is called "behavior-channeling" (England, 1967).

Indirect effects of executives' values on their problem-solving, termed "perceptual screening," also are proposed by Hambrick and Brandon (1988). In this case, values influence the perceptual saliency of stimuli: Executives see or hear what they want to see or hear. Perceptual screening may have a dramatic influence on the problems executives choose to notice and how these problems are defined. Leithwood and Steinbach (1990) have reported significant differences between expert and typical secondary principals' definition of problems, partly due to differences in their value orientations.

Both the direct and indirect effects of values on problem-solving, proposed by Hambrick and Brandon (1988), are modified by the amount of discretion executives' environments permit. In general, the more discretion allowed executives, the greater the probable effect of executives' values. Assuming that discretion is greater in more senior roles, values are especially important to consider in the problem-solving of CEOs. Hambrick and Brandon's (1988) model also suggests that when discretion permits, strongly held values will have a more direct influence on problem-solving than will weaker values. Furthermore, particular types of values (e.g., duty) may influence problem-solving in unique ways (e.g., cause executives to be more or less aggressive about their own values). Accordingly, a better understanding of CEOs' values—their nature and development—seems critical to a fuller appreciation of CEOs' problem-solving processes.

Questions concerning the nature and development of CEOs' values were pursued in the research reported in this chapter. In the next section we review research pertinent to each of these questions. Then we describe the methods used to collect our own evidence about these questions. Results of our data analysis are reported and discussed in the final two sections of the chapter.

PREVIOUS RESEARCH

The Nature of Values Used in CEOs' Problem-Solving

A value in Hodgkinson's terms is "a conception, explicit or implicit, distinctive of an individual or characteristic of a group, of the desirable which influences the selection from available modes, means and ends of action" (1978, p.

121). Imbedded in this definition are attributes of values also evident in the work of Kluckhon (1951), Rokeach (1973), and Williams (1968). That is:

• A value is an enduring belief about the desirability of some means or end
• Once internalized, a value also becomes a standard or criterion for guiding one's actions and thought, for influencing the actions and thoughts of others, and for morally judging oneself and others.

As Rokeach (1973) suggests, a person's value system is a learned set of rules for making choices and for resolving conflicts.

To inquire about the values used by CEOs in problem-solving, we were guided by a classification of values developed in our previous work and summarized in Table 4.1. This classification of values is a synthesis and modification of two value frameworks—one proposed by Hodgkinson (1978), the other by Beck (1984a,b,c). Hodgkinson (1978) proposes four categories of values:

1. *Transrational values* grounded in principle;
2a. *Rational values* based on an individual's assessment of consequences, the attainment of what is perceived as right;
2b. *Rational values* based on an individual's assessment of consensus, again, the attainment of which is perceived as right;
3. *Subrational values* related to personal preferences or what is perceived as good.

Type 3 values represent an individual's conception of what is "good." Such values are grounded in affect or emotion and constitute the individual's preference structure. They are self-justifying and primitive. Each of the remaining categories of values describes a "rightness" that, according to Hodgkinson, is higher than the one below it. Type 3 values, unlike the others, represent what is good as opposed to what is right.

Type 2 values are subclassified: Type 2a values define rightness in relation to a desirable future state of affairs or analysis of the consequences entailed by the value judgment; Type 2b values attribute rightness to consensus or the will of the majority in a given collectivity. Type 2 values, as a whole, are rational; Type 3 values are subrational; and Type 1 values are transrational.

Hodgkinson (1978) argues that Type 1 values are superior, more authentic, better justified, or more defensible than the other types. Indeed, use of these "sacred" values in decision-making, according to Hodgkinson, is the hallmark of the ethical educational leader. Such a leader "seeks to increase his own degrees of freedom (a Type 1 value) and the degrees of freedom of those who function under his aegis" (p. 8). However, Hodgkinson also claims that values tend to lose their level of grounding with time, thereby reducing their authen-

Table 4.1 Categories of Values Used in Administrative Problem-Solving

Categories of Values	Illustrative Statement
Set 1 Basic Human Values	
• Freedom	• Staff is not forced to supervise dances by the Education Act ... I would not force people to do this
• Happiness	• Most people felt pretty good about those goals
• Knowledge	• I would collect as much information about the probable suspects as possible
• Respect for others	• In a blanket approach you could offend many teachers
• Survival	• I don't think you can let an issue like this dominate a lot of time
Set 2 General Moral Values	
• Carefulness	• [Check] to indeed see if whether or not we have a problem
• Fairness (or justice)	• Make sure that some people who are a little unsure of themselves also have an opportunity to speak
• Courage	• Their responsibility is to speak out when vandalism occurs
Set 3 Professional Values	
• General Responsibility as Educator	• Your value system is interfering with the mandate that we have in education
• Specific Role Responsibility	• Staff have to feel they are supported by the office
• Consequences for students	• Kids deserve a certain number of social events
• Consequences for others	• There's an impression that ... students aren't under control
Set 4 Social and Political Values	
• Participation	• Involve groups such as Head's Council, Special Education, Student Services
• Sharing	• Allow people to get things off their chests - talk about the problems they perceive
• Loyalty, Solidarity and Commitment	• We [admin. team] have to be seen as being philosophically in tune
• Helping others	• Let's help each other [school and parent] deal with that child

From Leithwood, Begley, & Cousins, 1992

ticity or their force of moral insight. He is critical, for example, of what he sees as the widespread use of Type 2 rational values in administration and attributes it to a positivistic, impersonal view of organizations and a natural desire to avoid the messiness and unpredictability associated with use of other types of values. This tendency toward rational values is greatly reinforced by the characteristics of contemporary culture, according to Hodgkinson.

Beck's (1984a,b,c) categories of values, not developed with administration in mind, are based on the premise that a fairly common set of universal values exists. Priorities and emphases may shift over time and with respect to specific circumstances, but a set of "Basic Human Values" can be identified, since values arise from need and many individuals have similar needs. These values are part of human nature and the human condition (Beck, 1984b) and include, for example, survival, health, happiness, friendship, helping others, respect for others, knowledge, fulfillment, freedom, and a sense of meaning in life. Some of these values are means to others, but this cluster of Basic Human Values, according to Beck, is mainly ends-oriented. Furthermore, these values are interconnected and are continuously being balanced, or traded off, with others. A sense of fluidity, openness, and flexibility exists within this formulation.

In addition to Basic Human Values, Beck (1984a) identifies four other categories of values: Moral Values (e.g., carefulness, courage, responsibility); Social and Political Values (e.g., tolerance, participation, loyalty); Intermediate-range Values (e.g., shelter, entertainment, fitness); and Specific Values (such as a car, a telephone, and a high school diploma). According to Beck's conception, none are absolute. Values are to be considered within their own system rather than in isolation. They are both means and ends. Viewing a value merely as a means is to deny its intrinsic worth. Viewing it merely as an end is to make it into an absolute. Even the Basic Human Values category forms a set, each of which has considerable importance in itself, but must also be weighed against other values (Beck, 1984c).

Results of research carried out using the Hodgkinson and Beck frameworks separately (Begley & Leithwood, 1989; Campbell-Evans, 1988) led to the four-category system of values described in Table 4.1.

The first category, "Basic Human Values," incorporates values at the apex of Hodgkinson's hierarchy, which he calls principles. These are primarily terminal values: They refer to "end states of existence" (Rokeach, 1973, p. 160). The remaining categories are more instrumental in nature. They represent preferable modes of conduct although, as Beck (1984a) warns, the distinction between means and ends may be inappropriate to maintain. People's values act as interdependent systems to influence their problem-solving. Categories entitled "General Moral Values" and "Professional Values" include norms of conduct or guidelines for judging the ethics of an individual's actions. "Professional Values," an addition to Beck's framework, includes values uniquely relevant to guiding decisions in one's work life; Hodgkinson's (1978) values of consequence are included here. As Bayles (1981) suggests, in order for Professional Values to be guides to ethical conduct, they must be consistent with and subordinate to Basic Human Values.

"Social and Political Values," incorporating Hodgkinson's (1978) values of consensus, recognize the essentially social nature of human action and the need for individuals to define themselves in relation to others to make their lives meaningful. There is also a close link between the specific values in this category and the basic human value of respect for others. The categories of values included in Table 4.1 do not include Beck's short- or intermediate-range values.

Other categories of values relevant to administrative problem-solving have been proposed. However, they share sufficient similarity with those outlined in Table 4.1, or are not sufficiently grounded in empirical data, so as not to challenge the defensibility of using the value categories in Table 4.1 as initial guides for our research. For example, from research on business executives, Hambrick and Brandon (1988) propose six categories of values important in their thinking, three of which have direct parallels in Table 4.1: collectivism (comparable to the two Professional Values in Table 4.1 dealing with consequences); duty (same as general and specific role responsibilities); and rationality (some similarity with knowledge). The remaining three—novelty, materialism, and power—are not in Table 4.1 nor are they evident in the results of our previous research with educational administrators.

Another classification of values, proposed by Ashbaugh and Kasten (1984), is grounded in evidence collected from a sample of principals. As with our framework, Ashbaugh and Kasten's categories were influenced by Hodgkinson (1978). They propose a category of Transcendent Values very similar to Hodgkinson's "transrational" and our General Moral Values categories. A category labeled Personalistic Values includes subcategories concerning personal style, human relations, and nature of schooling; the first two of these are very similar to our Social and Political Values. An Organizational Values category is also proposed; it overlaps with a significant proportion of what we have included in our category Professional Values.

Development of CEOs' Values

Influences that shape the values used by administrators in their problem-solving seem likely to be found in both personal and professional life experiences. Prior evidence concerning these value-shaping influences is meager, however. For example, Miklos' (1988) review concluded that most studies of the recruitment, formal education, and employment of educational administrators have been doctoral dissertations about the experiences of women, only. Nevertheless, this research did offer some direction for our research. Most of this evidence was concerned with socialization processes—those processes by which an individual selectively acquires the knowledge, skills, and dispositions (including values) needed to effectively perform in a role, such as that of CEO.

Greenfield's (1985) research, with vice-principals, suggested that values are more likely to be the product of informal experiences rather than such formal mechanisms as training. Formal programs designed for educational administrators traditionally have devoted little attention to values, ethics, or moral reasoning (Blumberg, 1984; Corson, 1985; Farquhar, 1986; Greenfield, 1986).

Leithwood, Steinbach, and Begley (1992) developed a framework for studying the socialization of school leaders based on research in several fields of study. This framework included the nature of administrators' experiences with school districts and their policies, formal education, and relationships with peers, subordinates, and superordinates. Further, they conceptualized the process of socialization as being divided into three stages: initiation, transition, and incorporation. Five studies were done with school leaders seeking answers to four questions regarding socialization experiences and their perceived usefulness in leaders' development. Many, but not all, socialization experiences were considered helpful by principals and vice-principals, and there were variations among perceptions according to gender, geographical location, and whether people were already in administrative roles or working toward them. One of the specific suggestions for improvement that emerged from this research was the need for more opportunities for on-the-job leadership experiences in which the skills and attributes required for the position could be acquired and practiced.

Ashbaugh and Kasten (1984) inquired directly about influences on the values used by school administrators to make difficult decisions. Results suggested that both personal and professional life experiences conspire, in a blended fashion, to shape administrators' values. Specific influences on values identified by these researchers were religion, educational training, school district philosophy, and role models. Also shaping administrators' values were parents and mentors, experiences as a teacher, personal life events, and parental experiences.

Research on values in the area of leadership, however, is extremely thin and none of it addresses the development of CEOs' values in particular. At best, it offers hunches about some possible influences on the formation of values, but no clear framework of the sort available to guide our inquiry about the nature of CEOs' values.

METHOD

This study was part of a larger project examining several aspects of the thinking and practices of chief education officers in Ontario, Canada (equivalent to U.S. superintendents). Only the methodology relevant to data reported in this chapter is described. These data were provided by responses of CEOs to a survey about their values. The survey was sent to all 113 Ontario CEOs (except for 10 reputationally effective CEOs involved in the larger study). Items for the survey were developed from the research reviewed in the previous section. The final survey required approximately 35 minutes to complete. Frequency counts of CEO responses to closed questions were calculated. CEOs' short answers to open-ended questions were analyzed for evidence of values in two ways: use of specific words from the values framework (Table 4.1) and indications of values associated with the framework through use of words that implied those values; for example, if a CEO said a problem solution included meetings or discussions with other people, that was interpreted as expressing the value of Participation.

The survey was mailed to 66 CEOs of public school boards, of which 27 (42 percent) were returned, and 47 CEOs of Roman Catholic separate school boards, of which 24 (51 percent) were returned; two of the surveys were filled out anonymously. A total of 53 (47 percent) surveys were completed and returned. The larger percentage of Roman Catholic separate school board CEOs responding to a survey on values may be explained by the explicit emphasis on formal religion and Christian values in the policies and functions of the school systems they administered.

RESULTS

Of the 112 CEOs (including five women) who were sent the survey, 51 males and 2 females participated. Six (11 percent) of the responding CEOs were between the ages of 40 and 45; 18 (34 percent) were 46 to 50 years of age; 22 (42 percent) were 51 to 55 years of age; and 7 (13 percent) were between 56 and 60 years old. Forty of the 53 participating CEOs were between 46 and 55 years of age. Most of the CEOs (74 percent) had a master's degree, 21 percent also had a doctoral degree, and 6 percent had only a bachelor's degree. Eighty-one percent of the CEOs had a career path that involved moving up the traditional steps of the educational hierarchy (teacher, vice-principal, principal, etc.). Nineteen percent had skipped stages of the hierarchy, had held jobs outside the school board (e.g., at a faculty of education), or had interrupted their careers to take jobs outside of education. Thirty percent had held full-time jobs outside education, many of which were first careers that did not involve interrupting their work in education. Most CEOs (80 percent) grew up in families that lived in cities or towns rather than in rural settings. Occupations of male adults in CEOs' families were most often in trades and services (63 percent) and farming (14 percent), while the main occupations of female adults were homemaker (59 percent) and jobs in trades and services (31 percent). Very few CEOs came from professional families.

Nature of CEO Values

What are the values CEOs consider most important in their problem-solving and to what extent do CEOs share similar values? Four different approaches were used to answer these questions. One approach, using our values framework, asked respondents to indicate what values they considered most, second-most, and third-most important. Only those values they considered important were to be ranked and no context was provided within which to respond. Responses were ranked in order of frequency of selection (first-, second-, and third-most important selections were combined). CEOs could also add values they considered important but that did not appear in the framework. In total, 10 "Other" values were added.

Table 4.2 shows that 50 (94 percent) of the CEOs responding to the survey ranked the specific value of Respect for Others (a Basic Human Value) as either most, second-most, or third-most important. The value chosen next most often was Loyalty, Solidarity, and Commitment (a Social and Political Value), by 49 or 92 percent of the respondents; Fairness/Justice (a General Moral Value) and Consequences for the System (a Professional Value) were both chosen by the same number of participants (48 or 91 percent). Carefulness (a General Moral Value) was chosen as an important value least often (by 32 percent of the participants). The value most often ranked first was Respect for Others, followed by Integrity and then Loyalty, Solidarity, and Commitment. The value of Carefulness was not ranked most important by any of the CEOs.

CEOs agreed in their ranking of values. The first 11 items were all selected by well over 50 percent of the participants, while only five of the values were selected by less than 50 percent. A second approach to the nature of values held by CEOs was provided by responses to survey questions concerning the values considered most important for staff and students (not shown in Table 4.2). For students, CEOs named, in order of frequency, Integrity (fourth in Table 4.2), Respect for Others (first), Honesty (seventh), and Caring (not in the framework). For staff, the values considered most important were, in order of frequency, Integrity (ranked fourth in Table 4.2) and Honesty (seventh); Caring (not in the framework); Respect for Others (first); and Loyalty (second). Several other values that are not in the framework were mentioned. These included Faith, Work Ethic, and Open-mindedness. Again, CEOs were reasonably consistent in the values they selected as important using our first and second, context-free, approaches.

Our third approach to CEO values provided a context and yielded different results. The provision of a context for studying values acknowledges Kaminski's argument that "in the realm of complex social problems, values never occur singly; they always occur within a complex matrix of social, anti-social, moral and immoral relations" (1986, p. 22). The most likely way to clarify administrators' marginal values, then, is to describe the policies (or selections) they choose to achieve them (Lindblom, cited in Kaminski, 1986). As a result, our third approach asked CEOs to describe a specific recent conflict situation and their solution to the conflict. Answers were analyzed by looking for use of specific words from our values framework (e.g., Integrity or Fairness).

Table 4.2 Overall Ranking of Values by Frequency of Selection: First-, Second-, and Third-Most Important Combined

Rank	Value	Valid Responses (Maximum of 53)	% of Total Responses
1	Respect for others	50	94%
2	Loyalty, solidarity, commitment	49	92%
3	Fairness/Justice	48	91%
3	Consequences for System	48	91%
5	Integrity	47	87%
6	Helping others	46	87%
7	General responsibility as educator	42	79%
7	Consequences for clients	42	79%
9	Honesty	41	77%
10	Knowledge	39	74%
11	Happiness	37	70%
11	Sharing	37	70%
13	Participation	36	68%
14	Freedom	34	64%
15	Courage	23	43%
15	Consequences for society	23	43%
17	Role responsibility	22	42%
18	Survival	18	34%
19	Carefulness	17	32%

Values were also inferred from words used by CEOs when describing what they said they did that implied those values from this analysis. Participation (a Social and Political Value) and Knowledge (a Basic Human Value) were referred to most often, followed by Specific Role Responsibility (or Duty) (a Professional Value) and Fairness/Justice. Several values emerged, not explicit in Table 4.1, which are closely related to Participation: Consultation, Compromise, and Consensus.

As a fourth, context-imbedded, approach to identifying the values that prevail in CEO problem-solving, respondents were asked to rate, first of all, whether they never, seldom, occasionally, often, or always experienced each of the four following types of value conflicts.

1. External Value Conflict in which the CEO is not included; for example, a conflict among board administrators who disagree about the possible consequences for students of a long-range planning direction;
2. External Value Conflict that includes the CEO, such as a conflict between the CEO and the Chair of the Board of Trustees regarding the importance of Solidarity;
3. Internal Value Conflict (within CEO) where there is a conflict in organizational values; for example, a conflict between Honesty and the CEO's Role Responsibility regarding disclosure of confidential information;

4. Internal Value Conflict (within CEO) where there is a conflict between or among organizational values and personal values. An example of this is a conflict between a CEO's general responsibility as an educator and values espoused by a new school program (e.g., teaching the use of birth control methods).

Ratings indicated agreement with Blumberg's (1985) conclusion that conflict is part of the job. None of the CEOs said they never experienced conflicts of the first and second type. Four percent and 15 percent respectively never experienced the third and fourth types of conflict. When the response categories "often" and "always" were combined, the respective percentage of responses to categories one through four was 38, 29, 13, and 10 percent. This suggests that external value conflicts not including the CEO were perceived as most frequent. External value conflicts including the CEO were also fairly frequent. But the remaining two types of value conflicts were fairly rare, suggesting that these CEOs were not engaged in serious personal dilemmas.

More information about types of conflicts was available from CEOs' brief descriptions of problem situations (see approach three, above). Open-ended responses were categorized according to the four types of conflict described above. Of the 34 problems described by the 54 respondents, 18 could be classified as conflicts of the first type; 11 were conflicts of the second type; 2 were of the third type; and 3 were of the fourth type. In general, these results confirm CEOs' earlier estimates of how often these types of conflicts occurred. Twenty-two of the 34 problems described involved board policies, 7 concerned programs, 4 were disputes over budget (one of the problems lacked sufficient detail to make a judgment about the underlying issue). Of the 32 CEOs who indicated how they had resolved the problems they described, the largest number (12) said that board policy had prevailed in the final resolution. Assuming that board policy has been created to help the system as a whole function well, this reflects the value Consequences for the System—ranked third on Table 4.2. Three of the situations had been resolved by enforcing Ministry of Education policy (Consequences for Society—twelfth on Table 4.2), and three had involved compromise. One solution had been arrived at by consensus and one CEO had chosen to "back off." Several of the situations (8) were ongoing and remained unresolved at the time of the survey, and 4 of the solutions lacked sufficient detail to be analyzed.

In sum, our evidence concerning the nature of CEO values indicates

• A high degree of emphasis on Basic Human and General Moral Values when CEOs identified their values in response to context-free questions
• A high degree of emphasis on Professional and Social and Political Values

when CEOs' values were identified in the context of solving particular problems
• Most value conflicts experienced by CEOs did not challenge their personal values or create tension between organizational and personal values.

Influences on Values

Who are the people and what are the situations that have influenced the development and shaping of CEO values? To answer this question, participants were asked to consider a list of 18 possible influences (including both people and contexts), to select the ones they considered important, and then to rank the three most important. They did not have to rank items on the list they did not consider important. Ratings of first-, second-, and third-most important were combined to determine the total number of CEOs who selected each influence, keeping personal and professional values separate. As Table 4.3 indicates, a substantially larger number of influences contributed to the development of personal as compared with professional values.

A small number of common influences appeared to contribute to the development of both personal and professional values. This becomes evident when the rankings of influences for the two categories of values are combined. Three of these influences are personal in origin: parents (overall rank=1), spouses (overall rank=6), and adult friends (overall rank=7). Work contexts provide the origin of four of these influences: educational work experience and on-the-job leadership (tied for second overall), mentors (overall rank=4), and peer groups (overall rank=5). This suggests highly permeable boundaries around personal and professional values categories. CEOs' practices, to the extent that they are influenced by values, appear to be a product of their whole life experience. Such evidence would not support a claim that CEOs can keep their personal and professional lives separate.

Formal religious training had quite different impacts on the development of personal as compared with professional values. It ranked third as an influence on personal values but only fourteenth as an influence on professional values. This was especially surprising given the number of CEO respondents (24 of 51) from Roman Catholic separate school systems where such teaching is held in high regard. A small number of influences appeared to have relatively little influence on the development of either personal or professional values. These included childhood friends (overall rank=18); other relatives (overall rank= 17); and networking, noneducational work, and secondary teachers (tied overall rank=16).

"People" is a category of influence, in Table 4.3, worth special analysis. We asked which people influenced which values. Most often mentioned as having

Table 4.3 Influences on CEOs' Personal and Professional Values by Frequencies: Ratings of Importance (First, Second, Third) Combined

Types of Influences	Rank of Influence		
	Professional Values	Personal Values	Combined
Parents	6	1	1
Spouse	9	2	2
Educational work experience	3	4	3
Mentor	3	5	4
On the job leadership	1	7	4
Peer group	1	7	4
Learning by observation	5	9	7
Formal religious teaching	14	3	8
Adult friends	8	5	8
Professional development	6	9	8
Elementary teachers	10	11	11
Your children	14	12	12
Post-secondary teachers	11	15	13
Networking	14	13	14
Non-educational work	12	16	15
Secondary teachers	12	17	16
Other relatives	17	14	17
Childhood friends	18	18	18

influenced personal values were parents, spouse, and adult friends. These people increased CEOs' sensitivity to Integrity and Honesty (both General Moral Values). People mentioned most often as having influenced professional values were colleagues, teachers, and mentors. Colleagues were considered to have influenced CEOs' sensitivity to Justice, while teachers and mentors were credited with influencing CEOs' sensitivity to Integrity (both General Moral Values). Comparing the values ranking in Table 4.2 with the values just mentioned, Integrity is ranked fourth in the framework, Honesty seventh, and Justice/Fairness third. Interestingly, in the context of problem-solving, Integrity and Honesty did not appear to be very important. General Moral Values, development of which were influenced by the people mentioned above, may exist prior to other values and serve as a point of departure for the exercise of Professional Values.

CONCLUSION

Fifty-three CEOs responded to a survey designed to "triangulate" on questions concerning the nature and development of their values. Both open and closed questions were included in the survey. Responses were required sometimes without providing any context and sometimes in a specific problem-solving context. Professional values and the Social and Political value Participation were especially evident in the context of solving particular problems. Two of our four Professional Values concern general and specific role responsibility and correspond to Hambrick and Brandon's (1988) value Duty. A concern for consequences of several sorts make up the remainder of the Professional Values category. Such concerns are part of the broader philosophical tradition called Pragmatism. Pragmatism, Participation, and Duty, then, are strong value themes recurring throughout CEO problem-solving.

The dominance of Pragmatism in CEO problem-solving causes us to reconsider our earlier classification of the value Knowledge. A value that appeared to be important in the context of solving particular problems, Knowledge was classified in our initial framework as a Basic Human Value. But an overriding concern for the consequences of a particular solution by CEOs depends on knowledge of what such consequences might be. Knowledge, therefore, appears better conceptualized as an instrumental in the service of a fundamental concern for consequences, a Professional Value. Such an interpretation is also consistent with Begley and Leithwood's (1989) findings. When principals in their study became more knowledgeable about computer technology, they were increasingly likely to base their adoption decisions on the consequences of such technology for their students.

Participation, a specific value within the category we have labeled Social and Political values, acknowledges the importance of other stakeholders' being involved in problem-solving. Holding such a value seems especially important in light of our previous evidence about expert administrative problem-solving. Expert principals, we have found, work toward collaborative processes in most of their work (Leithwood & Steinbach, 1990). While acknowledging that they did not begin their administrative careers that way, most claim increasingly to solve virtually all significant problems through such means, time permitting (Leithwood & Steinbach, 1990). Their reasons are several, but among the most important is a genuine belief that the result will be not only greater commitment on the part of participants but better solutions as well. Nonexperts valued participation less. They appeared to believe that the reason for participation was only to foster greater teacher commitment to implementing a solution they had already identified. Better solutions were unlikely through participative processes, from their point of view. CEOs and expert principals are much alike on this matter (Leithwood & Steinbach, 1989).

Duty and Pragmatism were widely endorsed values by CEOs in the context of solving particular problems. Evidence about CEOs' values out-of-context, however, painted a modest role for these values, indicating a discrepancy between CEOs' "espoused theories" and "theories-in-use" (Schön, 1983). According to their espoused theories, CEOs' problem-solving is largely guided by Basic Human Values and General Moral Values (and, to a lesser extent, Social and Political values other than Participation). CEOs' espoused theories conform more closely, for example, to Hodgkinson's (1978) values hierarchy, which places general moral principles at the apex. As Begley and Leithwood (1989) discovered with principals, however, in a context approximating real problem-solving, Pragmatism and Duty emerge as increasingly influential.

Contrary to Hodgkinson (1978) we argue that such values not only are, but ought to be, at the apex of CEOs' theories-in-use. For example, considerations of consequence, based on empirical evidence, may ameliorate the problems that Holmes (1991) associates with major differences that appear to exist between CEOs' espoused educational philosophies and the philosophies of the larger public served by those CEOs. Hambrick and Brandon (1988) hypothesized that when Duty was a strongly held value, its effect was to reduce the forcefulness with which executives used their other values in group problem-solving. We suspect this also may be the effect of Participation, when it is strongly held.

Should this be the case, CEOs may have found a parsimonious solution to what some suggest is a fundamental dilemma for administrators: finding a defensible balance between being true to their own values and serving the values of the organization. The solution is to hold a set of values that honor the values of others. Participation reflects this position, especially in combination with the value of Respect for Others—the most frequently selected value, out of context, by CEOs in our study. Furthermore, Social and Political values such as Participation and Consensus are sometimes considered morally trivial by educational philosophers (e.g., Hodgkinson, 1978). But their concerns seem not to consider the instrumental advantage of such values in overcoming the "bounded rationality" (Newell & Simon, 1972) of individual human problem-solving.

How do CEOs come to the values they hold and think about while solving problems? While people (parents, spouses, adult friends) are prominent influences in the development of values, it may be that they largely shape only CEOs' espoused value systems. Our evidence suggests that such people helped increase CEOs' sensitivity to General Moral Values, in the main, and to a lesser extent Basic Human Values (especially Justice). But these were not the dominant values-in-use as CEOs solved problems. Rather, the work setting was the most powerful force in the development of CEOs' values-in-use, an answer to questions about the influence of school districts raised as a result of Ashbaugh and Kasten's (1984) study. That is, CEOs' own direct experiences about what values are "best," most "sensible," "successful," and the like in solving problems (through on-the-job leadership experiences, for example) may be the most powerful influence on the development of their professional values-in-use. This explanation of how values actually used in solving problems develop is the same as the explanation, offered by contemporary theories of situated cognition (Brown,

Collins, & Duguid, 1989) and practical problem-solving (Rogoff & Lave, 1984), of how authentic knowledge develops. Professionally relevant values and useful procedural knowledge develop through grappling with the authentic challenges of day-to-day leadership and administration.

REFERENCES

Ashbaugh, C. R., & Kasten, K. L. (1984). A typology of operant values in school administration. *Planning and Changing, 15*(4), 195–208.

Barnard, C. I. (1938). *The functions of the executive.* Cambridge: Harvard University Press.

Bayles, M.D. (1981). *Professional ethics.* Belmont, CA:Wadsworth.

Beck, C.M. (1984a). *The nature of values and implications for values education.* Unpublished paper.

Beck, C. M. (1984b, July 12–14). *The nature of teaching of moral problem solving.* Paper presented at a meeting of the Institute for Logic and Cognitive Studies, University of Houston, Houston, TX.

Beck, C. M. (1984c, November 7). *Our faith confronts differing life styles and value systems.* Presented to the Islington United Church School of Religion.

Begley, P. T., & Leithwood, K. A. (1989). The influence of values on the practices of school administrators. *Journal of Educational Administration and Foundations, 4*(1), 25–39.

Blumberg, A. (1984). The craft of school administration and some other rambling thoughts. *Educational Administration Quarterly, 20*(4), 24–40.

Blumberg, A. (1985). *The school superintendent: Living with conflict.* New York: Teachers College Press.

Brown, J. S., Collins, A., & Duguid, D. (1989). Situated cognition and the culture of learning. *Educational Researcher, 18*(1), 32–42.

Campbell-Evans, G. H. (1988). *Nature and influence of values in principal decision making.* Unpublished doctoral dissertation, University of Toronto, Toronto.

Corson, D. (1985). Quality of judgment and deciding rightness: Ethics and educational administration. *The Journal of Educational Administration, 23*(2), 122–130.

DeBono, E. (1985). *Six thinking hats.* Boston: Little, Brown & Co.

England, G. W. (1967). Personal value systems of American managers. *Academy of Management Journal, 10,* 53–68.

Farquhar, R. H. (1981). Preparing educational administrators for ethical practice. *The Alberta Journal of Educational Research, 27*(2), 192–204.

Fox, W. M. (1987). *Effective group problem solving.* San Francisco: Jossey-Bass.

Frankena, W. K. (1973). *Ethics* (2nd ed.). Englewood Cliffs, NJ: Prentice-Hall.

Greenfield, T. B. (1986). The decline and fall of science in educational administration. *Interchange, 17*(2), 57–80.

Greenfield, W. D. (1985). The moral socialization of school administrators: Informal role learning outcomes. *Educational Administration Quarterly, 21*(4), 99–119.

Hambrick, D. C., & Brandon, G. L. (1988). Executive values. In D. C. Hambrick (Ed.),

The executive effect: Concepts and methods for studying top managers (pp. 3–35). Greenwich, CT: Jai Press.

Hodgkinson, C. E. (1978). *Towards a theory of administration.* New York: St. Martin's Press.

Holmes, M. (1991). The values and beliefs of Ontario's Chief Education Officers. In K. A. Leithwood & D. Musella (Eds.), *Understanding school system administration* (pp. 154–174). London: The Falmer Press.

Kaminski, J. S. (1986). Legal reasoning, recipes, ethics, values, educational administration and applied philosophy. *The Journal of Educational Thought, 20*(1), 20–30.

Kepner, C. H., & Tregoe, B. B. (1981). *The new rational manager.* Princeton, NJ: Kepner-Tregoe, Inc.

Kluckhon, C. (1951). Values and value-orientations in the theory of action: An exploration in definition and classification. In T. Parsons & E. A. Shils (Eds.), *Toward a general theory of action* (pp. 388–433). Cambridge: Harvard University Press.

Leithwood, K. A., Begley, P. T., & Cousins, B. (1992). *Developing expert leadership in future schools.* London: The Falmer Press.

Leithwood, K. A., & Stager, M. (1989). Expertise in principals' problem solving. *Educational Administration Quarterly, 25*(2), 126–161.

Leithwood, K. A., & Steinbach, R. (1990). Characteristics of effective secondary school principals' problem solving. *Journal of Educational Administration and Foundations, 5*(1), 24–42.

Leithwood, K. A., Steinbach, R., & Begley, P. (1992). Socialization experiences: Becoming a principal in Canada. In F. W. Parkay & G. E. Hall (Eds.), *Becoming a principal: The challenges of beginning leadership* (pp. 284–307). Boston: Allyn & Bacon.

Miklos, E. (1988). Administrator selection, career patterns, succession, and socialization. In N. J. Boyan (Ed.), *Handbook of research on educational administration* (pp. 53–76). New York: Longman.

Newell, A., & Simon, H. A. (1972). *Human problem solving.* London: Prentice-Hall.

Rogoff, B., & Lave, J. (Eds.). (1984). *Everyday cognition: Its development in social context.* Cambridge: Harvard University Press.

Rokeach, M. (1973). *The nature of human values.* New York: The Free Press.

Schön, D. (1983). *The reflective practitioner.* New York: Basic Books.

Simon, H. A. (1976). *Administrative behaviour* (3rd ed.). New York: The Free Press.

Weber, M. (1949). *The methodology of the social sciences.* New York: The Free Press.

Williams, R. M. (1968). Values. In *International Encyclopedia of the Social Sciences.* New York: Macmillan.

PART II

The Nature of Administrative Expertise

Interest in the nature of expertise in various professional domains has increased dramatically over the past decade. Inquiry into the thinking that underlies the observable performance differences of novices and experts forms the foundation of much of this work. Recent work by educational psychologists studying expertise in teaching is but one example of this general trend in the cognitive science and professional education literatures.

We believe that a cognitive perspective holds a similar potential to make a unique contribution to our understanding of expertise in leadership and school administration. To date, empirical inquiry into the nature of expertise in educational administration has been sparse. Thus this section, devoted to the nature of expertise, draws heavily on what has been learned from investigations in other fields. Our goal in this section of the book is to examine how this body of work can further our understanding of the nature and development of expertise in the domain of educational leadership.

During the 1980s, much of the literature in educational administration was concerned with defining the characteristics of "effective principals." Behavioral descriptions were sought that might distinguish between the actions of more and less effective principals. Researchers sought to quantify and describe what effective principals do in the hopes that such knowledge might be used to increase the effectiveness of other school leaders. The results of this research were subsequently incorporated into training programs for principals, though the outcomes of these efforts remain in question.

The findings from this research literature on principal effectiveness represented an advance over the anecdotal and prescriptive literature that previously dominated the field. At the same time, however, the quest to discover the behaviors of effective leaders suffered from serious conceptual and technical limitations. An almost exclusive focus on overt behaviors left unanswered important questions about why and under what conditions educational leaders performed the observed behaviors.

Increasingly, those involved in research and training in educational leadership have acknowledged the need for better information on how expert school leaders think about what they do. This is essential to understanding the conditions under which they take action, a prerequisite to the design of effective training. Similarly, interest has increased in learning more about how the thinking of leaders changes as expertise develops. Inquiry into the covert processes that motivate the actions of leaders is a defining characteristic of a cognitive perspective on educational leadership.

Kathleen L. Ohde and Joseph Murphy open this section by reviewing the general literature on expertise and its development. They note that "experts differ from novices in the knowledge they possess, in the patterns of their thinking, and in the performance of their actions." They use these differences to frame their discussion of expertise while introducing many of the key concepts and issues that underlie a cognitive perspective (e.g., the role of domain-specific knowledge versus general problem-solving skills). They synthesize these findings and discuss their implications for how we think about the nature and development of expertise among educational leaders.

Richard K. Wagner extends the discussion of administrative expertise by analyzing two long-competing schools of administrative thought: management-as-science and management-as-craft. The comparative analysis is grounded in the theoretical and empirical literature that has come to be known as "cognitive science." Wagner's contribution is significant in that he reexamines the empirical basis for taking meta-rational views of leadership seriously. This chapter pays due respect to the work of Herbert Simon, but extends earlier contributions with reference to a significant body of recent empirical studies of managerial problem-solving. Thus, the chapter reengages a long-standing set of questions in the field of management.

Some of the most influential applications of the cognitive science literature to the field of educational administration and leadership have been conducted at the Ontario Institute for Studies in Education. The chapter by Kenneth A. Leithwood and Rosanne Steinbach builds on their earlier work that sought to explain differences in the problem-solving expertise of school leaders. In this inquiry, Leithwood and Steinbach focus on the increasingly important domain of group problem-solving. They examine how the same set of school leaders proceed to solve problems in collaborative settings. Their findings add insight to our understanding of expertise in the realm of educational leadership broadly defined, as well as in the specific domain of instructional leadership.

Derek J. Allison and Patricia A. Allison employ a cognitive perspective toward understanding how school leaders approach problem-solving tasks.

Specifically, their empirical analysis focuses on the "conceptual maps" used by administrators in addressing complex problems. An important question raised by the Allisons involves the role of experience in managerial problem-solving expertise, an issue previously engaged by both Glidewell and Wagner. The study reported here raises interesting implications for how we think about the selection and training of school leaders.

The final chapter in this section examines the development of expertise in a field of management that at first glance differs radically from school administration: credit administration in a bank. Yet, as Frank R. Yekovich observes, the two fields have an important facet in common: Managers in both fields must address complex problems armed with limited and often ambiguous information. With this in mind, Yekovich draws on empirical data to explore both the constituent cognitive features that underlie expert problem-solving and the processes by which expert administrators acquire their knowledge and skills. He provides compelling evidence concerning the development of expertise and challenges some of the basic assumptions on which our administrative preparation programs are grounded. His chapter provides an appropriate transition into the final section of the book, which focuses on the development of expertise in educational leadership.

5 The Development of Expertise: Implications for School Administrators

Kathleen L. Ohde and Joseph Murphy

A taxi driver effectively negotiating the streets of Chicago, a housewife skillfully balancing the family budget, and a radiologist astutely diagnosing a disease from chest x-rays all share a common bond. This bond is the ability to efficiently perform a particular complex activity in a capable, accurate, yet almost instinctive manner. In other words, these three individuals are experts within the activity they are performing. As can be seen from these examples, expertise can take many forms, ranging from common activities to specialized tasks. From a simplistic perspective, expertise may be viewed as a combination of practice, knowledge, and innate ability. The nature of expertise, however, is a complex issue that has spawned a body of scholarly research resolved to clarify exactly what expertise is and how it is acquired.

Over the past two decades, a growing body of knowledge has developed on the concept of expertise. Research into the nature of expertise has spanned a wide variety of fields and has utilized numerous investigative procedures and techniques, the most traditional being that of comparing the performance of experts with that of novices. Despite their many differences, these investigations have generated a volume of consistent and interrelated findings that now can afford a broader understanding of expertise. These findings include the following:

1. An expert within a specific domain will have amassed a large yet well-organized knowledge base. (Berliner, 1986)
2. This extensive body of knowledge allows experts to classify problems according to principles, laws, or major rules rather than surface features found within the problem. (Chi, Glaser, & Rees, 1983)
3. The knowledge base is highly organized, allowing experts to quickly and accurately identify patterns and configurations. This ability reduces cognitive load and permits the expert to attend to other variables within the problem. (Frederiksen, 1984)

4. The problem-solving strategies of experts are proceduralized. Experts can automatically invoke these skills while novices often struggle with the problem-solving process. (Dunn & Taylor, 1990)
5. The acquisition of this complex knowledge base takes a long time. Expertise within a domain is linked to years of practice, experience, or study. (Frensch & Sternberg, 1989)

In summary, these findings suggest that experts differ from novices in the knowledge they possess, in the patterns of their thinking, and in the performance of their actions. These three qualitative differences provide the frameworks from which the nature and acquisition of expertise will now be examined.

THE ROLE OF KNOWLEDGE IN EXPERTISE

Expertise has been identified in a variety of domains ranging from perception-based fields such as chess or electronics to comprehension-based pursuits such as medicine or teaching. Comparing experts with novices allows us to discover the numerous changes that occur as expertise is acquired (Lesgold, 1984).

One necessary characteristic of expertise is the acquisition of an extensive knowledge base that pertains to the area of competence. In examining the need for content knowledge in the development of competence, Simon (1980) commented that "we cannot produce physicists without teaching physics, or psychologists without teaching psychology" (p. 82). In the view of Simon and others who have compared the performance of experts with that of novices, a knowledge base that is both extensive and accessible is a necessary requisite for the development of expertise (Berliner, 1986; Chi, Feltovich, & Glaser, 1981; Glaser, 1984; Lesgold, 1984). In fact, few researchers would dispute the integral role knowledge plays in the acquisition of expertise.

Domain-Specific Knowledge

For expertise to develop within a domain or a field of study, a certain amount of knowledge about that area is needed. For example, how can one begin to solve a physics problem (Chi et al., 1981), debug a computer program (Klahr & Carver, 1987), play in a chess tournament (Chase & Simon, 1973), or diagnose a disease (Feltovich & Patel, 1984) without some knowledge of physics, computer programming, chess, or medicine?

Experts within any domain possess two types of knowledge: declarative and procedural (VanSickle & Hoge, 1989). Declarative knowledge is actually domain-specific knowledge or "knowledge about" the particular area of study

(p. 5). Declarative knowledge includes definitions of concepts, specific factual information, and generalizations. Procedural knowledge is "knowledge of how to" (Voss, 1989, p. 264). Experts differ from novices in their ability to transform declarative knowledge into procedural knowledge.

Sources of Knowledge

Two components are necessary for the development of a domain-specific knowledge base. First, specific facts, definitions, and rules about the domain must be acquired, synthesized, and organized by the learner. During this process, knowledge is acquired from both classroom instruction and everyday, real-life experiences (Lesgold, 1984; Voss, Greene, Post, & Penner, 1983).

The second component in the acquisition of the knowledge base is practice. Considerable practice is necessary to become an expert (Lesgold, 1984). Glaser (1984) supports this premise and contends "that a significant focus for understanding expert thinking and problem solving and its development is investigation of the characteristics and influence of organized knowledge structures that are acquired over long periods of time" (p. 99).

The tacit knowledge needed to recognize thousands of meaningful board positions in chess or to effectively manage a classroom is not gleaned from merely observing or from just textbook instruction, but rather from actively practicing the targeted performance. Experience allows acquired knowledge to be applied, permitting improvement in both accuracy and the qualitative nature of the performance (Lesgold, Glaser, Rubinson, Klopfer, Feltovich, & Wang, 1988).

Experience also expands and refines the knowledge base. As experience is acquired, a large, differentiated store of models, patterns, and configurations is amassed in an individual's memory (Feltovich & Patel, 1984). When this occurs, the expert "seldom has to deal with novelty, having brought much of his work-world into the realm of the familiar" (p. 3).

The Synthesis of Knowledge and Practice

Anderson (1982) has developed a theory of skill acquisition that explains how knowledge is acquired in a stagelike process and how practice affects and refines performance. He contends that the learning process can be broken into three phases: the declarative stage, the knowledge-compilation stage, and the procedural stage. Each stage builds on the previous one. Consequently, the types of knowledge learned and the concomitant skills that are acquired are transformed and refined as the learner moves from stage to stage.

During the initial stage of learning, declarative knowledge is utilized to direct performance. Declarative knowledge refers to the facts, concepts, and rules about a domain. This knowledge is encoded by the learner into sets of data that are stored in a networklike manner within declarative memory (Yekovich, Thompson, & Walker, 1991). Performance at this stage is slow, often repetitive, and subject to error because heavy demands are placed on working memory. A considerable portion of the training time invested at this stage involves the conversion of slow declarative-knowledge interpretations into the faster compiled procedures of the next stage (Lesgold, 1984).

The second stage is that of knowledge compilation, the process by which "the skill transits from the declarative stage to the procedural stage" (Anderson, 1982, p. 369). In this stage, domain-specific productions are formed after the learner repeatedly applies step-by-step rules on domain-specific facts (Yekovich et al., 1991). Productions can be likened to a routinized set of behaviors or procedures. These procedures are developed to perform specific tasks and their use fosters efficiency "both in terms of time and working memory demands" (p. 381).

In Anderson's (1982) third stage, the procedural stage, problem-solving procedures become refined and tuned. This refinement process allows experts to judiciously choose the path to a problem's solution, thereby replacing trial-and-error exploration with insight and selectivity. At this stage in the skill-acquisition process, domain-specific knowledge becomes directly embedded within the procedures for performing the skill.

THE ROLE OF THINKING IN EXPERTISE

Kolodner (1983) explains the intertwining of knowledge and experience as a novice evolves into an expert:

> Two things happen in that evolution. First, knowledge is built up incrementally on the basis of experience. Facts, once unrelated, get integrated through occurrence in the same episodes. Second, reasoning processes are refined, and usefulness and rigidity of rules is learned. . . . Because experience is vital to the evolution from novice to expert, experience is organized in long-term memory, and guides reasoning processes. . . . When a person has only gone to school and acquired book knowledge, he is considered a novice. After he has had experience using the knowledge he has learned, and when he knows how it applies both to common and exceptional cases, he is called an expert. . . . Experience serves to turn unrelated facts into knowledge. (p. 498)

As the knowledge base is acquired and expanded and as domain-specific skills are performed and refined, changes also occur in the ways an individual thinks. The cognitive processes of the expert become "more sophisticated, more efficient, and more useful" (Berliner, 1987, p. 76). Consequently, experience actually transforms three cognitive components integrally linked to the knowledge base: perception, memory, and specific thought processes.

Changes in Perception

Central to understanding the cognitive skills of experts is the concept of schema. Anderson (1982) defines a schema as an abstract knowledge structure that summarizes information about many particular cases and the relationships among them. Schemata, consequently, are organized collections of perceptions and thoughts that guide an individual through tasks ranging from routine, everyday occurrences to unique problem-solving situations. Schemata can also contain action plans or domain-specific problem-solving strategies. In the field of medicine, these action plans have been identified as "illness scripts" (Boshuizen & Schmidt, 1990; Schmidt & Norman, 1990). Similarly, in the area of teaching, three types of action plans have been identified: scripts, scenes, and propositional structures (Borko & Livingston, 1989).

An expert's schemata perform two important functions. First, schemata provide an effective means by which the knowledge base can be organized (Lesgold, 1984). Since the knowledge base of an expert is extensive, schemata not only organize the particular facts, principles, and experiences of the domain, but also provide a flexible framework into which new information and experiences can be integrated. Second, an expert's schemata are rich, elaborate causal networks whose usage reduces memory load (Owen & Sweller, 1989), resulting in faster responses (Lesgold et al., 1988), and responses that are flexible and sensitive to the specific demands of the task (Frensch & Sternberg, 1989; Voss, 1989). These perceptual changes, in turn, impact how and what an expert remembers.

Changes in Memory

Because the knowledge base of an expert is organized differently from that of a novice, *what* an expert remembers is different. What experts remember appears to be more functional and more focused on events and behaviors that have been reinforced through experience and practice (Berliner, 1987). Because experts perceive facts and events differently, *how* they remember is different from the way of novices. An expert's memory for information is different from the memory of a novice.

Two basic changes take place in memory as one becomes an expert. From the perspective of information-processing theory, these changes take place in long-term memory (LTM) as well as in working memory. First, information stored in long-term memory becomes integrated into clusters, chunks, patterns, and networks (Frederiksen, 1984). When one element of a cluster, for example, is triggered, "all are likely to be activated" (p. 364). This chain of events allows for the development of automaticity or the proceduralization of activities, especially those of a routine nature (Lesgold, 1984). According to Anderson (1982), an automated response is analogous to proceduralized knowledge, a network of information that is operable without the conscious control of the individual. From this perspective, learning can be "characterized as a process of acquiring a set of domain-specific facts and through practice transforming this knowledge into sets of fine-tuned, domain-specific procedures that are applied with little mental effort" (Yekovich et al., 1991).

The second transformation is occurring within working memory. The recognition of patterns, the ability to recall chunks of information, and the use of automated responses all reduce cognitive processing in an expert (Berliner, 1986). Working memory "contains all the information that is actively being used . . . [and] maintains an internal representation of what is going on" (Frederiksen, 1984, p. 365). Since the capacity of working memory is limited, the amount of information it can process is greatly increased by "chunking" pieces of information through collections, sets, and patterns of facts (p. 365). Consequently, the development and subsequent use of these refined abilities allow experts to efficiently recall and synthesize information from their knowledge base.

The use of chunking permits large amounts of information to be processed automatically (Frederiksen, 1984). In turn, this ability reduces cognitive load, freeing the individual from attending to routine elements of an activity and allowing attention to be focused on the "novel aspects of problem solving" (p. 365). These changes in both long-term and working memory permit the expert not only to process more information, but also to process that information quickly and accurately.

Changes in Thought Processes

Because of the changes that have occurred in the organization of the knowledge base and in the ways that specific information is remembered and retrieved, transformations can also be identified in the thinking patterns and reasoning abilities of an expert. Three significant changes are of particular importance. First, an expert's declarative knowledge, the collection of facts and concepts about the domain, is better organized than that of novices (Yekovich et al., 1991), permitting the expert to efficiently access and then to apply this knowledge (VanSickle & Hoge, 1989). This development facilitates the encoding of information held in working memory, allowing the expert to think and, subsequently, to work quickly and spontaneously.

Second, as more domain-specific declarative and procedural knowledge is acquired and rich schemata are cultivated, patterns of meaningful information are stored and classified (Chase & Chi, 1981). Mental catalogues of patterns, categories, and models enable the expert to classify, compare, and, ultimately, apply the appropriate chunk of information during the decision-making process (Papa, Shores, & Meyer, 1990). Finally, domain-specific schemata permit experts to make inferences, especially within novel situations. Schemata can represent knowledge about events we experience (Glaser, 1984). These schemata allow experts to fill in the information that may be missing or unstated within the situation, to integrate new information with prior knowledge, and then to make inferences or assumptions that go "beyond the observations that are available in any one stance" (p. 100).

In summary, as knowledge is integrated with experience, the evolving expert develops the appropriate schemata to record the interrelationship between the events taking place and the information that is used. These schemata are modified, refined, and, ultimately, become reflections of expertise as they are associated with successful problem-solving experiences. Just as time and experience transform the cognitive processes of an individual, changes are also unfolding in the actions and performance level of the aspiring expert.

ROLE OF ACTION IN EXPERTISE

The evidence of expertise is manifested through the performance of a task or skill. The performance of this action is characterized by accuracy and efficiency. As an extensive knowledge base is blended with efficient and highly organized thinking patterns, the outcome exhibited is a distinctive change in the actions of the emerging expert. Frensch and Sternberg (1989) have defined expertise as "the ability, acquired by practice, to perform qualitatively well in a particular task domain" (p. 158). This operational definition of expertise is directly tied to performance and is framed by three significant parameters.

First, practice appears to be linked to the development of competent performance. In discussing how expertise is acquired, Chase and Chi (1981) conclude:

> The most obvious answer is practice, thousands of hours of practice....
> There may be some as yet undiscovered basic abilities that underlie the attainment of truly exceptional performance . . . but for the most part practice is by far the best predictor of performance. (p. 112)

The expert chess players studied by Chase & Simon (1973) had more than ten years of experience in playing the game. Lesgold and his co-authors (1988) investigated the nature of expertise in the domain of radiology and determined that an average resident may see 40 cases per day while a senior staff radiologist may see on the order of 65 to 70. If each case counts as a trial in the sense of a classical psychological learning study, then the work described here can be seen as dealing with the 10,000th to 200,000th trials. (p. 312)

These examples point to the importance of time spent learning and perfecting a skill. Although the amount of time will vary from domain to domain and from individual to individual, practice is a universal requisite to the development of expertise.

The second parameter concerns the quality of the performance. Performance may be defined in two ways: the enactment of reasoning abilities or the execution of a particular skill. On the one hand, "experts are considered experts . . . because the products of their reasoning are qualitatively superior to those of nonexperts" (Frensch & Sternberg, 1989, p. 159). On the other hand, proficient performers exhibit a fluid, seemingly effortless performance (Berliner, 1988). These experts no longer must think about their actions because they intuitively "seem to know where to be or what to do at the right time" (p. 5).

The third parameter that characterizes expert performance concerns the domain-dependent nature of expertise (Frensch & Sternberg, 1989). This characteristic implies that an individual becomes an expert in the domain in which the necessary knowledge base and the appropriate and well-rehearsed skills have been acquired. Although proficiency may be cultivated in a number of different areas, "expertise in one domain does not necessarily follow from expertise in another domain" (p. 160). The demands and particular features of each domain determine the specific skills and actions that characterize expert performance. Quality of performance, however, is the pervasive attribute that is common to all areas of expertise. The development of expertise not only affects the outward actions of an individual, but also influences the problem-solving strategies utilized by experts across all domains.

The Role of Action in Problem-Solving

In a description of the differences in actions between novices and experts, research on the problem-solving characteristics of these two groups has shown several striking differences. First, experts and novices differ in the way they mentally represent problems. A problem representation is the solver's internal model of the problem, consisting of the stated and unstated variables of the problem as well as any embellishments that can be supplied by the solver's domain-related knowledge. The quality of this internal prototype is determined not only by the knowledge available to the problem-solver, but also by the way that knowledge is organized.

Problem representation is facilitated by the extensive and well-organized knowledge base of the expert (Alexander & Judy, 1988; Frederiksen, 1984; Glaser, 1984; Voss et al., 1983). Moreover, the structure of this knowledge base mirrors the abstract principles of the particular domain (Frensch & Sternberg, 1989). Experts, consequently, tend to focus on the semantics or underlying principles of the problems, while novices concentrate on the surface or superficial aspects (Voss, 1989). For example, experts in the field of physics "organize information in relation to higher level laws and principles . . . and use this knowledge to classify and solve physics problems. Novices, on the other hand, tend to organize information at a lower level such as that of specific variables" (p. 265). By focusing on principles, rules, and laws, experts are able to make high-level inferences from their knowledge base and are more capable of "separating relevant information from irrelevant information" (Carter, Sabers, Cushing, Pinnegar, & Berliner, 1987, p. 147).

Second, experts tend to establish a context for the problem. Establishing context facilitates problem representation because it allows the expert to place a "text-based problem" into a meaningful solution-based framework (Alexander & Judy, 1988, p. 392). The context for the problem varies with the domain. In social studies, experts may link the problem to a historical or political context (Voss et al., 1983), while expert legal analysts may categorize cases according to the type of court or the judge of the case (Lundeberg, 1987).

Third, experts and novices use different thinking and reasoning skills to solve problems. For example, experts tend to work in a forward fashion and novices work problems from a backward approach (Larkin, McDermott, Simon, & Simon, 1980). In forward thinking, the hypothesis is generated from actual information within the problem statement. Backward thinking is characterized by first creating the hypothesis and then attempting to fit the facts of the problem into that hypothesis. This method is cumbersome not only because of the mental backtracking involved, but also because of the additional burden placed on the capacities of short-term memory (Frederiksen, 1984).

Finally, findings across a variety of tasks and domains have documented that experts employ different strategies to shape, to frame, and ultimately to solve problems (Chi et al., 1981; Larkin et al., 1980; Voss et al., 1983). For example, in the initial stages of the problem-solving process, experts take more time to plan, to review, and, finally, to construct an abstracted version of the problem (Alexander & Judy, 1988). The completeness and coherence of the initial stages of problem-solving can ultimately affect the efficiency and accuracy of further thinking (Glaser, 1984). Furthermore, Voss and his colleagues (1983) observed that experts engaged in more problem analysis and solution evaluation than novices. For example, experts tended to systematically evaluate, support, and reflect on their solutions. The thinking patterns and reasoning abilities of experts, consequently, can lead to better and more successful solutions than those of novices.

Capabilities of Expert Problem-Solvers

There are no shortcuts to becoming a sophisticated problem-solver. Voss (1989) contends that developing problem-solving skills is a gradual process requiring the individual to "build up a knowledge base of both declarative and procedural knowledge" (p. 275). Because experts can recognize and respond to a variety of problem situations, their problem-solving capabilities incorporate both flexibility and opportunistic planning.

Voss (1989) maintains that a major characteristic of a good problem-solver is flexibility. This flexibility emerges only after a substantial knowledge base is acquired and is "integrated with knowing how to use such knowledge in a wide range of problem contexts" (p. 285). The highly organized knowledge base allows experts to respond flexibly to the demands of the problems by permitting them to select "those procedures that optimally reflect the problem-solving situations" (Frensch & Sternberg, 1989, p. 180). Furthermore, these procedures are domain-specific strategies. Recent research "suggests that superior problem-solving skill does not derive from superior heuristics, but rather from domain specific skill" (Owen & Sweller, 1989, p. 327).

Expert problem-solvers are also opportunistic planners (Berliner, 1986; Voss, 1989). Opportunistic planning refers to solving a problem by first setting up a sequence of subgoals (Hayes-Roth & Hayes-Roth, 1979). As the opportunity arises, a subgoal is solved, regardless of the original order of the subgoals. The solution sequence for sophisticated problem-solvers is not a fixed or unalterable path, but rather a changing and evolving process. This capability to easily alter the solution path is a characteristic of expert problem-solvers and demonstrates the interconnectedness of declarative and procedural knowledge.

CONCLUSIONS

The development of expertise is a gradual process that is characterized by the integration of an extensive and cognitively well organized knowledge base with experiences in applying that knowledge. The transition from novice to expert is facilitated by practice, with appropriate feedback. Regardless of the domain, experts across a variety of areas exhibit similarities in the characteristics of their knowledge base, in their thinking patterns, and in their skilled performance. Three conclusions can be derived from synthesis of this information on expertise.

First, past discussion of expertise has centered on the differences between novices and experts. On the one hand, this analysis is necessary in order to understand how experts think and act as well as to develop instructional techniques to facilitate the development of expertise in more novicelike individuals.

On the other hand, such an analysis dichotomizes expertise into extreme polarities. The acquisition of expertise should be viewed as a journey along a continuum. Dreyfus and Dreyfus (1986) have adopted this perspective in their general theory about the development of expertise. Their model provides a set of five categories that more precisely identify the various levels of expertise: novice, advanced beginner, competence, proficiency, and expertise. By breaking down expertise into these five steps, this theory not only clarifies the "fuzzy" areas that occur as a novice is transformed into an expert, but also provides a framework for explaining why all novices do not become experts.

Research into domain-specific and strategic knowledge has powerful implications for future studies of expertise, especially in educational leadership. Because the interaction of content and strategic knowledge is a phenomenon that is context-dependent, studies of educational administrators must take place in the environment in which this interaction occurs—the school. When studies of administrative expertise operate within the context of the school milieu, important social–contextual variables such as motivation and values can be identified, evaluated, and understood.

Finally, a cognitive analysis of administrative expertise will help in identifying those specific experiences that facilitate the integration of knowledge about with knowledge of how-to. These experiences can serve as guideposts for the structuring and sequencing of in-service programs, field experiences, and pre-service preparation. The careful and thoughtful development of such learning experiences will engender and maximize expertise in administrative knowledge, thinking, and actions.

NOTE

Support for this research was provided by the National Center for Educational Leadership (NCEL) under U.S. Department of Education Contract No. R117C8005. The views in this report are those of the authors and do not necessarily represent those of the sponsoring institution nor of the universities in the NCEL Consortium—The University of Chicago, Harvard University, and Vanderbilt University.

REFERENCES

Alexander, P., & Judy, J. (1988). The interaction of domain-specific and strategic knowledge in academic performance. *Review of Educational Research, 58*(4), 375–404.

Anderson, J. R. (1982). Acquisition of cognitive skill. *Psychological Review, 8*(4), 369–404.

Berliner, D. C. (1986). In pursuit of the expert pedagogue. *Educational Researcher, 15,* 5–13.

Berliner, D. (1987). Ways of thinking about students and classrooms by more and less experienced teachers. In J. Calderhead (Ed.), *Exploring teachers' thinking* (pp. 60–83). London: Cassell.

Berliner, D. (1988, October). *Implications of studies of expertise in pedagogy for teacher education and evaluation.* Paper presented at the Educational Testing Service Invitational Conference, New York.

Borko, H., & Livingston, C. (1989). Cognition and improvisation: Differences in mathematics instruction by expert and novice teachers. *American Educational Research Journal, 26*(4), 473–498.

Boshuizen, H., & Schmidt, H. (1990, April). *The role of biomedical knowledge in clinical reasoning by experts, intermediates, and novices.* Paper presented at the annual conference of the American Educational Research Association, Boston.

Carter, K., Sabers, D., Cushing, K., Pinnegar, S., & Berliner, D. (1987). Processing and using information about students: A study of expert, novice and postulant teachers. *Teaching and Teacher Education, 3,* 147–157.

Chase, W., & Chi, M. (1981). Cognitive skill: Implications for spatial skill in large-scale environments. In J. Harvey (Ed.), *Cognition, social behavior, and the environment* (pp. 111–136). Hillsdale, NJ: Lawrence Erlbaum Associates.

Chase, W., & Simon, H. (1973). A perception in chess. *Cognitive Psychology, 4,* 55–81.

Chi, M., Feltovich, P., & Glaser, R. (1981). Categorization and representation of physics problems. *Cognitive Science, 5,* 121–152.

Chi, M., Glaser, R., & Rees, E. (1983). Expertise in problem solving. In R. Sternberg (Ed.), *Advances in the psychology of human intelligence* (pp. 7–75). Hillsdale, NJ: Lawrence Erlbaum Associates.

Dreyfus, H., & Dreyfus, S. (1986). *Mind over machine.* New York: The Free Press.

Dunn, T., & Taylor, C. (1990). Hierarchical structures in expert performance. *Educational Technology Research and Design, 38*(2), 5–18.

Feltovich, P., & Patel, V. (1984, April). *The pursuit of understanding in clinical reasoning.* Paper presented at the annual conference of the American Educational Research Association, New Orleans.

Frederiksen, N. (1984). Implications of cognitive theory for instruction in problem solving. *Review of Educational Research, 54*(3), 363–407.

Frensch, P. A., & Sternberg, R. J. (1989). Expertise and intelligent thinking: When is it worse to know better? In R. J. Sternberg (Ed.), *Advances in the psychology of human intelligence: Volume 5* (pp. 157–188). Hillsdale, NJ: Lawrence Erlbaum Associates.

Glaser, R. (1984). The role of knowledge. *American Psychologist, 39*(2), 93–104.

Hayes-Roth, B., & Hayes-Roth, F. (1979). A cognitive model of planning. *Cognitive Science, 3,* 275–310.

Klahr, D., & Carver, S. (1987, April). *Cognitive objectives in a LOGO debugging curriculum: Instruction, learning, and transfer.* Paper presented at the annual meeting of the American Educational Research Association, Washington, DC.

Kolodner, J. (1983). Towards an understanding of the role of experience in the evolution from novice to expert. *International Journal of Man–Machine Studies, 19,* 497–518.

Larkin, J., McDermott, J., Simon, D., & Simon, H. (1980). Expert and novice performance in solving physics problems. *Science, 208,* 1335–1342.

Lesgold, A. (1984). Acquiring expertise. In J. R. Anderson & S. M. Kosslyn (Eds.), *Tutorials in learning and memory* (pp. 31–60). San Francisco: Freeman.

Lesgold, A., Glaser, R., Rubinson, H., Klopfer, D., Feltovich, P., & Wang, Y. (1988). Expertise in a complex skill: Diagnosing x-ray pictures. In T. Chi, R. Glaser, & M. Farr (Eds.), *The nature of expertise* (pp. 311–342). Hillsdale, NJ: Lawrence Erlbaum Associates.

Lundeberg, M. (1987). Metacognitive aspects of reading comprehension: Studying understanding in legal case analysis. *Reading Research Quarterly, 22,* 407–432.

Owen, E., & Sweller, J. (1989). Should problem solving be used as a learning device in mathematics? *Journal for Research in Mathematics Education, 20*(3), 322–328.

Papa, F., Shores, J., & Meyer, S. (1990). Effects of pattern matching, pattern discrimination, and experience in the development of diagnostic expertise. *Academic Medicine, 65*(94), S21-S22.

Schmidt, H. G., & Norman, G. R. (1990, April). *Transitory stages in the development of expertise in medicine: Review of the evidence.* Paper presented at the annual conference of the American Educational Research Association, Boston.

Simon, H. (1980). Problem solving and education. In D. Tuma & F. Reif (Eds.), *Problem solving and education: Issues in teaching and research* (pp. 81–96). Hillsdale, NJ: Lawrence Erlbaum Associates.

VanSickle, R. L., & Hoge, J. D. (1989, November). *Problem solving in social studies: Concepts and critiques.* Paper presented at the annual meeting of the College and University Faculty Assembly of the National Council for the Social Studies, St. Louis, MO.

Voss, J. F. (1989). Problem solving and the educational process. In A. Lesgold & R. Glaser (Eds.), *Foundations for a psychology of education* (pp. 251–294). Hillsdale, NJ: Lawrence Erlbaum Associates.

Voss, J., Greene, T., Post, T., & Penner, B. (1983). Problem solving skill in the social sciences. In G. Bower (Ed.), *The psychology of learning and motivation: Advances in research theory, Vol. 17* (pp. 205–232). New York: Academic Press.

Yekovich, F., Thompson, M., & Walker, C. (1991). Generation and verification of inferences by experts and trained nonexperts. *American Educational Research Journal, 28*(1), 189–209.

6   Practical Problem-Solving

Richard K. Wagner

For the past 80 years, the field of administrative management has been split in two. The split is between those who view administrators as rational technicians who solve problems by applying general principles of problem-solving and managerial science, and those who view administrators as craftsmen whose art cannot be reduced to a set of scientific principles (Schön, 1983). The split between those who view administrative management as a science and those who view it as a craft is reflected in a division that spans theory, practice, and training.

Researchers who view management as a science are interested in the study of relatively formal models of problem-solving, including models that can be implemented by a computer, such as Ernst and Newell's (1969) General Problem Solver (GPS). GPS now has a number of more sophisticated competitors, but remains the most widely known program of its kind. The purpose of developing GPS was to show that a set of powerful and general problem-solving techniques could be applied to a wide range of problems, and that the techniques were explicit enough to incorporate into a computer program. When GPS solves a problem, it does the following: (1) translates the problem into an initial state, a desired end state, and permissible operators that can be used to move from the initial to the end state; (2) breaks the problem down into a hierarchy of subgoals and goals; and (3) applied means-ends analysis—performing operations that reduce the distance between the present state and the end state, until the problem is solved. GPS has been able to solve a series of traditional problems such as the tower of Hanoi problem, water jug problems, letter series completion problems, and the three-coin problem. All of these problems are characterized by well-defined initial and end states, and a limited set of well-defined operators. Taking the three-coin problem as an example, the initial state is three coins on a table showing a tail, a head, and another tail. The task is to end up with all coins showing the same—either heads or tails—by turning over any two coins at a time. GPS can solve the problem by translating it into ten subgoals that can be traversed using means–ends analysis.

Researchers who view management as a craft are more likely to study experienced administrators rather than computer programs. The studies are more likely to be somewhat less formal and more descriptive, with a goal of capturing some of the complexities of problem-solving by experts. For example, Scribner (1986) carried out a relatively intensive study of how "unskilled" milk-processing workers fill orders. Filling an order involves retrieving appropriate quantities of goods, including different-sized cartons of milk stored in stacks. Although relatively unsophisticated from the point of view of formal mathematics, experienced workers have surprisingly effective and ingenious ways for completing orders that involved mentally adding and subtracting items to create partial stacks of known quantity, and then carrying out the mathematical manipulations of stacks and partial stacks as opposed to individual counts of cartons.

An example of how the science–craft split has affected managerial practice is provided by the emergence of the general manager. If the crux of problem-solving can be reduced to a set of principles that apply almost regardless of the particular context in which the problem is found, then having general managers makes sense. General managers are individuals whose training and experience are designed to turn them into problem-solving "generalists"—individuals who have mastered the principles of scientific problem-solving that can be brought to bear on a wide variety of problems, even problems for which the general manager has little direct experience.

The other side of the coin for managerial practice is what I refer to as "situated" leadership. The basic idea is that competence is confined to domains of experience. Rather than merely mastering a set of general problem-solving principles, individuals become effective administrators and leaders by learning from their experience within a given content area. Competence is "situated" within a domain as opposed to residing in domain-general principles.

An example of how the split has affected training is whether the emphasis in training is on the scientific method of problem-solving or on the study of problems as they occur in particular contexts. Deans of business schools wrestle with the question of whether to feature theories and principles that are presumed to generalize across many problem types or to feature intensive examination of individual problems presented on a case-by-case basis. Deans of medical schools have, for the most part, landed squarely on the fence. The first two "preclinical" years are devoted to study of the basic principles of science contained in academic subjects such as physiology and chemistry. The second two "clinical" years are devoted to more practical training about how to do family practice or internal medicine, training that takes place not in the formal classroom but in hospital clinics.

By way of organization, I will review the development of each view of management, and then conclude by considering implications of these views for administrative problem-solving.

MANAGEMENT AS SCIENCE

Historically, the view of managers as craftsmen predates the view of managers as scientists. The split can be traced to the beginning of the present century when Taylor (1911/1947) popularized the view that one could explain management in terms of a set of scientific principles just the way one might attempt to explain digestion or gravity. Early proponents of this view include Charles Babbage (1771–1858), a British professor of mathematics who sought to apply scientific principles in the factory to improve productivity and to lower expenses; Frederick Taylor (1856–1915), whose guiding philosophy was published in two books, *Shop Management* and *The Principles of Scientific Management,* reprinted together in Taylor (1911/1947); and Henri Fayol (1841–1925), who attempted to apply the principles of scientific management to increase the productivity not of the individual worker but of entire organizations.

Simon's (1977) influential book *The New Science of Management Decision,* coupled with increasingly powerful and available computers, provided a catalyst for even greater reliance on principles of management science. In the organizations that Simon envisioned, the traditional reliance on judgment, intuition, and creativity was replaced by a reliance on heuristic problem-solving techniques, applied by humans and also by computers using routines such as the General Problem Solver mentioned previously.

Heuristic problem-solving techniques when applied by human managers have collectively been referred to as rational approaches to problem-solving (Isenberg, 1986). A widely implemented rational approach to problem-solving called the rational manager was proposed by Kepner and Tregoe (1965) in what has become a classic text on rational management. This approach was embodied in five principles:

1. *Problems are identified by comparing actual performance to an expected standard of performance.* The existence of a problem is determined by a significant discrepancy between what is happening and what should be happening.
2. *Problems are defined as deviations from expected standards of performance.* The problem is defined by the discrepancy between actual and expected performance that alerted a manager to the existence of a problem in the first place. If, for example, the average verbal SAT for students in the state of Florida has been at the 500 mark for the past ten years, but it dropped to the mid-400 mark this year, a problem is defined as "the average SAT score has dropped by approximately 50 points."
3. *A precise and complete description of the problem is the first step to solution identification.* Included here is a description of precisely what

is happening, where it is happening, when it is happening, and to what extent it is happening.

4. *The cause of the problem will be found by comparing situations in which the problem is found to similar situations in which the problem is not found.* Problems rarely affect everything. In keeping with Plunkett and Hale's (1982) reliance on seeking out differences between situations in which a problem is found and those in which it is not, determining what differentiates the situation in which the problem is found from similar situations in which the problem is not found is the key to determining the cause of the problem.

5. *Problems are the result of some change that has caused an unwanted deviation from expectations.* Assuming the problem is of recent origin, something must have changed to produce it.

Turning to heuristic problem-solving techniques embodied in computer programs, a variety of artificial-intelligence-based problem-solving programs have supplanted earlier heuristic problem-solving programs such as the General Problem Solver. Although many of these programs are based on more complicated heuristics, one most recent approach is based on artificial neural networks. Artificial neural networks are not based on a priori derived heuristics or even identifiable symbol systems. Rather, they consist of richly interconnected sets of simple processing units that learn by example. Thus, an artificial neural network program runs through thousands or hundreds of thousands of training trials in which the network learns to produce a desired output for a given pattern of input data.

Evaluation

After over a half-century of experience with managerial-science-based approaches to problem-solving, a number of strengths and weaknesses have become apparent. Beginning with strengths, the methods are based on sound logic and scientific principles that have some generality. Because the methods "boil down" the essence of problem-solving into a manageable set of basic principles, the methods are easy to communicate and relatively easy to learn.

In spite of these significant strengths, the management-science approach to problem-solving is holding its own at best, and may be in something of a retreat. To take one telling though not very scientific piece of evidence, rational approaches receive little consideration in recent handbooks of managerial problem-solving (e.g., Albert, 1980; Virga, 1987).

Part of the problem for rational approaches to management is a growing body of evidence that suggests that even the most effective managers often deviate from rational methods. The start of this critique of rational management was a series of influential studies by Mintzberg (1973) of what managers actually do, as opposed to what they are supposed to do or what they say they do. Mintzberg found, for example, that even the most effective managers are more likely to grope along with only a vague impression of the problem to be solved than to follow a step-by-step sequence from problem definition to problem solution (Mintzberg, Raisinghani, & Theoret, 1976; see Isenberg, 1986 for similar results). Another problem for rational approaches to managerial problem-solving is a growing recognition that concomitant with generality is a lack of power for solving intractable problems. As mentioned previously, a strength of these approaches is that they can be applied with little or no modification to a wide range of problems. An important limitation, however, is that they are not sufficient to solve difficult or complex problems. Finally, there is a growing recognition that even if managers wanted to follow rational methods faithfully, human reasoning and judgment are characterized by a number of well-entrenched biases that affect problem-solving (see, e.g., Hogarth, 1987; Kahneman, Slovic, & Tversky, 1982; Nisbett & Ross, 1980; Tversky & Kahneman, 1983, 1986). Hogarth (1987) provided a catalog of common biases that affect the acquisition of information, the processing of information, and response selection, which I have summarized in the context of managerial problem-solving (Wagner, 1990).

Acquisition Biases. Managers must acquire a tremendous amount of information as they attempt to understand the problems they confront and to identify potential solutions. Biases that affect the acquisition of information include the following:

1. *Managers overestimate the frequency of occurrence of highly salient or publicized events and underestimate the frequency of occurrence of less salient or publicized events (i.e., the availability heuristic).* Consequently, their view of events associated with the problem to be solved may be distorted.
2. *Information acquired early in the problem-solving process receives too much weight; information acquired late in the problem-solving process receives too little weight.* Managers conceptualize their problems (i.e., develop a problem-solving "set") on the basis of the initial information that is available to them. Subsequent information is interpreted in terms of the conceptualization that emerged from analysis of the initial information, and thus subsequent information may not receive the weight it should receive.
3. *Managers have difficulty conceptualizing problems in ways that transcend their own prior knowledge and experience.* Consequently, every problem a marketing manager is given is seen as a marketing problem,

every problem that a personnel manager is given is seen as a personnel problem, and so on.

4. *Managers discover what they expect to discover.* What managers anticipate influences what they perceive. In addition, managers seek out information that is consistent with their views, and disregard or suppress information that is inconsistent with their views.

5. *When making comparisons, managers give greater weight to the total number of successes rather than to a ratio of the number of successes to the number of successes and failures.* When, for example, managers must decide whom to promote, they tend to evaluate candidates on the basis of the absolute number of previous "hits" (i.e., times when the candidate really came through on an assignment), forgetting to consider a candidate's "misses." Thus, a newer candidate who has had more hits per assignment will lose out to a candidate with a longer, yet poorer, track record.

6. *Concrete information (e.g., personal experience) is given more weight than abstract information (e.g., evaluative reports), even when the abstract information is likely to be much more valid.* Managers pay more attention to things they observe firsthand, even when what they can observe first-hand presents a less representative picture than that obtainable from other sources.

Processing Biases. Once relevant information has been acquired, it must be processed. Due to limitations in managers' ability to process information, a number of biases influence their performance:

1. *Managers apply evaluative criteria inconsistently when they must evaluate a number of courses of action.* Because evaluative criteria shift, comparable courses of action are unlikely to be valued equally.

2. *Once an opinion has been formed, it is not likely to be changed even in the face of new information.* Managers quickly become invested in their opinions. New information that suggests the need to revise prior opinions tends to be discounted.

3. *Managers are not able to estimate the products of nonlinear relations.* For example, a cost that increases exponentially will be underestimated.

4. *Managers are likely to continue using an alternative that has worked before even when it is no longer appropriate.* Personnel managers rely on selection tests as predictors of managerial performance. The predictive power of such tests is modest, at best, yet managers will rely on test scores when making decisions about individuals for whom criterion information is available.

5. *Managers overestimate the stability of data based on small samples.*

When managers go beyond qualitative opinion and collect data relevant to solving a particular problem, they are likely to overestimate the stability of the data they have collected.

6. *Managers make predictions by adjusting expectations relative to an anchor without questioning the continued validity of the anchor.* For example, sales managers may set a goal of increasing sales by 10 percent over last quarter, without considering any special circumstances that might have affected last quarter's sales figures.

Response Biases. Managers are prone to two biases that affect their selection of responses to problems:

1. *Managers are prone to engage in wishful thinking.* As a consequence, they judge the probability of outcomes they favor to be greater than the data warrant, and the probability of outcomes they fear to be less than the data warrant.

2. *Managers succumb to the illusion of control.* The illusion of control refers to an overestimation of the potency of one's actions. By planning for the future, managers may come to believe that they have more control over future outcomes than they in fact have, and to underestimate the importance of factors such as luck and economic conditions over which they have no control.

Concomitant with a growing dissatisfaction of management science has been the reemergence of interest in approaches to understanding managers as practitioners of a complex craft that may not be reducible into sets of general principles.

MANAGEMENT AS CRAFT

Rather than making a half-hearted attempt at covering a burgeoning area of very active research, I will begin by making brief reference to three influential approaches and then describe in relatively more detail an approach that Robert Sternberg and I have taken in our investigations of practical problem-solving.

What the three influential approaches have in common is that they show that managers, typically including very effective managers, rarely if ever follow rational methods of problem-solving. Isenberg (1984, 1986) has documented the degree to which managers, in contrast to the sequence advocated by rational approaches, take some action very early in the problem-solving process as opposed to waiting until "the correct solution" has been identified. A similar point has been made in a series of studies by Mintzberg and colleagues (Mintzberg et al., 1976), in which managers have been found to attack problems recursively—attempting a formulation, trying out a solution, revising the formulation, trying out another solution, and so on.

Schön's (1983) careful descriptions of managers and other professionals suggest that managers do not face simple, isolated problems, but rather dynamic situations involving complex, interwoven problems. Schön argues that given such a turbulent environment, rational-analytic methods will not suffice. Rather, managerial competence appears in the guise of nearly spontaneous action that is based more on tacit intuition than on rationality. Quoting from Schön, "Our knowing is ordinarily tacit, implicit in our patterns of action and in our feel for the stuff with which we are dealing. It seems right to say that our knowing is *in* our action" (p. 49).

If Schön is correct about the fact that much of problem-solving knowledge is tacit, then simply asking managers to describe what they know will result in an incomplete and probably erroneous picture of managerial competence. A more subtle approach is called for.

Tacit Knowledge in Practical Problem-Solving

In a series of studies done in collaboration with Robert Sternberg, I have explored the role of tacit knowledge—practical know-how that rarely is taught directly or even verbalized—in solving the kinds of practical problems found in the everyday world (including the everyday world of work) as opposed to the typical kinds of academic problems found in the classroom and on IQ tests (Wagner, 1987, 1990, 1991a; Wagner & Sternberg, 1985, 1990).

A number of characteristics differentiate academic and practical problems, several of the more salient of which are presented in Table 6.1.

Academic problems tend to be well defined. When you were struggling with an algebra problem in high school or college, you may not have known how to obtain the correct answer but you were clear about the problem that you were supposed to solve. Practical problems, on the other hand, tend to be ill defined. Often, it may not even be clear that there is a problem, let alone just what the problem is. Academic problems are formulated by others, typically teachers and authors of textbooks and IQ tests. Practical problems typically must be formulated by oneself. Either the nature of the problem has yet to be determined, or there is reason to question a problem formulation provided by others. For example, a supervisor may ask you to help solve the problem of a lack of participation in meetings on the part of subordinates. However, the real problem may be that the supervisor actually is not receptive to constructive criticism—even though the supervisor claims to be—and the subordinates have decided not to risk getting burned a second time. Academic problems

Table 6.1   Differences Between Academic and Practical Problems

Academic Problems	Practical Problems
1. Well-defined.	1. Ill-defined.
2. Formulated by others.	2. Formulated by self.
3. All information provided.	3. Additional information required.
4. One correct solution.	4. No single correct solution.
5. One method for obtaining correct solution.	5. Multiple methods for obtaining multiple solutions.
6. Everyday experience (i.e.,common sense) rarely useful.	6. Everyday experience (i.e., common sense) typically useful.

typically come complete with all necessary information. If you know the appropriate steps, no additional information will be required. On the contrary, finding solutions to practical problems often requires obtaining additional information, and knowing how much effort to expend seeking additional information as well as the most effective means for doing so can make all the difference in coming up with a satisfactory solution. Academic problems typically have a single correct answer, and a single method of obtaining the correct answer. Practical problems, on the other hand, typically have multiple partially correct solutions, each associated with liabilities as well as assets, and there may be multiple methods of obtaining each. Finally, it rarely helps to apply everyday knowledge or common sense to the solution of academic problems: Either you learned how to solve the problem in class or you did not. Practical problems, on the other hand, often are insoluble without the application of everyday knowledge or common sense.

The goal of the research I am about to describe has been to understand the nature and role of tacit knowledge in everyday intelligent behavior. For this purpose, we define tacit knowledge as practical know-how that usually is not openly expressed or stated (Oxford English Dictionary, 1933). Tacit knowledge can be classified according to its content, its context, and its orientation (Wagner, 1987).

The Content of Tacit Knowledge. Three contents of tacit knowledge have been identified. Tacit knowledge about *managing oneself* refers to practical know-how about self-organizational and self-motivational aspects of managerial performance. An example of tacit knowledge about managing oneself is knowing how to overcome the problem of procrastination. Tacit knowledge about *managing others* refers to practical know-how about managing one's subordinates, and one's relationships with peers and superiors. An example of tacit knowledge about managing others is knowing how to reward others in such a way that maximizes both productivity and job satisfaction. Tacit knowledge about *managing tasks* refers to practical know-how about how to perform specific tasks well. An example of tacit knowledge about managing tasks is knowing how to give an effective oral presentation.

The Context of Tacit Knowledge. Tacit knowledge with a *local* context refers to practical know-how concerning the short-term accomplishment of a task at hand. The focus is confined to the immediate task or problem, ignoring for the moment the larger context in which the problem exists. An example of tacit knowledge with a local context is knowing how to write an effective summary report. Tacit knowledge with a *global* context refers to practical know-how concerning long-term accomplishment. The focus is on how the present task or problem fits into the larger context. An example of tacit knowledge with a global context is knowing that assigning tasks to employees who have little experience with that particular task can pay off in the long run in terms of developing new skills even when another employee could do the task more quickly.

The Orientation of Tacit Knowledge. Tacit knowledge with an idealistic orientation refers to practical know-how concerning the ideal quality of an idea without regard to its practicality. Tacit knowledge with a pragmatic orientation refers to practical know-how concerning how workable an idea is, without regard to its ideal quality. Both ideal and pragmatic considerations usually matter in realistic problem-solving situations.

Combining Content, Context, and Orientation. By crossing the three contents, two contexts, and two orientations of tacit knowledge, we arrive at the framework portrayed in Figure 6.1. Consider an example of the kind of tacit knowledge represented by each block of the cube. For handling the problem of procrastination, forcing yourself to spend five minutes on a task in the hope that you will continue working once you have begun is an example of tacit knowledge about managing self, with a local context. If it so happens that the task is an important report to your superior, reminding yourself of the long-term consequences to your career of not completing the assignment also may help to avoid procrastination. This is an example of tacit knowledge about managing self, with a global orientation. Regarding making oral presentations, knowing that it helps to inform your audience in advance about what you intend to say is an example of tacit knowledge about managing tasks, with a local context. Recognizing the importance of doing well in an upcoming oral presentation to superiors in the organization whom you have not yet met is an example of tacit knowledge about managing tasks, with a global context. Regarding the unpleasant task of firing an employee, knowing how to fire the employee in a manner that is not unnecessarily punishing is an example of tacit knowledge about managing others, with a local context. Realizing that you may need to get feedback on your personnel practices because you have fired more employees

Figure 6.1 The Tacit-Knowledge Framework

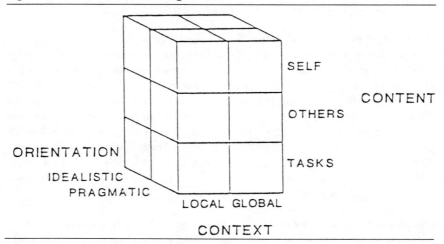

than your peers is an example of tacit knowledge about managing others, with a global context. Finally, for each of the judgments and decisions just mentioned, one might weigh separately how good each is ideally as well as practically.

In a series of studies, we have assessed tacit knowledge by presenting individuals with scenarios that depict practical situations and asking them to rate the quality of a variety of response alternatives. An example of such a scenario is presented in Table 6.2.

Across the studies, several key results have emerged with such consistency that we are confident about their validity (Wagner, 1987, 1990, 1991a, 1991b; Wagner & Sternberg, 1985, 1990, 1991a).

First, our measures of tacit knowledge differentiate groups whose members differ in amount of experience in a career domain. Interestingly, however, not everyone appears to acquire tacit knowledge from the experience at the same rate, and some appear to acquire very little. Apparently, it is not mere experience that matters, but what one learns from it.

Second, performance on measures of tacit knowledge is related to career performance as assessed by a variety of criterion measures of managerial performance. For example, in a study of a group of professional managers, significant correlations were found between tacit knowledge and the managerial criterion measures of salary (.46) and whether one's organization was at the top of the Fortune 500 list (.34). In a study of bank managers for whom more detailed indicators of performance were obtained, tacit knowledge was related significantly to criterion variables such as percentage of salary increase (based on

Table 6.2 A Scenario Used to Measure Managerial Tacit Knowledge

You have just been promoted to head of an important department in your organization. The previous head has been transferred to an equivalent position in a less important department. Your understanding of the reason for the move is that the performance of the department as a whole was mediocre. There were not any glaring deficiencies, just a perception of the department as so-so rather than as very good. Your charge is to shape up the department. Results are expected quickly. Rate the quality of the following strategies for succeeding in your new position.

_____a. Meet with your superiors to describe your strategy for improving the performance of the department.

_____b. Resist the pressure to turn things around in a hurry because quick improvements may come at the expense of long-term negative consequences.

. . .

_____g. Buy some time from your superiors by taking quick, but limited action, then consider what needs to be done in the long run.

merit) (.48) and a rating of the managers' success at generating new business for the bank (.56). In yet another study, we found a significant correlation (.61) between amount of tacit knowledge and rated performance in a managerial problem-solving situation for a group of managers who were participants in a leadership development program at the Center for Creative Leadership.

Third, our measures of tacit knowledge are not simply proxies for IQ tests or personality inventories. In the study of managers at the Center for Creative Leadership just mentioned, we were able to carry out a series of hierarchical regression analyses to determine whether tacit knowledge would predict performance in a managerial problem-solving simulation after partialling out the effects of IQ and personality measures including the California Personality Inventory, the Myers-Briggs, the Fundamental Interpersonal Relations Orientation-Behavior (FIRO-B), the Hidden Figures Test, and other measures. For every analysis, tacit knowledge was found to account for a significant and large proportion of the variance in managerial performance regardless of the other variables that were partialled out.

IMPLICATIONS FOR SCHOOL LEADERSHIP

Obviously, the intent of much of the research that was described in this chapter was not specifically to assess or improve the problem-solving skills of school administrators. Nevertheless, the sheer amount of research that has been carried out and the consistency of certain findings suggest that deriving implications for school leadership is not as wildly imprudent as such an enterprise often is.

One obvious implication of the resurgence of the view of administrative management as a craft that is not easily reducible to a set of principles concerns the feasibility of broad implementation of findings from "what-works" studies as a means to improve our schools. A relatively popular strategy for trying to improve schools has been to study schools that work well to distill characteristics that distinguish schools that work well from comparable schools that do not. This approach has been employed in various settings and at various levels over the years. For example, characteristics of "water-walkers"—superb managers— have been the basis for the critical-incident methodology in which superb managers and average managers are differentiated by the descriptions of how they handled critical tasks. Broad implementation of findings from recent what-works studies is likely to have some positive benefit, at least for schools that are doing things especially poorly, but there is little reason to hope that a majority of schools will be brought up to the level of the top-performing schools that were the basis of the original recommendations. What works is likely to depend as much on specific factors such as who is making what works "work."

A second implication is that effective administrative leadership is not likely to be reducible to a set of basic principles, as much as we would like to be able to do so (Blumberg, 1984). This is not to discount a role for guiding principles we use to organize our day or our approach to a given problem. The point is that such guiding principles are merely guides, and are not sufficient in and of themselves to accomplish the solution of real problems of the sort faced by school leaders.

A third implication is that attempts to measure and, if possible, to train aspects of managerial practical know-how or common sense for those who aspire to be school leaders may be beneficial. We have begun the measurement part of this for business managers with the recent publication of the Tacit Knowledge Inventory for Managers (Wagner & Sternberg, 1991b), a test to be used for selecting individuals who show promise as managers. The second part of this, training managerial tacit knowledge, has yet to be explored with any depth. An approach we have begun to study involves attempting to convey at least some general aspects of tacit knowledge using the vehicle of "rules of thumb." For example, a useful rule of thumb that distinguishes top performers from average performers in a variety of situations is to "think in terms of tasks accomplished rather than hours spent working." Average performers are likely to reward themselves for putting in long hours on a task. Top performers, who tend to be more goal or "throughput" oriented, are more likely to reward themselves for completing important tasks as opposed to merely working hard at them.

In the end, improving school leadership is likely to be a slow process that is not accomplished with any kind of quick fix no matter how scientifically sound the fix appears to be. Of course, this prediction can be made by anyone who knows that the best predictor of future behavior is past behavior. But what the research that has been reviewed shows is that one reason for the difficulty in applying quick fixes is that effectively school leadership is a complicated art and craft as much as it is a science, and becoming good at arts and crafts is not as easy as mastering a handful of principles with near universal generality.

REFERENCES

Albert, K. J. (Ed.). (1980). *Handbook of business problem solving.* New York: McGraw-Hill.

Blumberg, A. (1984). The craft of school administration and some other rambling thoughts. *Educational Administration Quarterly, 20,* 24–40.

Ernst, G. W., & Newell, A. (1969). *GPS: A case study in generality and problem solving.* New York: Academic Press.

Hogarth, R. M. (1987). *Judgment and choice.* New York: John Wiley & Sons.

Isenberg, D. J. (1984). How senior managers think. *Harvard Business Review, 62,* 81–90.

Isenberg, D. J. (1986). Thinking and managing: A verbal protocol analysis of managerial problem solving. *Academy of Management Journal, 4,* 775–788.

Kahneman, D., Slovic, P., & Tversky, A. (Eds.). (1982). *Judgment under uncertainty: Heuristics and biases.* New York: Cambridge University Press.

Kepner, C. H., & Tregoe, B. B. (1965). *The rational manager: A systematic approach to problem solving and decision making.* New York: McGraw-Hill.

Mintzberg, H. (1973). *The nature of managerial work.* New York: Harper & Row.

Mintzberg, H., Raisinghani, D., & Theoret, A. (1976). The structure of "unstructured" decision processes. *Administrative Science Quarterly, 21,* 246–275.

Nisbett, R. E., & Ross, L. (1980). *Human inference: Strategies and shortcomings of social judgment.* Englewood Cliffs, NJ: Prentice-Hall.

Oxford English Dictionary (1933). Oxford: Clarendon Press.

Plunkett, L. C., & Hale, G. A. (1982). *The proactive manager.* New York: John Wiley & Sons.

Schön, D. A. (1983). *The reflective practitioner.* New York: Basic Books.

Scribner, S. (1986). Thinking in action: Some characteristics of practical thought. In R. J. Sternberg & R. K. Wagner (Eds.), *Practical intelligence: Nature and origins of competence in the everyday world* (pp. 13–30). New York: Cambridge University Press.

Simon, H. A. (1977). *The new science of management decision.* Englewood Cliffs, NJ: Prentice-Hall.

Taylor, F. W. (1911/1947). *Scientific management.* New York: Harper & Row.

Tversky, A., & Kahneman, D. (1983). Extensional versus intuitive reasoning: The conjunction fallacy in probability judgment. *Psychological Review, 90,* 293–315.

Tversky, A., & Kahneman, D. (1986). Rational choice and the framing of decisions. *Journal of Business, 59,* 251–278.

Virga, P. H. (Ed.). (1987). *The National Management Association handbook for managers.* Englewood Cliffs, NJ: Prentice-Hall.

Wagner, R. K. (1987). Tacit knowledge in everyday intelligent behavior. *Journal of Personality and Social Psychology, 52,* 1236–1247.

Wagner, R. K. (1990). Products and processes of practical reasoning. *International Journal of Research in Education, 14,* 437–454.

Wagner, R. K. (1991a). Managerial problem-solving. In R. J. Sternberg & P. Frensch (Eds.), *Complex problem solving: Principles and mechanisms* (pp. 159–183). Hillsdale, NJ: Lawrence Erlbaum Associates.

Wagner, R. K. (1991b). Managerial tacit knowledge. *Consulting Psychology Bulletin, 43,* 55–58.

Wagner, R. K., & Sternberg, R. J. (1985). Practical intelligence in real-world pursuits: The role of tacit knowledge. *Journal of Personality and Social Psychology, 48,* 436–458.

Wagner, R. K., & Sternberg, R. J. (1990). Street smarts. In K. Clark & M. Clark (Eds.), *Measures of leadership* (pp. 493–504). Greensboro, NC: Center for Creative Leadership.

Wagner, R. K., & Sternberg, R. J. (1991a). Tacit knowledge: Its uses in identifying, assessing, and developing managerial talent. In J. Jones, B. Steffy, & D. Bray (Eds.), *Applying psychology in business: The manager's handbook* (pp. 333–344). New York: Lexington.

Wagner, R. K., & Sternberg, R. J. (1991b). *The Tacit Knowledge Inventory for Managers (TKIM).* San Antonio, TX: The Psychological Corporation.

7 The Relationship Between Variations in Patterns of School Leadership and Group Problem-Solving Processes

Kenneth Leithwood and Rosanne Steinbach

The field of educational administration has been inordinately late in recognizing the value of knowing more about how its practitioners think and the processes they use to solve problems central to their work. This is the case in spite of compelling evidence accumulating in closely allied, if not overlapping, fields (Schwenk, 1988). The present study is part of a larger program of research, begun in 1986, aimed at addressing this neglect. Many earlier products of the program have been described in Leithwood, Begley, and Cousins (1992), as well as elsewhere. Our most recent work (Leithwood, Steinbach, & Dart, in press) has explored directly the relationship between problem-solving processes and different patterns of administrative practice. This research reflects increased attention to the importance of domain-specific knowledge in explaining variation in the quality of administrators' problem-solving. Relationships between problem-solving expertise and length of administrative experience, gender, and organizational size have also been examined.

These several foci of our most recent work have been pursued in the context of school-improvement problems largely solved by principals individually. Evidence from earlier work, however, suggests that as administrative problems become more complex (many school-improvement problems are of this sort) and as administrators' experience and expertise increase, they are more inclined to involve others in solving problems collaboratively (Leithwood & Steinbach, 1990). This rise in collaborative problem-solving appears to be justified on the grounds that it leads to better solutions, increased commitment to those solutions, and long-term growth of participants (Leithwood & Steinbach, 1991). These benefits are due in large measure to evidence concerning the severe limits placed on an individual's processing of information by the restricted capacity of "short-term" or "working" memory. Simon (1957) captured this limitation concisely with the term "bounded rationality."

The study described in this chapter is a further exploration of the nature of collaborative problem-solving processes. It parallels Leithwood et al. (in press) using the same sample of administrators, but describing their problem-solving in collaboration with their staffs rather than by themselves. The sample consisted of selected principals in British Columbia, Canada, who were attempting to improve their schools through the implementation of a major Ministry of Education policy initiative. Called the Primary Program this initiative aimed to restructure the first four years of schooling through such organizational changes as ungradedness, continuous progress, and dual entry periods to kindergarten (Primary Program Foundation Document, 1990). Instructional changes were premised on a constructivist image of learning and aimed at the type of active participation of students in their own learning evident, for example, in "whole language" approaches to instruction (e.g., Watson, 1989). Anecdotal reporting to parents, greater parent involvement as "partners" in instruction, and a concern for better meeting the needs of a culturally diverse population of students were among the elements of the Primary Program. The program itself was part of a broader set of policies (Year 2000, 1989) to be implemented through the end of secondary school over a ten-year period.

FRAMEWORK

Patterns of School Leadership

One obvious explanation for variation in principals' contribution to school improvement is offered by research describing differences in the practices they use for this purpose (Blase, Dedrick, & Strathe, 1986; Blumberg & Greenfield, 1980; Brady, 1985; Hall, Rutherford, Hord, & Huling, 1984; Hoy & Brown, 1986; Leithwood & Montgomery, 1986; Salley, McPherson, & Baehr, 1978). Four distinct patterns of practice (or styles) are evident in this research, which Leithwood, Begley, and Cousins (1990) have summarized as follows:

> Leadership style [or pattern] A is characterized by a focus on interpersonal relationships; on establishing a cooperative and genial "climate" in the school and effective, collaborative relationships with various community and central office groups. Principals adopting this style seem to believe that such relationships are critical to their overall success and provide a necessary springboard for more task-oriented activities in their schools.
>
> Student achievement, well-being, and growth is the central focus of leadership Style B. Descriptions of this class of practices suggest that while such achievement and well-being are the goal, principals use a variety of means to accomplish it. These include many of the interpersonal, administrative, and managerial behaviors that provide the central focus of other styles.

Compared with styles A and B, there is less consistency, across the four dozen studies reviewed, in the practices classified as style C (programme focus). Principals adopting this style, nevertheless, share a concern for ensuring effective programmes, improving the overall competence of their staff, and developing procedures for carrying out tasks central to programme success. Compared with style A, the orientation is to the task, and developing good interpersonal relations is viewed as a means to better task achievement. Compared with style B, there is a greater tendency to view the adoption and implementation of apparently effective procedures for improving student outcomes as a goal—rather than the student outcomes themselves.

Leadership style D is characterized by almost exclusive attention to what is often labelled "administrivia"—the nuts and bolts of daily school organization and maintenance. Principals adopting this style, according to all four studies, are preoccupied with budgets, timetables, personnel administration, and requests for information from others. They appear to have little time for instructional and curriculum decision making in their schools, and tend to become involved only in response to a crisis or a request. (pp. 12–13)

There is considerable evidence to warrant the claim that patterns B and C make the greatest contribution to school improvement—especially pattern B (e.g., Heck, Larsen, & Marcoulides, 1990; Leithwood & Montgomery, 1982). Indeed, these four patterns appear to represent a hierarchy in terms of their contribution to school improvement with the student-growth focus (B) making the greatest contribution followed in diminishing order by the program focus (C), the interpersonal-relationships focus (A), and the building-manager focus (D) (Hall et al., 1984; Leithwood & Montgomery, 1986; Stevens & Marsh, 1987; Trider & Leithwood, 1988). Such differences in effectiveness are partly explained by the increased inclusivity of patterns closer to the student-growth focus; this focus, for example, also includes attention to building management, school climate, and school programs but as "means" to the student-growth "end," not as ends themselves.

The prior study out of which this one builds most directly (Leithwood et al., in press) found evidence of all four patterns of practice in principals' school-improvement efforts. In that study, both patterns B and C were considered to be variations of "instructional leadership." Among principals demonstrating such leadership, some did so in a very direct way—through modeling new forms of teaching, for example; others provided such leadership indirectly by ensuring, for instance, that new forms of instruction were modeled but not doing the modeling themselves. Both forms of instructional leadership included concern for creating conditions in the school (second-order changes) that would give teachers the best chance of successfully implementing the Primary Program. Three principals were classified as direct instructional leaders (DIL) and five were classified as indirect instructional leaders (IIL).

The third pattern of practice corresponds to leadership style A (interpersonal-relationship focus). We labeled it "teacher-centered management" (TCM). These principals were supportive of the school-improvement effort and reasonably knowledgeable about the Primary Program. They were also intellectually engaged in the improvement process, interacting from time to time with teachers. But their involvement was neither intensive nor particularly direct. Two principals in our study demonstrated this pattern.

The fourth pattern of practice closely corresponds to what was described earlier as leadership D (building-manager focus). Two of the twelve principals in our study demonstrated such a focus, which we labeled "building-centered management" (BCM). These principals, concerned mainly with budgets, timetables, and so forth, were only minimally involved with the Primary Program.

Evidence from the Leithwood et al. (in press) study also supports the claim that the four patterns of practice constitute a hierarchy of effectiveness. Dependent variables in that study included the form of the schools' culture, changes in the attitudes and behaviors of teachers, and teachers' perceptions of the helpfulness of the principals' leadership. So, for example, the school-improvement efforts of direct instructional leaders (Style B) as compared with building managers (Style D) were associated with greater professional collaboration among teachers. Those efforts were also associated with more positive attitudes on the part of teachers toward the improvements being attempted in the school and more changes in teachers' classroom practices reflecting the intentions of such improvements. Teachers working with instructional leaders also valued more highly those leaders' assistance in implementing school improvements.

Problem-Solving Processes

What principals do depends on what they think. More specifically, the patterns of practice used for school improvement are products of how principals think about and approach not just the overall problem of school improvement but also the multitude of smaller, imbedded subproblems. Only recently, however, has systematic research begun to be devoted to the thinking and problem-solving of educational administrators and accumulated evidence to date is quite small. Considerably more research has been reported on the problem-solving and strategic thinking of managers and leaders in noneducational organizations (Schwenk, 1988; Srivastva, 1983). Without a better understanding of principals' thinking and problem-solving, it is difficult to explain differences in their school-improvement practices; nor are attempts to assist principals in acquiring more effective patterns of practice likely to be especially successful. Further, a significant number of school-improvement problems are unpredictable and must be solved in contexts that are highly variable. Under such contingent circumstances, it is unlikely that any single set of specific interventions will be reliably effective (Leitner, in press). Much more important is the quality of those problem-solving processes (or thinking) giving rise to practice.

The present study inquired about principals' thinking and problem-solving using theoretical orientations to and results from our own program of research in this area. Taking contemporary cognitive science theory as a point of departure (e.g., Chi, Feltovich, & Glaser, 1981; Frederiksen, 1984; Voss, Greene, Post, & Penner, 1983), this research has investigated differences in the problem-solving processes of "expert" and typical principals. Among the most significant results of this research to date is a model of educational administrators' problem-solving consisting of six constructs defined as follows:

Interpretation: a principal's understanding of the specific nature of the problem, often in situations where multiple problems may be identified;

Goals: the relatively immediate purposes that the principal is attempting to achieve in response to his or her interpretation of the problem;

Principles/Values: the relatively long-term purposes, operating principles, fundamental laws, doctrines, values, and assumptions guiding the principal's thinking;

Constraints: "barriers or obstacles" that must be overcome if an acceptable solution to the problem is to be found;

Solution Processes: what the principal does to solve a problem in light of his or her interpretation of the problem, principles, and goals to be achieved and constraints to be accommodated;

Affect: the feelings, mood, and sense of self-confidence the principal experiences when involved in problem-solving.

Leithwood and Stager (1989) and Leithwood and Steinbach (1990) described processes associated with each of these constructs used by both expert and typical samples of administrators solving problems individually. Leithwood and Steinbach (1991) provided similar data but in a collaborative problem-solving context. Table 7.1, summarizing the results of that study, was used as a starting point for coding and analyzing data in the present study. Aspects of collaborative problem-solving described in Table 7.1 and signified with an asterisk were incorporated into the coding form for the present study. As the asterisks indicate, emphasis in the present study was on the solution process component, in particular.

Building on this prior research, the study described in this chapter addressed three sets of questions:

• Are variations in school-improvement leadership practices associated with variation in group problem-solving processes?

Table 7.1　Principals' Problem-Solving Processes with Others: A Comparison of Expert and Typical Principals

Components	Experts	Typical
Interpretation	• understands importance of having a clear interpretation of problem	• does no conscious reflection on this matter
	• seeks out and takes into account the interpretation others have of the problem	• assumes others share same interpretation
	*• immediate problem usually viewed in its relation to the larger mission and problems of school	• has tendency for problems to be viewed in isolation
	• has a clear interpretation which he/she can describe to others and rationalize	• has less clarity about the interpretation; difficulty in explaining it to others
	*• has multiple goals for problem solving	• has multiple goals for problem solving
	• shares own goals with others involved in problem solving	• shares own goals with others involved in problem solving
Goals	• has goals for both the problem and the meeting in which collaborative problem solving occurs	• has goals for both the problem and the meeting in which collaborative problem solving occurs
	• has a strong concern for the development of goals both the principal and staff can agree to	• is concerned with achieving only own goals and getting staff to agree to those goals
	*• has less of personal stake in any preconceived solution; wants the best possible solution the group can produce	• is often strongly committed to a preconceived solution and attempts to manipulate group problem solving to result in support for the preconceived solution
Principles/Values	• order of frequency of mention of value categories: Professional Values, Basic Human Values, Social and Political Values, and General Moral Values	• order of frequency of mention of value categories: Professional Values, Basic Human Values, Social and Political Values, and General Moral Values
	• most frequently mentioned specific value: Specific Role Responsibilities	• most frequently mentioned specific value: Specific Role Responsibilities
	• mean total of 21 value statements	• mean total of 16.6 value statements
	• high use of specific values: Respect for others, Participation Consequences for clients, Knowledge - in that order	• high use of specific values: Consequences for clients, Respect for others, Loyalty, Happiness - in that order
Constraints	*• accurately anticipates obstacles likely to arise during group problem solving	• does not anticipate obstacles or identifies relatively superficial ones
	• plans in advance for how to address anticipated obstacles	• rarely considers in advance how to respond to obstacles that are predicted
	*• adapts and responds flexibly to unanticipated obstacles which arise	

Table 7.1 Continued

Components	Experts	Typical
	• views obstacles not as major impediments to problem solving	
Solution process	*• has well-developed plan for collaborative problem solving (meeting)	• rarely plans for collaborative process and may value "spontaneity"
	*• provides clear, detailed introduction to problem and its background to collaborators	• introduces problem unclearly and occasionally misses altogether
	*• outlines clearly the process for problem solving (e.g. how meeting will be conducted)	• is not likely to share plan for meeting with collaborators if plan exists
	*• carefully checks collaborators' interpretations of problem and own assumptions	• assumes others have same interpretations of problem; does not check
	*• without intimidating or restraining others, clearly indicates own view of the problem and relationship with larger problems	• argues stubbornly for own view or "orchestrates" meeting so that it supports such a view
	*• remains open to new information and changes views, if warranted	• adheres to own view in the face of competing views
	*• assists collaborative problem solving by synthesizing, summarizing, and clarifying as needed and by keeping group (gently) on track	• uses limited action to assist collaboration and may seriously underestimate time required for collaborators to explore problem as principal has
	*• ensures that follow-up is planned	• rarely considers plans for follow-up
Affect	*• always appears to be calm and confident	• usually appears calm but frustration may occasionally become visible
	• hidden anxieties usually the result of inability to find a workable solution	• frequently feels frustrated, especially by unwillingness of staff to agree with principal's views
	*• invariably treats others politely [shows respect and courtesy to staff]	• shows occasional signs of insecurity about own ability to solve problems
	• uses humor to diffuse tension and to clarify information	• uses humor to diffuse tension and to clarify information

From Leithwood & Steinbach, 1991

- Within which aspects of group problem-solving do principals demonstrate greatest variation?
- To what extent are variations in leadership practices and group problem-solving processes associated with principals' age, administrative experience, and gender?

Method

Twelve schools in three districts (four schools per district) were selected for the study. Eight of these schools had volunteered to be pilot schools ("Lead Schools") for implementing the new Primary Program policy. Four were chosen from the seven elementary schools in one district that were initiating activities related to the policy.

Data related to principals' thinking and problem-solving were collected at two points in the year (fall and spring). At the beginning of the school year (about 2 1/2 months after the start of implementation) principals were asked how they were going about solving the current school-improvement problem (i.e., implementing the Primary Program policy). In a semi-structured interview schedule, principals were asked to describe the problem and then discuss what they wanted to accomplish, the values that might be influencing them, constraints that might be impeding progress, and the specific steps taken to solve the problem. These interviews provided the data for the study reported in Leithwood et al. (in press). As discussed earlier, that study described the four patterns of practice exhibited by the 12 school leaders.

Toward the end of the school year principals were interviewed again. This time they were asked to reflect on their thinking during a previously taped staff meeting called to address a problem related to implementation of the school-improvement policy. Instead of having principals rely on their memories of what occurred at the meeting, an audiotape was used to "stimulate recall."

Data for this set of interviews were collected on three occasions. Prior to the staff meeting, principals were interviewed about the nature of the problem they would be working on, what they expected and wanted to happen at the meeting, and what they were planning to do. Next, an audiotape recording was made of the portion of the staff meeting addressing the chosen problem. Finally, after some preliminary instructions, the principal and interviewer listened to the tape of the meeting together, stopping frequently to ask questions or offer information about intentions and thought processes. This discussion was recorded on a separate tape, which was subsequently transcribed carefully to eliminate all identifying characteristics. These transcripts provided the data for the present study.

Based on the findings of our previous research on the collaborative problem-solving of expert and typical principals (see Table 7.1), along with some additional insights, a coding form for analyzing the data was developed including 18 determinants of collaborative problem-solving. This coding form focused most heavily on the solution process steps used by principals, although key items related to the interpretation, goals, constraints, and mood components of our problem-solving model were also included. New components examined were principals' use of problem-relevant knowledge, the degree/quality of self-reflection, and staff development as a goal for staff meetings. In order to quantify the analysis, responses were classified according to the coding form and rated on a five-point scale (expert=5 points, typical=1 point). To earn a rating of 5, responses had to be explicit and/or appear three or more times.

Each transcript was divided into relevant statements made by the principal, which were then numbered sequentially. Two researchers worked together, using two training protocols, to classify and rate each statement. Once the raters felt comfortable with their degree of understanding, they coded and rated the 10 remaining protocols independently. Interrater reliability was .73 (Pearson Product Correlation). Although this is an acceptable level of reliability, a check of the data indicated that it did not adequately reflect the extent of rater agreement. Except for a very few occasions, ratings never differed more than one point and a test failed to identify any significant differences between the raters (t=0.99, p=0.32). In addition, when mean scores given by each rater for each principal were compared, the correlation was .87. All differences in ratings were discussed, disputes were resolved, and principals were assigned a single score for each of the 18 items on the coding form. A mean score was also computed for each principal.

RESULTS

This section summarizes data collected in response to the three questions guiding the study.

Patterns of Practice and Group Problem-Solving Processes

Are different patterns of practice or approaches to school improvement by principals associated with or perhaps even partly explained by differences in the processes used to solve problems in groups? To answer this question, differences in the total mean ratings for the group problem-solving processes of principals engaged in each of the four patterns of practice were compared. As Table 7.2 indicates, DILs and IILs exhibited greater expertise than did TCMs or BCMs. A one-way analysis of variance was followed by a Tukey post-hoc procedure to locate pairs of means that differed significantly. Differences in expertise between BCMs and each of the other patterns were significant [$f(3,8)=14.18$, $p < .05$]. Principals engaged in both instructional leadership patterns also demonstrated substantially greater problem-solving expertise than did teacher-centered managers, but that difference did not reach significance. In sum, then, differences in patterns of practice are associated with differences in group problem-solving processes.

Table 7.2 Mean Ratings of Group Problem-Solving Expertise for Principals Engaged in Four Different Patterns of Practice

Style	N	Mean	SD
		Scale (1=typical; 5=expert)	
Direct Instructional Leader (DIL)	3	4.02	.27
Indirect Instructional Leader (IIL)	5	4.08	.49
Teacher-Centered Manager (TCM)	2	3.53	.35
Building-Centered Manager (BCM)	2	2.03	.04

Aspects of Greatest Differences in Principals' Problem-Solving Processes

Table 7.3 reports the total mean ratings on each of the 18 aspects of problem-solving examined in this study for principals engaged in each of the four patterns of practice. It is clear from this table that the scores for the building-centered manager pattern are substantially lower than those of the other three patterns on nearly every item. A one-way analysis of variance showed that those differences were significant ($p < .05$) for items 9, 13, 16, and 17. BCM scores were also significantly lower than DIL and IIL (but not TCM) scores on items 1, 4, 14, 15, and 18. BCM and IIL leaders differed significantly on item 3. And for item 18, TCM scores were significantly lower than those for IILs. The nature of these statistically significant differences falls into three main categories (goals, skills and knowledge, and disposition/attitudes), which are described in more detail in the remainder of this section.

Goals

Goal setting is vitally important in the running of any meeting and shared understanding of goals is of particular importance in collaborative problem-solving. A prior study (Leithwood & Steinbach, 1991) suggested that expert and typical principals were equally adept at sharing their own goals with others involved in problem-solving. Similarly, all principals in the present study at least mentioned the purposes for problem-solving at the outset of their meetings with staff. However, three goal-related dimensions of group problem-solving did show significant variation among principals—items 1, 17, and 18.

Item One. The impact of instructional leadership on students is indirect. Among the most powerful mechanisms for exercising this leadership is influencing what teachers focus on by ensuring that the school's mission is clearly defined (Hallinger, Bickman, & Davis, 1990; Leitner, in press). Group problem-solving provides school leaders with an opportunity to draw attention to the school's mission and to assist staff in finding meaning in that mission by showing its relevance in the solution of everyday problems. Given the importance of the

Table 7.3 Dimensions of Group Problem-Solving: Mean Ratings for Each Pattern of Practice

ITEMS		DIL (n=3)	IIL (n=5)	TCM (n=2)	BCM (n=2)
		MEANS (scale=1-5)			
*1	Immediate problem viewed in relation to the larger mission and problems of school	4.3	4.8	3.5	2.0
2	Less of a personal stake in pre-conceived solution; want best possible group solution	4.3	3.4	4.5	2.5
*3	Anticipates obstacles, responds flexibly to unanticipated obstacles, deals with constraints	3.7	3.6	3.5	1.5
*4	Has well developed/prepared plan for meeting	4.7	4.8	3.5	2.0
5	Provides clear, detailed introduction to problem and its background to collaborators	4.3	3.8	3.5	2.5
6	Outlines clearly the problem solving process	3.7	3.6	3.5	2.5
7	Without intimidating or restraining others, clearly indicates own view of problem	3.7	3.0	3.5	2.5
8	Remains open to new information (flexibility)	3.7	4.0	4.0	3.0
*9	Assists collaborative problem–solving by synthesizing, summarizing and clarifying	3.7	4.6	4.5	2.0
10	Has strategies for keeping group focused and allowing discussion	3.7	4.2	3.5	3.0
11	Checks for consensus, agreement, understanding, commitment	3.7	4.0	3.5	2.0
12	Ensures that follow-up is planned	3.3	4.0	2.5	2.0
*13	Always appears to be calm and confident	4.0	4.2	3.5	1.5
*14	Respect and courtesy shown to staff during meeting and interview	4.7	4.2	4.0	1.5
*15	Use of problem related knowledge	4.0	4.2	3.0	1.5
*16	Indication of self-reflection, self-evaluation	4.7	3.6	3.5	1.5
*17	Broad range of goals (includes program/student goals)	4.3	4.6	3.5	1.5
*18	Staff development an explicit goal of meeting	4.0	4.8	2.5	1.5

school's mission, more expert principals would be expected to invest more effort in helping staff place the immediate problem being addressed in relation to the larger mission and problems of the school (item 1). Such was the case with principals in this study.

Each DIL and IIL received a rating of 4 or 5 on this aspect of their problem-solving. To illustrate, one principal introduced the problem to be addressed by staff in this way:

> The topic of retention is a contentious one for primary grades or any grades . . . and it forces us, as teachers, to examine the reasonings behind recommending retention or promotion. So we need to think about whether a student's education career should be driven by competence, by readiness, by age, or group solidarity, or whatever. It makes us— pushes us really to think about why we do certain things.

The mean score for the TCMs was 3.5. This indicated that the problem was seen in a larger context, but that the context often was limited to staff opinions or feelings. The problem of class assignment might be viewed just from the perspective of personnel, for example:

> So, that was a factor that they had, which impinged on their decision-making, because they were not only thinking of the classes, they were thinking of personnel as well. Little factors such as, Mrs. M.—her last year's coming, she's going to retire. She doesn't want to do any major changes in the time of her career.

Each BCM received a score of 2 for this item. This means that the immediate problem was viewed in isolation. For example, one principal who was dealing with complaints of limited resources kept the problem at that level.

> So a lot of money has gone into it; it's really disappointing to see boxes of the same stuff arriving for each classroom . . . that's just my personal opinion.

Item Seventeen. Research on social cognition places individuals' internalized goals at the center of explanations of self-motivation (e.g., Showers & Cantor, 1985). As Bandura (1977) explains:

> [they] represent future consequences in thought. . . . Many of the things we do are designed to gain anticipated benefits and to avert future difficulties. When individuals commit themselves to explicit goals, perceived negative discrepancies between what they do and what they seek to achieve create dissatisfactions that serve as motivational inducements for change. (p. 161)

In order for a school to pursue a common mission, individual staff members' practices have to be motivated by at least a significant core of common goals related to that mission. Among the especially important aspects of school leadership expertise, then, is the effort devoted to and success in creating that common core of goals among staff. Expertise is a function of both the nature of the goals school leaders assist staff to adopt and the extent to which a common core of goals is actually internalized by staff.

Significant differences were found among principals in relation to the nature of the goals espoused for problem-solving, particularly in their breadth and in the incidence of program and student goals (item 17). Such goals are one of the defining features of instructional leadership (Leithwood & Montgomery, 1982, 1986) and principal expertise (Leithwood & Stager, 1989). All DILs and IILs in the present study were rated either 5 (explicit mention) or 4 (implicit mention) on this item. Student growth and/or program goals were used as benchmarks to help guide problem-solving. For example, one principal set student needs as a goal by saying:

> So I think what we have to look at is what makes the best sense for the kids at this school.

To help reach consensus about how to evaluate students using the new reporting procedure, another principal said:

> What we have to do here is get really clear in our minds that the report has got to enhance the learning of the child.

TCMs were weaker on this dimension (mean = 3.5): One TCM had several goals but none were related either explicitly or implicitly to what was best for children. He received a score of 3. The second TCM did indicate that reporting procedures should be a fair assessment of the child's development or potential. This implicit goal gave him a score of 4.

The main goal of both BCMs was to comply with the researchers' request. As one BCM said to his staff:

> I believe what the [research team] would like us to do is to hear us talking over the difficulties of implementation (score = 1).

The second BCM's goal was to discuss what was good and bad in the past year so priorities could be set. There seemed to be no higher-learning goals—only task goals (score = 2).

Item Eighteen. The extent to which staff development explicitly was considered to be a goal by principals in solving school-improvement problems with their staff was an aspect of problem-solving not examined in our previous research. It was included in this study for two reasons. Our choice of a focus on the domain of school-improvement problems, in particular, was the first reason. Inferences about effective practice derived from recent research on school improvement (reviewed by Fullan, 1991) argue that it is more productive to focus broadly on capacity-building within the school rather than more narrowly on the implementation of specific innovations.

A second reason for attending to staff development as a goal is inherent in the meaning of collaboration. Authentic collaboration depends on a belief in the value of the contributions that can be made by one's collaborators. Such a belief requires principals not only to view staff as possessing capacities critical to the solution of school-improvement problems but to aim at improving those capacities, as well.

Most DILs and IILs received high scores (4 or 5) on this dimension (one received a 3). They seemed to see their roles as instructional leaders for teachers as well as for students. The three DILs had a mean score of 4. The five IILs had a mean score of 4.8. These are principals attempting to accomplish student goals through staff development and they use staff meetings as opportunities to do this. Four of these five principals were very explicit about having staff development as a goal for the staff meeting (score = 5), the fifth was slightly less explicit. Comments such as the following illustrate how this goal was expressed:

> I wanted them to understand the process that one goes through when you start putting a class group together.

> So I wanted all of this [talk] so that they could know what each other is thinking, where they're coming from.

The mean score for TCMs on item 18 was 2.5. While there was definitely concern for teacher feelings, teacher development was not so clearly a goal. One TCM received a score of 2. He wanted to understand the staffs' rationale for their choice of class configuration and he wanted to ensure that staff were satisfied with their choice. The second TCM received a score of 3. He turned the meeting over to the teacher who had initiated the topic and attempted to ensure everyone had an opportunity to speak. The tenor of the meeting was very "empowering."

BCMs had a mean score of 1.5. One BCM received a score of 1 because his only real goal was to comply with the researchers' request for him to tape a meeting. The second principal received a score of 2. His goals were to comply with the researchers' request, to make sure class lists were in order, to make certain that staff were organized to advise the new principal, and to discuss what was good and bad in the past year so priorities could be set. The score of 2 was given because, at the end of the meeting, he said to the interviewer: "I just expected them to be able to have a free expression of views more than any-thing."

Skills and Knowledge

The limits on individual problem-solving, which Simon (1957) described as "bounded rationality," are due to short-term (or working) memory capacity; individuals are able to process or think about only five to seven separate items of information at a time. For this reason, individuals may (1) consider only a small number of the actually available alternative solutions to a problem; (2) possess less than adequate information about these alternatives; (3) consider the problem from narrowly biased perspectives; (4) overlook relevant criteria in decision-making. Each of these limitations on individual problem-solving can be overcome in a collaborative context—two (or more) heads are better than one, *under the right circumstances.*

Our prior research on group problem-solving (see Table 7.1) described some of the specific skills used by expert administrators to ensure such circum-stances during their meetings. Results of the present study point to many of the same skills with differences between patterns of practice reaching significance on four items: 3, 4, 9, and 15.

Item Three. The ability to anticipate obstacles and deal with them if they arise unexpectedly is a component of individual problem-solving expertise. It is an important feature of collaborative problem-solving as well.

DIL, IIL, and TCM mean scores were very similar: 3.7, 3.6, and 3.5, re-spectively. All of these principals either anticipated obstacles and prepared themselves for them ("And so I had to be prepared for reluctance initially") or else responded casually and flexibly to unanticipated constraints. While there was some frustration, it was not apparent to the staff.

In contrast, building-centered managers received a 2 and a 1 for this item (mean = 1.5). For these two principals, obstacles were seen as anything that impeded the desired smooth path of the meeting and they reacted to these stumbling blocks with poorly disguised anger.

> The [partner school] issue is a separate issue, J. and I'd like to talk to you about it, because you may not be aware of the time that [your school] is getting. So, I'll talk to you later. (Interviewer: You sound a little bit an-noyed.) I am.

Item Four. "A plan," as Shank and Abelson explain, "is a series of projected actions to realize a goal" (1977, p. 71). Prior research on both individual and group problem-solving by administrators suggested that experts, as compared with nonexperts, verbalized more detailed plans for how to solve their problems. In some cases, they were able to anticipate a series of a dozen or more actions they would take. Often they considered alternative steps in response to different possible outcomes of a given action (Leithwood & Stager, 1989; Leithwood & Steinbach, 1991). In a group context, such detailed contingent planning has both instrumental and symbolic value. Instrumentally it increases the probability of reaching one's goals and makes for a well-run meeting. Such planning also signals to staff that the issue being addressed in the meeting is important and that the principal does not want to waste their time.

DILs and IILs scored high on this dimension (mean scores were 4.7 and 4.8, respectively). Each of these principals had spent considerable time preparing for the meeting either by gathering materials (e.g., unifix cubes, research articles), or by making extensive notes summarizing the results of a previous meeting. As one principal noted:

> What I've done since that last meeting was . . . to take all the items listed on the board that members raised and try to cluster them into some kind of logical grouping.

TCMs did plan, but their plans were less elaborate; the mean score for this group was 3.5.

> Those are my plans on paper, which they have a copy of . . . I gave each of them . . . the three scenarios [they had arrived at].

BCMs appeared to value spontaneity (although they reacted with annoyance if things did not go according to their own internal agenda); planning was kept to a minimum. For example, as one BCM said to his staff:

> Umm, I guess they [the researchers] want to know how I deal with problems so I'll just toss it open for discussion.

Item Nine. This item, perhaps more than the others, captures the critical skills necessary to facilitate collaborative problem-solving. Except for the two BCMs, scores were consistently high (DIL = 3.7; IIL = 4.6; TCM = 4.5; BCM = 2). Most principals frequently summarized, synthesized, and clarified what had been said. Differences between scores of 4 and 5 indicated the degree of frequency with which they carried out these functions. Leaders who diligently synthesize, summarize, and clarify are letting their staff know that what is happening is important, that they want to make sure all understand what is being said so the best possible solution can be developed.

One principal said of her role in the meeting:

> I kind of clarified, I kind of restated, I kind of asked them to substantiate what they were saying if somebody else didn't.

During the staff meeting, another principal said, at various points:

> What kind of stuff are you implying? (asking for clarification)
>
> Okay, learning difficulties. (restates for clarification)
>
> What do you mean by that? By the teacher's ability to handle the children?
>
> Do you think those characteristics fit into different categories? You know, you have short attention span, you have lack of social skills, you [have] chronologically young . . . are all those things to do with maturation? (synthesizing)

In contrast, the BCMs were more likely to prevent teachers from having the opportunity to vent their frustrations (even though this was part of what both meetings were set up to do) by cutting off discussions prematurely. For example:

> I felt we were sort of beginning to drift from what was close to the [school]. I'm quite happy with what goes on in school and you can see I'm not happy with what's gone on provincially.

And this from the second building manager:

> I'm saying we could sit around and chat about this ad infinitum and I want to close it off so I think they've talked about that particular thing enough.

Item Fifteen. Evidence from many domains stresses the importance of problem-relevant knowledge in accounting for expertise (e.g., Chi, Glaser, & Farr, 1988; Lesgold, 1984). Indeed, Johnson-Laird (1990) claims that, in the study of intellectual development, emphasis has shifted from changes in cognitive structures and processes "toward the view that what really changes is the content of knowledge" (p. 485). Our prior research had paid little attention to domain-specific knowledge, but its importance could not be overlooked in the present study, especially in the face of the instructional modeling practices of the DILs.

All but one of the direct and indirect instructional leaders exhibited considerable problem-relevant or domain-specific knowledge. The one who did not was working on a problem that did not call for much display of such knowledge. The knowledge used by these principals was mainly about a specific, short-term problem faced in the schools but these principals were also knowledgeable about the Primary Program.

The scores of TCMs on this item showed wide variation. One received a 2 and one received a 4.5. The score of 2 could be explained by the nature of the problem-solving session, which did not require the display of much knowledge.

Building-centered managers exhibited little problem-relevant knowledge. Teachers were responsible for program-relevant knowledge, as this comment by one of the principals suggests:

> Well do we know much money is being allocated to the books? To the school? I said to them, when do you see a kindergarten becoming what is in fact a K-1?

Dispositions/Attitudes

Three personal characteristics were significantly linked with expertise in collaborative problem-solving: appearing calm and confident (Item 13), demonstrating genuine respect for staff (Item 14), and exhibiting habits of self-reflection (Item 16).

Item Thirteen. Research in the field of social cognition identifies mood, along with goals and existing knowledge, as a variable directly influencing the flexibility of one's thinking (Showers & Cantor, 1985). Cognitive flexibility, in turn, is central to expert problem-solving. Schwenk's (1988) review of research provides evidence of this claim in relation to senior managers in private corporations, for example.

Our prior research found that expert administrators remained more calm and confident during problem-solving than did nonexperts (Stager & Leithwood, 1989). In the present study, although all IILs and DILs overtly appeared calm and confident (all received scores of 4 or 5), four of the eight admitted to feelings of anxiety or frustration. As one said after listening to the tape recording of their staff meeting:

> . . . this may sound strange to you [but I'm] always so worried about talking too much in the meetings and I don't feel as badly as I thought I would.

Another said:

> I felt rather frustrated at this point in the conversation because they wanted to talk about specifics. (But frustration was not apparent in the meeting.)

Both teacher-centered managers admitted to being a little uncomfortable at some points in the meeting. With one principal, it was not evident (score = 4); it was slightly more evident with the other because of his excessive talking (score = 3).

> Okay now probably it's my personality but the fact that they aren't talking in this meeting bothered me . . . they didn't feel comfortable to open up and talk. (This principal did not give the teachers much of a chance to talk.)

One of the most obvious differences between the BCMs and those in the other patterns is in the degree of annoyance felt and shown; the building-centered managers were frequently perturbed and were not concerned about hiding their anger.

> I would think I sounded a bit peremptory [at this point in the staff meeting]. And, if that's how I sounded, that's how I meant to sound.

Item Fourteen. One of the best ways to empower teachers is for principals to directly demonstrate their respect. However, it is crucial that this respect be genuine; teachers will know the difference.

For the most part, DILs and IILs were genuine and consistent in the high regard they showed their staff members (five received scores of 5, one received a score of 4). They knew their teachers well, valued their contributions, and praised them during and after the meeting. Attention to this factor is crucial for creating an atmosphere of trust in which teachers feel free to express themselves honestly. The following quotes illustrate how this respect was expressed in interviews with the researchers:

> Time is really precious to them and that's something else that is really important for an administrator to remember—don't waste their time.

> This is a very good staff, a very confident staff, and I think, for any misgivings they have about it, once they got into it, I think they would make it really work.

With the teachers, you can't expect them to read everything, but at least you have to have it in a form so it's available . . . and, of course, it keeps the interest up when you give them a chance to do [something] . . . they've all signed up for another summer institute.

Terrific teacher! She's really very very good and tremendously conscientious, so this is why there's a bit of hesitancy on her part all of a sudden.

. . . and M. was the one, by the way, who had all negative responses and it wasn't her fault. This is her first year in the school and she has just a very powerful class and a very powerful set of parents.

Two of the indirect instructional leaders, however, were less consistent and they each received a score of 3. To illustrate:

Well . . . one thing that was striking me obviously because it's bugging me again, there are a couple of people in there who are always wanting, whining. . . . And I have a hard time valuing their opinions sometimes.

Item Sixteen. A central difference between experts and nonexperts in "knowledge-rich" domains of problem-solving is that experts possess substantially more problem-relevant knowledge. This often allows experts to solve problems readily, primarily by recognizing them as instances of familiar problem types; in contrast, lack of problem-relevant knowledge requires an often difficult search for a solution. But what explains the knowledge possessed by the expert? As VanLehn argues: "The ultimate explanation for the form and content of the human expert's knowledge is the learning processes that they went through in obtaining it. Thus the best theory of expert problem solving is a theory of learning" (1990, p. 529). Self-reflection and evaluation (item 16) are habits of mind that allow one to learn from experience. In the case of principals, those with greater expertise would be expected to demonstrate, in their problem-solving in groups, more self-reflection and evaluation and this would help explain their expertise. Our data conformed to this expectation.

The scores of DILs differed substantially from those of IILs (mean = 4.7 vs. 3.6) on this item. DILs were very quick to notice errors they might have made. Perhaps they are always vigilant for opportunities to improve their practice. This vigilance is illustrated in the following comments on their own problem-solving as they listened to the taped staff meetings:

I should have jumped in here. Part of it, I was feeling a little bit of tension . . . part of it is that I'm not sometimes as aggressive as I should be in certain situations.

And from another:

> Okay, that was my first mistake . . . if I had to do it over again, I would have deleted it completely.

> I'm coming out of this meeting feeling, you know, I really haven't handled this very well because, in the end, I didn't get them thinking "Hooray, let's just go for this!" But that may be a stage.

And this, from an IIL:

> I don't think I handled it particularly well because I'm a bit ambiguous on the topic.

TCMs were similar to IILs. Their mean score of 3.5 indicates a medium amount of self-reflection. BCMs, with a mean score of 1.5, showed little reflection.

Problem-Solving Expertise and Its Relationship to Age, Experience, and Gender

Table 7.4 reports level of problem-solving expertise, pattern of practice, estimated age (we did not request this information directly), years of experience as a principal, and gender for each of the 12 principals in the study. These data are reported for principals in descending order of their expertise.

There were seven female and five male administrators. All instructional leaders but one (an IIL) were female; all teacher-centered and building-centered managers were male. This lends support to the finding that female administrators, on average, devote a greater amount of and more direct attention to classroom instructional practices than do males (e.g., Hallinger, Bickman, & Davis, 1990; Shakeshaft, 1987). Gender alone, however, is not a sufficient explanation for leadership style. In addition to being female, all three direct instructional leaders were also first-year administrators. Two related interpretations are possible.

First-year principals may be more inclined to model instructional strategies in the classroom not because they are women, but because they are very familiar with the strategies and feel confident to teach them. This may well be the situation here, since the Primary Program policy encourages instructional practices that are quite different from those considered effective a decade ago and, thus, would not be as familiar to principals who had been in the role for a long time. A related explanation concerns the notion that new administrators

Table 7.4 Relationship Between Problem-Solving Expertise, Age, Experience, and Gender

	Ratings of Expertise					
S#	Total Score	Mean Score	Patterns of Practice	Age	# Yrs. as Princ.	Gender
8	83	4.61	IIL	56+	4	F
3	79	4.39	IIL	56+	28	F
11	78	4.33	DIL	46-55	1	F
7	76	4.22	IIL	36-45	2	F
10	70	3.89	DIL	36-45	1	F
9	69	3.83	DIL	36-45	1	F
12	68	3.78	TCM	46-55	12	M
5	68	3.78	IIL	36-45	7	M
6	61	3.39	IIL	36-45	5	F
2	59	3.23	TCM	46-55	28	M
4	37	2.01	BCM	56+	15	M
1	36	2.00	BCM	46-55	18	M

may be in a "transition" year and are finding a way to bridge the gap between the teacher's classroom and the principal's office. Support for this notion is provided by the fact that indirect instructional leaders were also relatively new to the role in contrast with those adopting the two other styles. Whether it is due to reluctance to break with the past, a love of teaching, a strong belief that he or she knows how to do it best, or an awareness that teachers learn best when new strategies are modeled for them, number of years in the role may provide some of the rationale for leadership style.

The two anomalies in the sample tend to confirm the above interpretation. The one male instructional leader is from a district where all of the principals in our sample were indirect instructional leaders (a possible district effect); however, he had also been a principal for a relatively short time (7 years). One instructional leader was in a district that had no other instructional leaders and had been a principal for 28 years, but this leader was female.

While these data are far from conclusive, they do indicate some interesting connections and perhaps point the way to future research.

CONCLUSION

Building on our recent prior research and concerned with how principals solved school-improvement problems with their staff, this study explored three questions. We inquired, first, about the relationship between variations in patterns of leadership practices and expertise in group problem-solving processes. Paralleling results of our research on individual problem-solving (Leithwood,

Steinbach, & Dart, in press), principals engaged in both the direct and indirect forms of instructional leadership demonstrated significantly higher levels of group problem-solving expertise than did building-centered managers and substantially higher levels than teacher-centered managers. Teacher-centered managers also demonstrated significantly greater group problem-solving expertise than did building-centered managers. Clearly, the thinking giving rise to instructional leadership practices is similar to the thinking that creates an expert collaborative problem-solver. These results may help explain some of the variation in impact of different patterns of leadership practice. They also add validity to our growing accumulation of evidence about the links between problem-solving and administrative expertise. At a minimum, these results offer a more complete understanding of what is involved in each pattern of practice.

To add further depth to our understanding of leadership patterns, we asked, second, about aspects or dimensions of group problem-solving within which principals differed most. There were ten such dimensions. Differences among principals in these dimensions of group problem-solving were most evident in the purposes, skills and knowledge, and dispositions principals brought to the process. With respect to purposes, higher levels of expertise were associated with the pursuit of student, program, and staff-development goals and the ability to help staff place immediate problems in the context of the school's broader mission. Higher levels of expertise were associated with a larger stock of domain-specific knowledge and more refined skills in planning for group problem-solving and assisting staff in being as productive as possible during their deliberations; this was accomplished through clarifying, synthesizing, and summarizing activities during those deliberations. Finally, dispositions associated with greater group problem-solving expertise included at least the *overt* management or control of intense personal moods, a high regard for staffs' potential contribution to problem-solving, and habits of self-reflection and evaluation of one's thinking and practices.

Relationships between problem-solving processes and three "demographic" variables—age, experience, and gender—was the third question. Each of these variables appeared to explain some of the differences in problem-solving expertise and leadership patterns. The most effective forms of leadership were associated with women's having limited formal experience as principals. But marked exceptions were evident, indicating that much still has to be learned about variables that give rise to, or interact with, problem-solving processes and leadership patterns.

Implications for Research and Theory

Although this study is limited to 12 elementary principals solving school-improvement problems in a common provincial educational context, there are relatively obvious implications for future research related to external validity. These implications raise such questions as the following: Would similar problem-solving processes be used by school administrators in a different educational context? Is there something about the secondary school leadership role that stimulates the use of processes unlike those used by elementary school leaders? Would variations in particular problem domain (school improvement) result in the use of processes different from those observed in this study?

Several questions other than those concerned with external validity are also prompted by the results. First, this study and its immediate predecessors inform us more fully about the nature of problem-solving expertise. Nevertheless, little is known about the development of the purposes, skills, knowledge, and dispositions around which administrators differed most. Recent research has begun to explore this question (e.g., Leithwood, Steinbach, & Begley, 1992) but much remains to be done.

Although problem-relevant knowledge is known to have an influence on problem-solving expertise, as yet there has been little attention devoted to identifying the important problem domains for school administrators (for one example, see Leithwood, Cousins, & Smith, 1990). This question has radical implications for administrator preparation curricula. It suggests that the propositional knowledge offered by such curricula could be organized, more meaningfully, around a grounded (or more phenomenological) conception of the principal's world than is presently the case. This would go some distance toward avoiding the acquisition of inert knowledge by aspiring administrators—knowledge stored in memory but of little practical value since the appropriate occasions for its application are not usually recognized.

Finally, results of the study raise questions about the stability of problem-solving processes across different school contexts. Hallinger, Bickman, and Davis (1990) report, for example, that principal leadership practices are best understood through contingency models. Variations in student socioeconomic status (SES), as well as such variables as gender and parental involvement, change what principals do. But do such variables have a bearing on how principals think—the processes they use to solve problems in groups, for example? Perhaps the thought processes remain stable and the changed practices are only the result of such processes' responding to different "information." Were this the case, the value of contingency models of leadership would need to be reconsidered.

Implications for Practice: An Observation About Being Premature

Psychology's greatest disservice to nonpsychologists in the past has been to render, through its concepts, language, and methods, understandings of how the human mind functions as opaque, irrelevant, and boring. Otherwise, it is hard to imagine a discipline more exciting and more useful. Recent work in cognitive science begins to demonstrate this promise and nowhere more vividly than in research on practical problem-solving (e.g., Rogoff & Lave, 1984; Sternberg & Wagner, 1986). From research with this focus, for example, novice writers are able to make dramatic strides in their own development (Scardamalia, Bereiter, & Steinbach, 1984) and individual students are able to monitor and refine their own learning more autonomously and intentionally (Steinbach, Scardamalia, Burtis, & Bereiter, 1987). Such research also enables us to appreciate the roots and explain the overt practices of those in a variety of professional roles, such as teachers and business executives. This knowledge may have considerable value, for example, in future efforts to systematically stimulate the development of expertise in many areas of human enterprise.

But as we begin to inquire more closely into the thinking of educational administrators, we should avoid the temptation to assume what we will learn and what its value will be for practice. While the theoretical case for great practical significance is a compelling one, we should stand ready to be surprised—both pleasantly and not so pleasantly. The results of further research are patently unpredictable, the real consequences for practice largely circumstantial. All we can really claim at this time is that what we will learn ought not to be boring.

NOTE

This research was funded by the Social Sciences and Humanities Research Council of Canada, the Ontario Ministry of Education through its block transfer grant to OISE, and the British Columbia Ministry of Education. We appreciate Tiiu Raun's contribution to data analysis.

REFERENCES

Bandura, A. (1977). *Social learning theory*. Englewood Cliffs, NJ: Prentice-Hall.

Blase, J., Dedrick, C., & Strathe, M. (1986). Leadership behavior of school principals in relation to teacher stress, satisfaction and performance. *Journal of Humanistic Education and Development, 24*(4), 159–171.

Blumberg, A., & Greenfield, W. (1980). *The effective principal: Perspectives on school leadership*. Boston: Allyn & Bacon.

Brady, L. (1985). The supportiveness of the principal in school-based curriculum development. *Journal of Curriculum Studies, 17* (1), 95–97.

Chi, M. T. H., Feltovich, P. J., and Glaser, R. (1981). Categorization and representation of physics problems by experts and novices. *Cognitive Science, 5*, 121–152.

Chi, M. T. H., Glaser, R., & Farr, M. J. (1988). *The nature of expertise.* Hillsdale, NJ: Lawrence Erlbaum Associates.

Frederiksen, N. (1984). Implications of cognitive theory for instruction in problem solving. *Review of Educational Research, 54*(3), 363–407.

Fullan, M. (1991). *The new meaning of educational change.* New York: Teachers College Press.

Hall, G., Rutherford, W. L., Hord, S. M., & Huling, L. L. (1984). Effects of three principal styles on school improvement. *Educational Leadership, 41*(5), 22–31.

Hallinger, P., Bickman, L., & Davis, K. (1990). *What makes a difference? School context and student achievement.* Cambridge, MA: National Center for Educational Leadership.

Heck, R., Larsen, T., & Marcoulides, G. (1990, April). *Principal leadership and school achievement: Validation of a causal model.* Paper presented at the annual meeting of the American Educational Research Association, Boston.

Hoy, W. K., & Brown, B. L. (1986, April). *Leadership of principals, personal characteristics of teachers and the professional zone of acceptance of elementary teachers.* Paper presented at annual meeting of the American Educational Research Association, San Francisco.

Johnson-Laird, P. N. (1990). Mental models. In M. I. Posner (Ed.), *Foundations of cognitive science* (pp. 469–500). Cambridge: The MIT Press.

Leithwood, K. A., Begley, P., & Cousins, B. (1990). The nature, causes, and consequences of principals' practices: An agenda for future research. *Journal of Educational Administration, 28* (4), 5–31.

Leithwood, K. A., Begley, P., & Cousins, B. (1992). *Developing expert leadership for future schools.* New York: Falmer Press.

Leithwood, K. A., Cousins, B., & Smith, M. (1990, January/February/March). Principals' problem solving (published in three issues). *The Canadian School Executive.*

Leithwood, K. A., & Montgomery, D. (1982). The role of the elementary school principal in program improvement. *Review of Educational Research, 52*(3), 309–339.

Leithwood, K. A., & Montgomery, D. (1986). *Improving principal effectiveness: The principal profile.* Toronto: OISE Press.

Leithwood, K. A., & Stager, M. (1989). Expertise in principals' problem solving. *Educational Administration Quarterly, 25*(2), 126–161.

Leithwood, K. A., & Steinbach, R. (1990). Characteristics of effective secondary school principals' problem solving. *Journal of Educational Administration and Foundations, 5*(1), 24–42.

Leithwood, K. A., & Steinbach, R. (1991). Indicators of transformational leadership in the everyday problem solving of school administrators. *Journal of Personnel Evaluation in Education, 4*(3), 221–244.

Leithwood, K. A., Steinbach, R., & Begley, P. (1992). Socialization experiences: Becoming a principal in Canada. In G. Hall & F. Parkay (Eds.), *Becoming a principal* (pp. 284–307). Boston: Allyn & Bacon.

Leithwood, K. A., Steinbach, R., & Dart, B. (in press). The consequences for school improvement of differences in principals' problem-solving processes. *Education Research and Perspectives.*

Leitner, D. (in press). Do principals affect student outcomes: An organizational perspective. *School Effectiveness and School Improvement.*

Lesgold, A. (1984). Acquiring expertise. In J. R. Anderson & S. M. Kosslyn (Eds.), *Tutorials in learning and memory.* New York: Freeman.

Primary Program Foundation Document (1990). Victoria, BC: British Columbia Ministry of Education.

Rogoff, B., & Lave, J. (Eds.). (1984). *Everyday cognition: Its development in social context.* Cambridge: Harvard University Press.

Salley, C., McPherson, R. B., & Baehr, M. E. (1978). What principals do: A preliminary occupational analysis. In D. A. Erickson & T. L. Reller (Eds.), *The principal in metropolitan schools* (pp. 22–39). Berkeley: McCutchan.

Scardamalia, M., Bereiter, C., & Steinbach, R. (1984). Teachability of reflective practices in written composition. *Cognitive Science, 8,* 173–190.

Schwenk, C. R. (1988). The cognitive perspective on strategic decision-making. *Journal of Management Studies, 25*(1), 41–56.

Shakeshaft, C. (1987). *Women in educational administration.* Beverly Hills: Sage.

Shank, R., & Abelson, R. (1977). *Scripts, plans, goals and understanding.* Hillsdale, NJ: Lawrence Erlbaum Associates.

Showers, C., & Cantor, N. (1985). Social cognition: A look at motivated strategies. *Annual Review of Psychology, 36,* 275–305.

Simon, H. (1957). *Administrative behaviour: A study of decision-making processes in administrative organizations.* New York: The Free Press.

Srivastva, S. (Ed.). (1983). *The executive mind.* San Francisco: Jossey-Bass.

Stager, M., & Leithwood, K. A. (1989). Cognitive flexibility and inflexibility in principals' problem solving. *The Alberta Journal of Educational Research, 35*(3), 217–236.

Steinbach, R., Scardamalia, M., Burtis, P. J., & Bereiter, C. (1987, April). *Childrens' implicit theories of knowledge and learning.* Paper presented at the annual meeting of the American Educational Research Association, Washington, DC.

Sternberg, R. J., & Wagner, R. K. (1986). *Practical intelligence.* Cambridge, UK: Cambridge University Press.

Stevens, W., & Marsh, L. D. D. (1987, April). *The role of vision in the life of elementary school principals.* Paper presented at the annual meeting of the American Educational Research Association, Washington, DC.

Trider, D., & Leithwood, K. A. (1988). Influences on principals' practices. *Curriculum Inquiry, 18*(2), 289–312.

VanLehn, K. (1990). Problem solving and cognitive skill acquisition. In M. I. Posner (Ed.), *Foundations of cognitive science* (pp. 527–579). Cambridge: The MIT Press.

Voss, J. F., Greene, T. R., Post, T. A., & Penner, B. C. (1983). Problem-solving skill in the social sciences. In G. H. Bower (Ed.), *The psychology of learning and motivation* (pp. 165–213). New York: Academic Press.

Watson, D. J. (1989). Defining and describing whole language. *The Elementary School Journal, 90*(2), 129–141.

Year 2000. (1989). *A curriculum and assessment framework for the future.* Victoria, BC: British Columbia Ministry of Education.

8 Trees and Forests: Details, Abstraction, and Experience in Problem-Solving

Derek J. Allison and Patricia A. Allison

In colloquial usage, the phrase "unable to see the forest for the trees" implies a dysfunctional preoccupation with details or immediate concerns. By this token, being able to rise above immediate details, to "step back" and "take the broad view"—to see the forest rather than just the trees—is implicitly recognized as a useful ability. In some discussions of administration and leadership, this capability has been dubbed the "helicopter factor," connoting an almost literal ability to rise above the immediate situation and look at things from a broader and more inclusive viewpoint (Bennis, 1984; Handy, 1976).

Yet at the same time it seems evident that good administration requires attention to detail. In other words, effective administrators—good leaders, if one prefers—cannot afford to spend all day in their helicopters. Not that their responsibilities allow them to do so, of course. The pressing demands of administrative work and the characteristics of "brevity, variety and fragmentation" highlighted in Mintzberg's (1973, p. 31) research are often cited as denying incumbents time for reflection and planning. But it is not "administrivia"—important as they may be—that we have in mind as the details to which good administrators seem likely to attend. The details of interest concern the specific elements, contours, and fine ingredients within administrative problems and leadership opportunities. This could involve attending to (rather than overlooking or ignoring) specific subproblems embedded within larger ones, following through a prolonged series of discrete steps in pursuit of a distant goal, or recognizing and providing for the particular interests or needs of individuals or groups that are important to the successful operation of the organization. In essence such attention to detail involves an alert and sustained coordination of organizational activities, opportunities, and resources in the pursuit of a desired goal.

In this chapter we describe and discuss a study undertaken to investigate how attention to detail and taking a broad view of a presented situation were associated with judged performance on a standardized problem-solving task.

Study participants who were judged as having handled the problem better than others appeared to take a broad, inclusive view of the problem and its context while also looking closely at specific details: They were aware of both the forest and the trees.

BACKGROUND

The study discussed here forms part of a larger investigation into the nature of administrative expertise that builds on the growing body of literature concerned with problem-solving within specific knowledge domains, key elements of which are summarized in other chapters in this volume. This larger project complements recent work by Leithwood, Begley, and Cousins (1992), but was conceived and conducted independently as an extension of earlier work by members of our research team (Allison & Nagy, 1989; Nagy, 1990, 1991; Nagy & Allison, 1988; Nagy & Moorhead, 1990).

An important concern in our more recent work (Allison & Allison, 1991; Allison & Nagy, 1991) has been the relationship between problem-solving expertise and experience. As noted by our colleagues Martin, Slemon, Heibert, Hallberg, and Cummings (1989),

> the role of experience in the acquisition of expertise is pivotal because it is through experience that experts acquire an adequate knowledge base for conceptualizing situational information in ways that permit effective conceptualization, problem solving and action. (p. 395)

Yet while experience appears to be an indispensable precondition for the development of expertise, by itself time-in-role will not necessarily produce experts, for "experience can only contribute to expertise if practitioners are capable of learning from it" (Kennedy, 1987, p. 148), a point that has also been discussed by Schön (1983, 1987) and Schwab (1978). Even so, experience and expertise appear to be highly correlated in knowledge domains where more highly structured problems tend to predominate, such as mathematics and physics (Larkin, McDermott, Simon, & Simon, 1980; Leinhardt & Smith, 1985). The relationship between these two concepts may well be less strong in "messier" knowledge domains such as school administration, but there has been little direct investigation of the matter.

CONCEPTUAL FRAMEWORK

Looking at the forest rather than the trees implies that a problem-solver is able to place the problem within a broader, more inclusive, conceptual context.

This in turn implies that the problem-solver possesses, or is able to construct, an appropriate conceptual setting or frame in which to place the problem. On the other hand, looking at the trees that make up the forest suggests that a problem-solver is examining constituent elements of the problem, which, in turn, implies an ability to first recognize the important elements in the problem and then not lose track of them as additional information is acquired. This implies that the problem-solver is able to build or draw on a reasonably detailed conceptual map of the problem that will help him or her to identify, remember, and connect important features.

Schema theory offers a useful framework for exploring both of these abilities. As discussed by Anderson, Spiro, and Anderson (1978) and Schallert (1982), schemata are mental structures used to organize knowledge in memory. As such they can serve as mental templates for imposing conceptual order on complexity, for linking isolated pieces of information together into more coherent wholes, and for recognizing nonobvious patterns in situations. Prolonged exposure to a given knowledge or action domain can reasonably be expected to provide opportunities for individuals to acquire information about phenomena, processes, and problems characteristic of that domain. Information captured through such experience forms the raw material, as it were, for the construction, modification, or elaboration of schemata, which then function to guide future perception, interpretation, and action. Some individuals, however, appear to construct and employ more complex schemata than others. Insofar as these more complex schemata provide effective and reliable guides for analysis and action, the possession of such schemata offers a basis for distinguishing between experience and expertise: Given two individuals with equal experience in a knowledge or action domain, one who has developed and is able to apply more complex schemata relevant to problems within the domain would probably be judged to have a higher level of expertise.

But what might be the nature of this greater complexity? In what ways, along what dimensions, might more complex or sophisticated schemata differ from others? The forest-and-trees analogy implies that more complex schemata will contain more discrete elements, this being the quality that assists more expert problem-solvers to recognize and attend to details embedded in problems and task-relevant situations. Further, the constituent elements comprising more complex schemata will undoubtedly be linked to each other in a more organized, more richly connected fashion, a quality that would assist problem-solvers in linking elements of problems together and remembering them. More highly organized schemata, particularly if they contain a higher level of interconnection between knowledge elements, could also help (but perhaps mislead) problem-solvers in looking for, and perhaps filling in, relevant factors that are initially hidden or missing in their first encounter with a problem. On the basis of such reasoning we concluded that more complex schemata of the kind likely to be held by experts could be plausibly expected to include more conceptual "pigeonholes" or "placeholders" linked together in richer ways, qualities that would enable problem-solvers to recognize, relate, and attend to a greater number of relevant constituent elements when thinking through and devising a response to a presented problem. Such a view is in accord with discussions of expert problem-solving offered by several researchers (Bereiter & Scardamalia, 1986; Berliner, 1986; Leithwood & Stager, 1986, 1987; Norris, 1985; Voss, Green, Post, & Penner, 1983).

Schemata that are more highly organized and contain richer interconnections between elements should also assist more expert problem-solvers to rise above the immediately given aspects of problems by providing a more comprehensive conceptual context in which to place and appreciate the problem and its elements. But while the possession of more complex schemata provides a theoretical foundation for postulating a linked ability to both attend to detail and take a broader view in expert problem-solving, it does not explain how this may work. The principle of increasing abstractness incorporated in various theories of cognitive development provides a promising way forward here. In Piagetian theory, for example, cognitive functioning is portrayed as developing through concrete to more abstract levels of operations (1960), and the higher levels of Bloom's learning taxonomy also involve high levels of abstract thought (1956). Expert problem-solvers appear to be able to think about problems in more abstract terms, suggesting that their more complex schemata incorporate or encourage the synthesis of problem elements at higher levels of abstraction than do those of nonexperts.

We have found that parts of Jaques' (1976, 1986) work, especially his outline of stratified systems theory, provide a useful framework in modeling how increasing levels of abstraction may be incorporated into schemata. Jaques' (1986) stratified systems theory builds on the claim that a person's cognitive power is directly related to his or her time horizon, which is understood as the maximum time over which an individual can actively plan into the future. Jaques' research has identified regular discontinuities in the structure of work and responsibility in formal organizations that appear to correspond to similar discontinuities in the range of time horizons held by different people. These discontinuities led him to identify a four-step hierarchy of cognitive functioning, proceeding from more concrete to more abstract levels. Individuals operating at the first, or *concrete shaping*, level work toward "goals described in concretely specified terms," and have time horizons extending from one day to three months (p. 364). At the second level, termed *task definition*, time horizons extend from three months to one year, and individuals are able to deal with aggregates of tasks and ideas. The third level is termed *task extrapolation* and is characterized by an ability to extrapolate from current trends and established rules over a time horizon of some two years. The fourth, or *transformative* level, encompasses time spans from two to five years; individuals operating at this level are able to make "paired comparisons of known systems" (such as schools, for example) and design and implement plans for transforming reasonably complex social systems to better conform to a preferred alternative (p. 366).

What is of prime interest here is the hierarchy of increasing cognitive complexity and abstractness extending through Jaques' shaping, definition, extrapolation, and transformative stages, and the way in which this adds another dimension of complexity in the consideration of schema theory. We may imagine that schemata held by individuals functioning at the lowest (shaping) level of Jaques' hierarchy will be primarily concerned with the elements of problems associated with the concrete work and goals characteristic of this level. It also seems reasonable to imagine that individuals functioning at higher levels will develop more abstract and complex schemata appropriate to working toward more distant time horizons and with more complex tasks and problems. Yet at the same time, individuals functioning at high levels will also need to possess a repertoire of more concrete schemata in order to deal with short-term tasks and problems they will inevitably encounter in their work. In particular, administrators capable of operating at higher levels of abstraction will necessarily need to maintain lower-level schemata in memory in order to direct and supervise the more concrete work engaged in by their subordinates. Consequently, it seems plausible that people functioning at the higher Jaqusian levels will hold what amounts to a hierarchical set of schemata arranged in increasing order of abstractness. An individual working at the transformative level, for example, will of necessity possess a set of abstract schemata required to operate at that level, but in addition will possess other sets or subassemblies of schemata arranged in layers of increasing concreteness. Such a cognitive hierarchy can be thought of as providing a "conceptual stepladder," as it were, that can be ascended or descended as required to obtain broader or closer views of problems and their contexts encountered during the course of administrative (or other) work. In accord with Jaques' theories, the vantage gained from the top of this stepladder expands the time horizon, allowing a person to see and plan further into the future: to gain a view of the forest rather than just the trees.

METHOD

Data

The study described here was based on the analysis of 39 transcribed think-aloud responses to a case study involving problems centering on a school library. Subjects contributing responses were recruited to represent a wide range of administrative experience distributed across five predetermined categories. The 8 subjects in the *Aspirant* category were elementary school teachers who had recently obtained the qualifications necessary for appointment to a principalship in Ontario, but had no direct experience as principals; the 8 *Rookies* were in the first or second year of their first elementary school principalship; the 7 principals in our *Seasoned* category all had 10–15 years experience as elementary school principals; and the 6 members of the *Veteran* category had all been elementary school principals for more than 20 years. The 10 subjects in our fifth experience category, dubbed *Entrant,* were postgraduate student teachers who were subsequently added to the data set to provide a true novice category.

Following Ericson and Simon (1984), subjects were prepared for the think-aloud activity through a brief training session designed to familiarize them with the procedure. They were then handed the case study and asked to read it aloud, interjecting their thoughts as they read, and then to "think aloud" about how they would respond to the situation described in the case. Finally, they were asked to recall their thought processes and reflect on how they had reacted to the case.

Measures

Quality of Response. Three professors of educational administration rated "action summaries" prepared from the 29 Aspirant, Rookie, Seasoned, and Veteran transcripts. These summaries listed, in the subjects' own words, the actions they proposed to take in responding to the case together with the immediately surrounding text. Ratings were out of 10, where 10 was judged as representing an excellent response. The full think-aloud transcripts from all 39 subjects were later read and rated by five graduate students, with the mean of these ratings being used as a more global measure of the quality of subject responses.

Subjects were grouped into one of four performance categories using the following procedure. The action and global rating means were ranked and then partitioned into quartiles. Subjects who ranked above the third quartile (seventy-fifth percentile) on *both* ratings were coded as having given a high-quality response to the case problem. Those who ranked below the first quartile (twenty-fifth percentile) on *both* ratings were classified as having rendered a low-quality response. All other subjects were classified as having given a medium-quality response, *unless* they appeared as marked outliers on a comparative plot of the ranked ratings, in which case they were coded as anomalies. As a result of applying these decision rules, 6 subjects were classified as having given a high-quality response to the case, 20 as having given a medium-quality response, and 7 as having rendered a low-quality response; there were 6 responses classified anomalous.

Attention to Detail. Our conceptual framework suggests that better problem-solvers will be able to recognize and attend to a greater number of details in a presented problem. To measure this variable we devised a coding sheet for the case based on the detailed schema analysis of responses created by another member of our original team (Nagy, 1991). This analysis showed that collectively our subjects focused on three main areas or subproblems within the case, namely the librarian, the library, and the professional staff (teachers). We identified five elements or points of concern in each of these focus areas and then coded whether subjects paid attention to these details. We also coded the level of attention paid to each of these predetermined elements using a three-point scale. One point was awarded if the element was *mentioned;* an additional point was awarded if a subject also *considered,* discussed, or reflected on the element concerned; and a further point was awarded if a subject also *addressed* the element by declaring or outlining what he or she would do about it.

We made no attempt to count the total number of times an element was mentioned by subjects, for we were interested in how many different elements attracted the attention of subjects and their level of response. Nor did we seek to identify all of the different elements mentioned by subjects in the three focus areas. Past experience has shown that this approach quickly overwhelms the analyst with complex detail and yields results that are difficult to interpret. Our technique of coding what is in essence a preselected sample of elements was devised partly as a way of avoiding such confusion. The other consideration was to create a readily interpretable measure of the degree of detail attended to across subproblem areas. As applied, the coding scheme yielded a maximum score of 15 "attention points" within each focus area, that is, five elements in each area with a maximum score of three points for each element. This provided a sample measure of the density of attention paid to each focus area that is readily compared across areas. For this reason, we call this technique "density sampling."

In addition to the three subproblem focus areas in the case study, we also coded the density of attention paid to five specific, but more isolated, elements in the case, all of which can be seen either as related to subproblems in the case or as signposts to other problems within the school. Finally, we coded the attention paid to five generic elements of school administration that are not directly mentioned in the case but would have a bearing on dealing with the problems raised. These elements were students, program, budget, external assistance, and time horizon. Transcripts were coded independently by two raters. Levels of agreement ranged from 73 to 86 percent across the five focus areas. Disagreements in the initial coding were subsequently discussed and consensus reached on the most appropriate scoring prior to entering the data for analysis.

Goal Abstraction. In order to obtain a measure of the broadness of view subjects displayed in their analysis of the case, we sought to relate their responses to the spectrum of abstraction underlying Jaques' levels of cognitive power.

After working with the transcripts for some time, we concluded that variation across this spectrum was most clearly evident in the overall objective subjects appeared to be pursuing in their analysis and proposed actions. This guiding objective or *implicit goal* was rarely articulated clearly by subjects during their analysis of the case, but was evident or could be imputed from what they appeared to be attempting to accomplish as they thought through the problem.

In working through this stage of the analysis we found it was relatively easy to identify responses that tended toward the extremes of the concrete–abstract continuum, but it was more difficult to differentiate between responses falling between these extremes. Subjects who gave what we judged to be more concrete responses focused on attempting to "fix" what they took to be the immediately presented problem or problems, and their proposed actions were directed at adjusting—or shaping, to use Jaques' apt term—more or less concrete things or concerns, such as the paperwork needed to facilitate the librarian's transfer or the books in library.

In contrast, the more highly abstract responses were concerned with "turning around" or transforming the situation, with the proposed solutions to the problems in the case being seen as part of a much more ambitious program of planned change. Responses of this kind typically identified short-term and long-term objectives, with the more distant objectives being envisaged within time horizons extending over more than one year, in some cases over three or more years. What Jaques (1986) describes as "the ability to compare known systems, usually in pairs" (p. 366) was clearly evident (although often implicit) in these more transformative responses as subjects verbally compared images of the staff, library, and school constructed from the case with their conceptions of how things should be, or how they wanted them to become.

Even so, some of these more transformative responses were broader in scope than others. We eventually distinguished between what we took to be more and less transformative responses on the basis of whether the implicit goal was to transform the whole school, with changes to the library and its role in the school program being seen as a subcomponent of this broader objective, or whether the implicit goal was to transform the library program, other changes in the school being seen as consequent to that main focus. Toward the more concrete end of the abstraction continuum we identified responses to the case that, while not preoccupied with concreteness, were limited to more immediate concerns. These transcripts typically focused on the personal needs of characters in the case (including the principal, or the subject in the role of the principal) and/or the school staff in general. Responses of this kind often embodied what appeared to be a sincere concern for meeting the personal needs of individuals, but in some instances subjects seemed more concerned with appeasement. Transcripts embodying these characteristics were classified as falling between the more concrete and the less abstract responses.

In sum, we classified the transcripts into one of four categories of goal abstraction by considering how the implicit goals held by subjects related to Jaques' theory of cognitive power. We neither assume nor claim that our categories display a one-to-one correspondence with Jaques' four levels. They were constructed to reflect the principle of progressive abstraction underlying his theory, but our categories were grounded in the transcript data and not taken from his theory. Consequently, while the subjects whom we classified as pursuing transformational goals were clearly operating at a much higher level of cognitive abstraction than those we classified at the concrete level, they would not necessarily qualify for inclusion in Jaques' transformative category as it appears in his theory. This is also the case with the middle categories of our scheme.

Once the four grounded categories of goal abstraction—which we termed concrete, personnel, program, and transformational—were finalized, the two authors independently reviewed and coded the transcripts once more. When results were compared, there were three instances of disagreement, which represents an agreement level of 88 percent. These disagreements, each of which involved a one-category difference, were resolved by consensus before the data were entered for analysis. Ten subjects were coded as having focused on concrete goals, 14 on people-oriented goals, 11 on program changes, and 4 on transforming the school.

RESULTS

Attention to Detail

The 6 subjects who were judged as having given a high-quality response to the case problem all paid markedly higher attention to the case elements sampled in the density analysis, except with regard to the more peripheral elements in the "other" focus area. The 20 subjects classified as having given a medium-quality response to the case had lower—but markedly consistent—density scores across the five focus areas, while the 7 subjects who were judged to have given a low-level response gave relatively little attention to any of the sampled case elements. One-way ANOVAS comparing the density scores for the performance groups within each focus area yielded significant F ratios ($p < .0001$) in four of the five focus areas, the "specific" area being the exception, where there was no significant difference between performance groups. Post-hoc analyses identified the density score of the high-performance group as being significantly different from that of all other performance groups, including the anomalous group (composed of subjects who had received discrepant ratings from the two sets of judges). Indeed, the anomalous group was essentially indistinguishable from the medium-performance group during this stage of the analysis.

A similar pattern emerged when we examined differences in the levels of attention within the focus areas: Subjects judged to have given higher-quality responses to the case not only mentioned more details; they consistently considered and then addressed more of these details than did subjects who were judged to have performed less well.

Goal Abstraction

We began this stage of the analysis by cross-tabulating level-of-abstraction and performance categories. All of the 6 subjects judged to have given high-quality responses to the case fell into the two more abstract goal categories, while the 7 subjects in the lowest performance category were all clustered in the two more concrete goal categories. The 20 subjects judged to have given a medium level of response to the case were distributed across all four abstraction categories, but with the majority clustering toward the concrete end of the continuum. Subjects in the anomalous performance group fell toward the middle of the goal-abstraction continuum. The cross-tabulation of level of goal abstraction by judged performance yielded a chi-square value of 27.85, (9df) with an associated $p = 0.001$. A similar result was obtained when the four levels of abstraction were collapsed into two: Chi-square was 14.9, (3df) $p = 0.0019$.

Subsequent graphical analysis provided additional insight into the relationships between judged performance, level of goal abstraction, and attention to detail. Subjects judged to have handled the case poorly not only pursued more concrete goals, they also had markedly lower density scores, indicating that they had paid much less attention to details in the case. In addition to being distributed across the abstraction continuum, subjects judged to have given a medium-quality response to the case had shown at least a moderate level of attention to detail. All subjects in the high-rated performance group had not only concentrated on more abstract goals but had also attended to more details in the case. The main finding, therefore, is that subjects rated highly by the two panels of judges were able to see both the forest and the trees: They attended to more details than did those who received lower ratings but they also held broader, more abstract, goals when creating their plans for dealing with the case problem.

The Role of Experience

The 20 subjects who received medium-performance ratings were distributed relatively evenly across our five experience categories. Six of the 7 subjects judged to have responded relatively poorly to the case were, as might be expected, student teachers in the Entrant category, who had had no direct experience of school administration or school teaching. Even so, 4 subjects in this novice group were judged to have responded to the case problem moderately well, which placed them in the same performance category as some principals with 10 or more years of administrative experience. Furthermore, 3 of the 6 subjects judged to have given high-quality responses to the case were Rookie principals, and one was an Aspirant principal. In other words, only 2 of the 6 subjects judged to have given high-quality responses to the case were experienced principals, both of whom had between 10 and 15 years of experience-in-role. Thus, while none of the Entrants were judged to have given a high-quality response to the case, neither were any of the Veteran principals who had 20 or more years experience. Interestingly, 4 of the 6 subjects receiving markedly divergent performance ratings from the two sets of judges were Veterans, a point we will return to later.

As sketched above, the relationship between experience and rated performance on the problem-solving task was neither simple nor direct. A cross-tabulation of the experience categories by performance categories yielded a chi-square of 35.7 (12df. $p = 0.0004$). A smaller but still significant ($p = 0.004$) chi-square was obtained when the anomalous performance category was collapsed into the medium category, an adjustment suggested by the earlier analyses reported above. The overall relationship, however, was highly dependent on the inclusion of the Entrant group, for when this category was dropped from the analysis, chi-square failed to reach significance (chi-square $= 6.7$, $p = .34$).

We also investigated attention to detail by level of abstraction across experience categories. Our most important finding here was the way in which attention to detail was related to both a more abstract approach to the problem *and* increased experience. Regardless of whether they pursued more abstract or more concrete goals in their response to the case, all of the Aspirants gave approximately the same level of medium-intensity attention to details. Marked differences emerged, however, within the Rookie experience group, that is, those who had recently been appointed to the principalship: Rookie principals who pursued more abstract goals paid considerably more attention to details in the case than those concerned with more concrete goals. A similar pattern was evident for the more experienced principals in our Seasoned category, but not for the most highly experienced Veterans, who were, once again, an exception. Leaving the Veterans aside, the key point appears to be that this pattern was only apparent for subjects who were principals. Thus, direct experience-in-role, even if this was relatively short, appeared to enable subjects who pursued more abstract goals to provide increased attention to details in the case problems.

DISCUSSION

The analyses outlined above suggest that there are at least two distinct elements at work in the development of problem-solving expertise: experience and cognitive ability. Experience as a principal was not by itself associated with improvements in the judged quality of responses to the case problem—even where one comparison group had no direct experience in the role. Experience in schools—the organizational context for the case problem—did, however, have an effect. Without the addition of the Entrant group composed of inexperienced student teachers we would have missed this point entirely. Our original design, although it was structured to capture a wide range of administrative experience, including a "novice" group of subjects who had not yet been appointed as principals, did not apparently capture "true" novices. It seems that teachers who have prepared themselves to be principals, even if they have no direct administrative experience, cannot be considered novices when it comes to dealing with at least certain kinds of administrative problems.

On the other hand, the student teachers comprising our Entrant group were true novices in the sense that they lacked both direct and contextual experience of administrative problems in schools. As such, most of them appeared to lack sufficient domain-specific knowledge to begin solving the problem presented to them. This was particularly evident in our analysis of attention to detail: Only one of the 10 Entrants scored above the third quartile on this measure, whereas half of the subjects in the Rookie and Seasoned groups did. Even so, a few of the Entrants were judged to have responded to the case problem quite well. Whatever generic skill these true novices had, it was sufficient to enable them to tackle the case as well as some principals with many years of school and administrative experience, but not sufficient to enable them to do outstandingly well.

But if contextual experience is important in approaching a domain-specific, ill-structured problem, how can we explain the failure of many highly experienced subjects to do well? Our analyses showed that subjects whose performance was highly rated were likely to have seen both the forest and the trees: They paid more attention to detail *and* gave evidence of being able to entertain and plan for the accomplishment of more transformative goals. Concentrating on either the forest or the trees was not in itself sufficient: Highly rated subjects did both. Yet while our findings suggest that experience is associated with both greater attention to detail and higher levels of abstraction in problem-solving, this was so only in some cases. Experience can help, but will not by itself ensure a high level of problem-solving expertise.

Limitations in our current data do not allow us to draw strong conclusions, but the patterns that emerged in our comparison of Aspirant and Rookie principals suggest that a capacity to approach and react to problems at more abstract levels is a potentially powerful ingredient in the development of administrative expertise. At the same time, the potency of this ability will apparently not be realized in the absence of direct domain-relevant experience. By themselves, neither experience nor a high level of abstract functioning seems sufficient for the development of expertise: Each appears to require the other. In essence, an ability to function at more abstract cognitive levels appears to enable experience to be transmuted into expertise; but without this ability, experience by itself may never produce expertise. This view is in accord with the discussion of schema theory presented in our framework section, but carries that discussion one step further by identifying a capacity for abstract cognitive functioning as a key factor in the organization of experience into more complex schemata. Furthermore, our findings from the Rookie principals imply that an ability to deal with problems on more abstract levels can enable individuals to develop complex schemata of task domains on the basis of relatively short periods of direct experience.

The principals in our Veteran group presented us with a number of anomalies that merit further consideration. These principals had more than 20 years of experience-in-role, but most had been appointed to principalships after only minimal classroom experience, with minimal academic qualifications and little, if any, preparative training. Many told us freely that they would not meet current appointment expectations if they were to be considered today. All, nonetheless, had sought at least some training after their initial appointment, and a few had completed graduate degrees. Even so, our Veterans represented an era that predates current expectations for the selection and training of principals.

Their approach to the case was, on the whole, quite different from that of the other experience groups. Only one of the six Veterans paid high attention to detail when responding to the case but two approached the case at what we judged to be a transformational level of abstraction, and two others analyzed the case at our somewhat less abstract program level. None, however, were judged to have provided a high-quality response to the case problem under the decision rules explained in the methods section, four of these six Veterans being classified in our anomalous category as a result of being rated highly by some judges and poorly by others. In an oversimplified generalization, most were rated poorly by the professorial judges (whose specialization is theoretical educational administration) but more highly by the graduate students (who are all experienced teachers). The professorial judges, however, saw only action summaries of the transcripts, and the Veterans generally described few specific actions, being more inclined not to commit themselves until they had "a feel" for the "real" situation. On the other hand, the graduate student judges read the entire transcripts, and, apparently, found much more than was conveyed in the summaries. In our own reading of the transcripts, we found that the Veterans, for the most part, talked knowledgeably about the case on the basis of their experience, often making reference to, but not committing themselves to, strategies they had used in the past, and this may have impressed our graduate student raters.

CONCLUSION

As with the forest and the trees, the importance of attending to detail in administrative matters is also recognized in colloquial language in phrases such as "getting the ducks lined up" or "taking care of the knitting." This latter phrase seems particularly apt in that it implies the importance of not "dropping stitches" in the pursuit of a larger goal. But the phrase with which we began can also be turned around to make the same point, for while it is important to gain a view of the forest, one cannot afford to ignore individual trees when attempting to traverse it.

If both experience and innate ability contribute to the development of expertise in problem-solving, there are many implications for the selection and training of future principals. Selection procedures that concentrate on the accumulation of experience without regard for innate ability (as one might argue the current Ontario regulations do) will achieve only serendipitous success. If, however, selection is to include an assessment of innate ability, then how might such ability be identified and measured?

Finally, the findings discussed here suggest a number of profitable lines of inquiry for future work. We plan to undertake a more detailed and focused study of the apparent levels of cognitive functioning, paying particular attention to the question of whether this seems to be an innate ability, as Jaques contends, or a skill that can be developed through training. Then there is the question of why some of our Entrants were able to perform as well as, or even better than, some trained and experienced principals: What background experiences and training or innate abilities were they able to draw on in the absence of domain-relevant experience? We hope to be able to explore this issue through more thorough studies of how principals, true novices, and experienced administrators from noneducational contexts respond to school problems.

REFERENCES

Allison, D. J., & Nagy, P. (1991, April). *A study of principal problem solving: An introduction to the study.* Paper presented at the Annual Meeting of the American Educational Research Association, Chicago.

Allison, P. A., & Allison, D. J. (1991, April). *Experience and expertise in administrative problem solving.* Paper presented at the Annual Meeting of the American Educational Research Association, Chicago.

Allison, P. A., & Nagy, P. (1989, April). *Analysis of problem solving in school administration: A comparison of methods.* Paper presented at the Annual Meeting of the Canadian Educational Research Association, Laval.

Anderson, R. C., Spiro, R. J., & Anderson, M. C. (1978). Schemata as scaffolding for the representation of information in connected discourse. *American Educational Research Journal, 15,* 433–439.

Bennis, W. (1984). The artform of leadership. In *The executive mind.* San Francisco: Jossey-Bass.

Bereiter, C., & Scardamalia, M. (1986). Educational relevance of the study of expertise. *Interchange, 17,* 10–19.

Berliner, D. C. (1986). In pursuit of the expert pedagogue. *Educational Researcher, 15*(7), 5–13.

Bloom, B. S. (1956). *Taxonomy of educational objectives. Handbook I: Cognitive domain.* New York: David McKay.

Ericson, K. A., & Simon, H. A. (1984). *Protocol analysis: Verbal reports as data.* Cambridge: The MIT Press.

Handy, C. B. (1976). *Understanding organizations.* Harmondsworth, UK: Penguin.

Jaques, E. (1976). *A general theory of bureaucracy.* London: Heinemann.

Jaques, E. (1986). The development of intellectual capability: A discussion of stratified systems theory. *The Journal of Applied Behavioural Science, 22*(4), 361–383.

Kennedy, M. M. (1987). *Inexact sciences: Professional education and the development of expertise.* East Lansing: National Center for Research on Teacher Education, Michigan State University.

Larkin, J., McDermott, J., Simon, D. P., & Simon, H. A. (1980). Expert and novice performance in solving physics problems. *Science, 208,* 1335–1342.

Leinhardt, G., & Smith, D. (1985). Expertise in mathematics instruction: Subject matter knowledge. *Journal of Educational Psychology, 77,* 247–271.

Leithwood, K. A., Begley, P., & Cousins, B. (1992). *Developing expert leadership for future schools.* New York: Falmer Press.

Leithwood, K. A., & Stager, M. (1986, April). *Differences in problem solving processes used by moderately and highly effective principals.* Paper presented at the Annual Meeting of the American Educational Research Association, San Francisco.

Leithwood, K. A., & Stager, M. (1987, November). *Components of expertise: "Artistry" in principals' problem solving.* Paper presented at the Annual Meeting of the Canadian Society for the Study of Education, Hamilton.

Martin, J., Slemon, A., Heibert, B., Hallberg, E. T., & Cummings, A. (1989). Conceptualizations of novice and experienced counselors. *Journal of Counseling Psychology, 36*(4), 395–400.

Mintzberg, H. (1973). *The nature of managerial work.* New York: Harper & Row.

Nagy, P. (1990, April). *Assessing thinking skills in social problem solving.* Paper presented at the Annual Meeting of the American Educational Research Association, Boston.

Nagy, P. (1991, April). *Using schema to map ill-structured problem solving: An applica-*

tion to school administration. Paper presented at the Annual Meeting of the American Educational Research Association, Chicago.

Nagy, P., & Allison, P. A. (1988, April). *School-level decision making: A cognitive perspective.* Paper presented at the Annual Meeting of the Canadian Society for the Study of Education, Windsor.

Nagy, P., & Moorhead, R. (1990). Administrative response to classroom testing data: A problem solving perspective. *Alberta Journal of Educational Research, 36,* 18–34.

Piaget, J. (1960). *The origins of intelligence in children.* New York: International University Press.

Schallert, D. L. (1982). The significance of knowledge: A synthesis of research related to schema theory. In W. Otto & S. White (Eds.), *Reading expository material.* Toronto: Academic Press.

Schön, D. A. (1983). *The reflective practitioner.* New York: Basic Books.

Schön, D. A. (1987). *Educating the reflective practitioner.* San Francisco: Jossey-Bass.

Schwab, J. J. (1978). *Science, curriculum and liberal arts: Selected essays.* Chicago: University of Chicago Press.

Voss, J. F., Green, T. R., Post, T. A., & Penner, B. C. (1983). Problem solving skill in the social sciences. In G. H. Bower (Ed.), *The psychology of learning and motivation: Advances in research theory* (pp. 165–213). New York: Academic Press.

9 A Theoretical View of the Development of Expertise in Credit Administration

Frank R. Yekovich

One task that administrators of all types—school administrators, credit administrators in banks, business managers, and so forth—have in common is that they are expected to solve complex problems regularly and effectively. The problems are complex in the sense that many ill-defined factors need to be considered in order for an effective solution to be found. Further complicating the situation is that one or more of the factors involved may be left open or unspecified by the situation. Additionally, the nature of these problems is such that administrators sometimes have a lot of information available to aid their decision-making and at other times they have access to very little information. Thus, not only are the problems complex in an absolute sense, but the informational resources available may vary.

Given the complexity of this kind of problem-solving activity, an important question becomes whether administrators can learn to be effective solvers of such problems. Put another way, can administrators become expert problem-solvers? A second important question is whether we can model the cognitive operations that describe both how administrators solve such problems and how they acquire the skill or expertise that underlies the ability to solve complex problems.

With respect to the first question, the answer appears to be yes, the problem-solving ability of administrators does get better with time and experience. A growing body of literature shows that school administrators (Leithwood & Steinbach, in press; this volume), business managers (Wagner, 1991; this volume), and bank credit administrators (Yekovich, Thompson, & Walker, 1991) can be differentiated on a continuum of expertise, and that experts are better, more efficient problem-solvers than their inexperienced counterparts.

The purpose of this chapter is to scrutinize some of the issues associated with the questions of the constituent cognitive features that underlie expert problem-solving and how expert administrators acquire their expertise. The chapter is divided into two major sections. The first section considers the cognitive characteristics that distinguish experts from nonexperts and subsequently discusses the transformation of these characteristics from their nonexpert form to their expert form. The development of expertise is viewed as a process of acquiring cognitive skill (i.e., the evolution of ability to think and reason effectively in a domain). In order to make the acquisition model meaningful, it is presented using a hypothetical case of a new loan officer who works in the credit administration department of a bank. Becoming a competent lending officer is a common prerequisite for promotion to the position of head of the credit administration function within a bank. The second section presents data that support the model's assumptions about the acquisition of expertise. This part is devoted to a brief summary of a study completed with some of my colleagues that looked at the problem-solving and reasoning capabilities of credit administrators with varying degrees of expertise.

COGNITIVE UNDERPINNINGS ASSOCIATED WITH EXPERTISE AND ITS DEVELOPMENT

Imagine the following situation: An inexperienced administrator reports for work and is faced with a moderately difficult problem to solve. As an employee who has the chance to observe, you notice that the newly hired administrator has considerable difficulty dealing with the informational load that accompanies the problem and that he or she appears to use information in a piecemeal and unsystematic way. The administrator seems to rely too heavily on irrelevant information and seems to ignore or overlook information central to the problem situation. The overall problem-solving episode is rather haphazard, and the quality of the decision is questionable at best. As an employee within the organization, you shake your head and pray that the whole enterprise does not come tumbling down. Now fast-forward to the future. The organization is still intact and somehow the administrator has managed to survive. You observe that when faced with a similar, moderately difficult problem, the more experienced administrator has become capable of recognizing complex patterns of information and using large amounts of information efficiently to reach a "coherent" or "integrated" solution to the problem. The person requests missing critical information, and discriminates between the relevant and the irrelevant. Moreover, the administrator appears to handle the problem with relative ease.

What happened over the period of time to produce such a dramatic change in the administrator's problem-solving ability? In order to understand the differences that exist between experienced (expert) and inexperienced (novice) administrators, one needs to understand the cognitive characteristics that accompany the problem-solving of each group. Further, one needs to be able to describe how the cognitive characteristics of inexperienced administrators evolve into the characteristics possessed by experienced administrators.

During the last 15 years, cognitive and educational psychologists have made considerable progress on these two issues. Let us now turn to what we know about each issue.

Characteristics Associated with Expertise

In a 1988 volume devoted to the nature of expertise, Glaser and Chi (1988) presented seven general characteristics of expert performance that have emerged from an extensive body of research on thinking, reasoning, and learning. These seven characteristics are listed and briefly described below.

1. *Experts excel mainly in their domains.* Expertise is basically a domain-specific phenomenon that requires an understanding of the domain itself. Further, being expert in one domain does not ensure expertise in another domain. For instance, being an expert school administrator does not ensure success at being a student in a graduate program.

2. *Experts perceive large, meaningful patterns in their domains.* When faced with large amounts of domain-related information, experts are able to organize the information into meaningful "chunks," thereby allowing the recognition of patterns rather than discrete pieces of information. Novices perceive information in a more piecemeal way.

3. *Experts are fast.* They are faster than novices at performing the skills of their domain, and they often solve problems with little error (see, however, statement 6 below).

4. *Experts have superior short-term and long-term memory.* When faced with domain-related descriptions of situations and problems, experts are better able than novices to recall both recent past events and events that occurred a moderately long time ago. The superiority is due to the fact that experts are able to encode and store large amounts of domain-related information whereas novices have a great deal of difficulty because the information is unfamiliar to them. The result of superior encoding and storage by experts is a highly enriched memory representation that produces superior recall.

5. *Experts see and represent a problem in their domain at a deeper (more principled) level than do novices. Novices tend to represent a problem at a superficial level.* For instance, expert administrators are likely to see problems as similar or different according to the principles that underlie the solution of the problems (e.g., organizational effectiveness, resource allocation) whereas novice administrators decide on similarity or difference

according to the surface features of the problems (e.g., broken equipment, angry employees).

6. *Experts spend a great deal of time evaluating the problem.* An interesting difference between novices and experts is that when presented with a problem, the novices often launch off quickly into attempts to solve the problem while experts spend time evaluating the nature of the problem and representing it correctly before attempting a solution. As one might expect, the novices' attempts often result in trial-and-error behavior and many failed attempts. In contrast, once an expert attempts a solution, the behavior is very goal-directed and contains relatively few errors. Thus, experts spend a large proportion of solution time generating the correct representation of the problem and a small proportion of time executing the solution. Novices do just the opposite: They spend a large proportion of time executing potential solutions and a small proportion of time generating the representation of the problem.

7. *Experts have strong self-monitoring skills.* Experts exhibit the ability to know when they do not understand and the capability to generate and evaluate alternatives that will lead to recovery. Novices tend not to be able to monitor their own understanding very well. Even when they notice comprehension failure, they do not know what to do to overcome the difficulty.

Given these seven performance characteristics, what are the corresponding cognitive characteristics that underlie expert performance? Basically, two general characteristics can be identified.

Experts possess a large amount of domain-related knowledge. This statement is a deceptive oversimplification. Put more precisely, experts possess extensive knowledge about the domain itself, and also about how to operate within the domain. Knowledge about the domain is called *declarative* knowledge (Anderson, 1982, 1983, 1987, 1990a). The declarative knowledge of experts is both vast and well organized, thereby allowing them to be very familiar with most of the domain-related information with which they come in contact. Knowledge about how to operate in the domain is called *procedural* knowledge (again cf. Anderson, especially 1983, 1987). Procedural knowledge provides experts with specialized mental algorithms and heuristics for dealing with domain-related information in efficient and effective ways.

The cognitive processes that underlie performance operate more effectively for experts than for novices. In the theory of skill proposed by Anderson (1983), cognitive processes are modeled as pieces of procedural knowledge known as production sets or production systems. Production sets "produce" cognitive or overt actions through a series of mental steps or operations. Cognitive processes (AKA production sets) require knowledge in order to produce an action. In other words, one cannot do any mental work if one does not have knowledge with which to do the work. One consequence is that having a large amount of domain-related knowledge may actually facilitate the way cognitive processes do their work. For instance, in reading, the cognitive processes responsible for word identification operate on the primitive features of letters for beginning readers (i.e., lines, angles). In contrast, those processes may operate on entire words or wordlike subunits in experienced readers (Just & Carpenter, 1987). The amount of knowledge of the language and the degree of experience with its written form change the processing units from elemental pieces of knowledge to larger, more complicated and informationally dense pieces. The result is that with the same amount of mental effort expended, more of the reading process is accomplished. Thus, in some sense the cognitive processes themselves benefit from one's knowledge of a domain.

These two cognitive characteristics can essentially account for or explain the seven performance characteristics described earlier. Table 9.1 presents each of the performance characteristics of experts and the associated cognitive characteristic that is primarily responsible for it. I use the term *primarily* because a complete distinction between structure and process cannot be made (Anderson, 1990b). However, for purposes of illustration one can say that some performance characteristics are primarily the result of domain knowledge (numbers 1, 2, 5); others are primarily the result of enhanced processing capabilities (numbers 3, 7), and others are the clear result of both knowledge and processing effectiveness working together simultaneously (numbers 4, 6). To give a concrete example, consider the first performance characteristic, *Experts excel mainly in their domains.* The cognitive underpinning primarily responsible is knowledge. Experts simply know so much more about the domain than novices do that the experts "excel" in the domain relative to the novices.

How do the cognitive characteristics underlying expert performance come to exist in expert form? Essentially, learners initially acquire knowledge about a domain and use that knowledge to begin reasoning in the domain. Eventually the repeated use of that knowledge leads to the formation of larger processing units and the formation and refinement of specialized processing capabilities. In order to gain a fuller understanding of this process, let us consider in some detail a theory that describes the acquisition of cognitive skill in a domain.

The Acquisition of Cognitive Skill

Anderson (1983) and others (see Anzai & Simon, 1979) have described the acquisition of skill as a process of "learning by doing." Anderson's theory, known as ACT° (read "Act Star" an acronym for Adaptive Control of Thought), has directed much of our work (e.g., Gagné, Yekovich, & Yekovich, in press; Walker,

Table 9.1 The Relation Between the Characteristics of Expert Performance Identified by Glaser and Chi (1988) and the Cognitive Characteristics Primarily Responsible for That Performance

Characteristics of Performance	Cognitive Features	
	Domain-Related Knowledge	Cognitive Processes
1. Experts excel mainly in their domains.	X	
2. Experts perceive large, meaningful patterns in their domains.	X	
3. Experts are fast.		X
4. Experts have superior STM and LTM.	X	X
5. Experts represent a problem in their domain at a deep (principled) level.	X	
6. Experts spend a great deal of time qualitatively.	X	X
7. Experts have strong self-monitoring skills.		X

1987; Yekovich et al., 1991; Yekovich, Walker, Ogle, & Thompson, 1990). The discussion that follows is a brief explication of his theory.

In order to make the presentation more concrete, I will describe the theory using expertise in credit administration in banks as an example. A credit administrator is responsible for the loan functions of a bank, and consequently is often the head of the loan department within the bank. So there will be no confusion, the credit administrator is not simply a glorified loan officer. Rather, the administrator's responsibilities include managing the loan department, setting loan policies, reconciling the changing asset size of the bank against the optimal loan liabilities in order to preserve the health of the institution, and interacting with other senior bank managers for the purpose of setting general bank policy. Although credit administrators vary in their backgrounds, a typical individual may have an undergraduate degree in Economics or Business, perhaps an advanced degree such as an MBA, experience in the loan department perhaps as a lending officer, specialized training in credit administration, and perhaps additional experience in other departments within the bank.

According to Anderson (1987, 1990a; see also Fitts, 1964), the acquisition of cognitive skill occurs in roughly three stages, known respectively as the declarative, the associative, and the autonomous stages. In the following sections, I outline the major performance and cognitive characteristics associated with each stage.

Declarative Stage. In the declarative stage, an individual learns concepts and facts about the domain and stores that information in memory as declarative knowledge. Declarative knowledge is stored in a semantic network in which the concepts and facts form nodes within the network and the nodes are linked or connected by relations. During this stage, a person's declarative knowledge grows and becomes organized in a rudimentary way. However, it is important to realize that at this early time, the declarative knowledge base about the domain is sketchy relative to what it will eventually become. The overall amount of knowledge is not great, the connecting relations are few and are not very strong, and the organization of the network (i.e., which facts and concepts go together and for what reasons) is primitive. Put simply, the declarative knowledge base is essentially a very loosely and sparsely connected set of information. The degree to which this knowledge state will change will be a function of the amount of use of the declarative knowledge base and the amount of new information input to the base. As individuals progress through the declarative stage, the progression can be characterized as moving away from "novice" in the truest sense (i.e., having no domain-related knowledge whatsoever) to some form of non-novice in the domain.

How do individuals in the declarative stage go about solving domain-related problems? In general, problem-solving is viewed as a process in which a person moves from a set of givens (also called the initial state of a problem) to an end or goal state (Newell & Simon, 1972). The problem-solving process includes, (1) forming a mental representation of the problem that includes the initial and goal states as well as the possible intermediate steps; (2) selecting a strategy for working through the possible steps in order to form a path between the initial and goal states; (3) making moves from one intermediate step to another; and (4) evaluating whether each move results in being closer to the goal. Success in solving domain-related problems depends on having the requisite knowledge to correctly represent the problem and on possessing the strategies and moves that are required for traversal through the problem representation.

Individuals who are in the declarative stage of learning a domain probably have only some of the declarative knowledge that will be required to solve a problem and will have only general methods (hereafter referred to as domain-general strategies or weak methods) available for use. The current state of their declarative knowledge will be such that the givens in the problem will appear to have no pattern and consequently no hints. This situation is due to both the small size of the declarative knowledge base (i.e., some pieces of the pattern will not exist in memory) and to its lack of connectedness (i.e., even if the givens of the problem are known to the problem-solver, they probably will not be related in memory). Further, the individual will not be able to determine whether some of the givens are irrelevant because the organization of the declarative knowledge base does not differentiate the importance of the information and the lack of connectedness again will not tell which information should go together.

Additionally, the problem-solver in the declarative stage will have only domain-general methods available for use. Domain-general methods are strategies that apply across a variety of domains. For example, the use of an analogy is a common method for solving a novel problem (see Anderson, 1987, or Gagne et al., in press, for a discussion of domain-general methods). Using an analogy basically involves determining whether a current problem maps onto one the problem-solver already knows how to solve. The solution to the new problem then becomes following the procedure that produced the solution to the already known or familiar problem. Domain-general methods are called "weak" because while they can be used in numerous domains, they will not always produce success. Domain-general methods, along with one's declarative knowledge of a domain, eventually combine to form methods that are *specialized* for use on a limited class of domain-specific problems. Unfortunately, the powerful, specialized, domain-specific methods develop and evolve only after considerable use of one's declarative knowledge of the domain. Thus, domain-specific strategies are not available to an individual in the declarative stage and consequently, she or he must resort to weak strategies to solve domain-related problems.

Consider the hypothetical case of a recent college graduate with a BA in English and limited experience as a bank teller, who assumes a job as a loan officer in a small, commercial bank. This credit administrator novice initially knows nothing about the domain of credit administration. In all likelihood, the bank will have a training program in which the novice learns a large number of concepts and facts about making loans, as well as general principles of banking and bank policies. The training program may consist of a set of self-instructional manuals and/or workshops in which lectures and exercises are the predominant forms of instruction. The new employee, being an especially good and recent student, takes notes faithfully and commits as much information as possible to memory.

Essentially, the new loan officer is acquiring declarative knowledge about one or two aspects of credit administration, namely, making loans and fundamental banking principles. Since most of the information is new and does not seem to make much sense, many of the concepts and facts are being stored in a sparsely connected, unintegrated network. Further, because the new loan officer has not had opportunities to practice, her knowledge of how to complete loan transactions is nonexistent.

Now suppose the trainee is faced with her first spreadsheet problem in which she is given the loan amount, the loan interest rate, and a series of loan payments and dates, and is asked to produce the outstanding balance. Having had little experience with the bank's loan accounting method (and having remembered almost none of it), the new loan officer thinks,

Well, the concepts of credit and debit remind me alot of the concepts of deposits and withdrawals that I used to keep my own checkbook, so I'll set up the spreadsheet with three columns, one for credits, one for debits, and one for the remaining balance. Now, I'll put the initial value of the loan in the debit column because the bank withdrew that amount and gave it to the customer.

So she diligently sets out to work. She also has difficulty with the concept of the interest rate and how much of each payment will cover the interest and how much will apply to the principal. Knowing that the interest rate is annual, she determines the interest due for a one-year period and divides the result by 12, thereby distributing the interest equally across the payments for a year.

Consider what happened in the two problem-solving episodes in this vignette. First, notice the use of analogy in the trainee's thoughts about setting up the spreadsheet. She maps her knowledge of balancing a checkbook onto the problem of setting up a loan balance sheet. This is an example, albeit a fictitious one, of how novices resort to domain-general methods in order to solve a domain-specific problem. Second, notice how the trainee solved the interest rate difficulty. Again she used general knowledge (annual = 12 months) and applied a weak heuristic to compute and distribute the interest costs.

In each problem-solving episode, the solution may be wrong. Suppose, for example, that the accounting method requires four columns: interest credits, principal credits, total credits (the sum of columns one and two), and debits. No outstanding balance column is needed because the debit column will provide the outstanding balance. Suppose further that interest is computed not only on that portion of the original principal still owed (the outstanding balance), but on the full amount of the original principal. Finally, suppose that a set of tables exists that provides a breakdown of interest and principal on a loan amount for a given term period. Essentially, the new trainee performed miserably on this problem because (1) she lacked the declarative knowledge about the bank's loan accounting format; (2) she misapplied a weak method as a result of her knowledge deficit; and (3) she lacked declarative knowledge about the tables that would have precluded the need for attempting to solve the interest rate dilemma.

While this example may make the new loan officer look like a poor performer, the illustration does in fact characterize the behavior of novices or near-novices in a new domain. Fortunately, this type of thinking and performance is supplanted as one gains increased declarative knowledge and repeatedly uses this knowledge base. The second stage of skill acquisition, known as the associative stage, is where this transformation occurs.

Associative Stage. The associative stage is characterized by two noticeable changes in the knowledge state of an individual. First, one's declarative-knowledge base continues to grow, but more importantly, it undergoes continual refinement so that eventually its organization and interconnectedness begin to approximate an expert form. Second, the continued development of the declarative-knowledge base results in the ability to "associate" facts and concepts with actions or operations in the domain. The associations between facts and actions form the building blocks for domain-specific procedural knowledge, the type of knowledge responsible for fast, efficient processing of large pieces of domain-specific declarative knowledge. Let us consider each of these changes in a little more detail.

At the beginning of the associative stage, one's declarative knowledge of a domain is sparsely connected and very loosely organized. The acquisition of new knowledge becomes somewhat easier because some domain-specific anchors are available in memory for appending the new information. Of course, as one acquires more knowledge, the process of acquiring yet additional knowledge will be further enhanced. During the acquisition process in the associative stage, repeated encounters with frequently co-occurring pieces of information lead to the formation and strengthening of links (or relations) between and among the pieces. Over time the connections and their strengths shape or define the organization of the declarative knowledge about the domain. Further, the interconnectedness of facts and concepts will eventually allow one to recognize a complex pattern, that is, a number of facts and/or concepts that go together or have meaning as a whole. These chunks of declarative information will exist in different-sized packages. The embedding of smaller chunks within larger chunks eventually produces an elaborately organized representation of one's knowledge about the domain. Finally, during the acquisition process, repeated encounters with identical or very similar sets of information will lead to the induction of schemata that can also be used to recognize patterns. Thus, during the associative stage of skill acquisition, one's declarative knowledge about a domain literally evolves from a sparse set of weakly related information into a larger, more integrated network that approximates expert knowledge. However, the refinement and elaboration of the network is not complete.

The second change that occurs during the associative stage is the formation of domain-specific procedural knowledge. As mentioned earlier, Anderson (1983) formally represents procedural knowledge as a series of productions. A production is a rule or contingency statement of the IF–THEN form. The IF portion of a rule contains one or more conditions that must exist or be satisfied, and the THEN portion contains one or more cognitive or overt actions that will be executed when the conditions are satisfied. To illustrate, a production for crediting a loan account might look like the following:

IF   The goal is to credit a loan account with a monthly installment
        and I have the check for the installment amount
        and the check has the loan account number written on it
THEN   Call up the computer file of the account
        and enter the installment amount in the Credit column
        and enter today's date in the Date of Payment column
        and satisfy the goal once the computer file is completely updated

Technically, the above production will produce the actions associated with crediting the account only when all three conditions are present simultaneously. Thus, if a person is holding a check but it does not have the account number on it, the production will not be used. Similarly, once the production executes, all of the actions will occur. So in the above example, both calling up the account file and working in it would occur.

Although a complete discussion of the nature of procedural knowledge is beyond the scope of the current chapter, two important properties are worth noting (for a detailed discussion of the representation and acquisition of procedural knowledge, see Gagné et al., in press). First, each condition and each action in a production is a declarative-knowledge structure. In the example production, the condition "and the check has the loan account number on it" is really a proposition or fact derived from our knowledge about writing checks to pay bills. For current purposes, the declarative structures will be domain-specific, and the resulting productions will make up domain-specific procedural knowledge. The acquisition of domain-specific procedural knowledge will thus require the existence of domain-specific declarative knowledge.

Second, productions are related to one another by goal–subgoal relations and the related productions are called a *set* or a *system*. For instance, if one has a goal of adding two three-digit numbers, one required subgoal must be to add each of the three columns. If one modeled the addition process using productions, a production set would be needed and the way the productions within the set would be connected would be through the goal–subgoal relations (i.e., the relation between producing the answer to the overall problem and producing the correct column sums). In the current vein, this means that domain-specific productions will be related together into sets that accomplish a domain-specific processing goal (e.g., setting up a spreadsheet for a specific type of loan). Once acquired, domain-specific production sets provide powerful but specialized means for reasoning and behaving in the domain.

During the associative stage, the recognition of frequently co-occurring information and the corresponding action(s) results in the formation of domain-specific productions. This process contrasts sharply with the way procedural knowledge was used in the declarative stage. In that stage all domain-specific declarative knowledge was interpreted by domain-general productions. Now, because the learner has acquired enough declarative knowledge to be able to recognize regularities, the cognitive system either "builds" new domain-specific productions using declarative knowledge as the source, or "modifies" a domain-general production set by building a special-purpose domain-specific version of it.

Since procedural knowledge is responsible for producing our cognitive and overt behavior, it is ultimately the controller of our actions. Consequently, the cognitive system builds procedural knowledge slowly and cautiously. This is the main reason that extensive practice opportunities and experiences are required for the construction of new procedural knowledge.

Return to our hypothetical loan officer who has been working in the small commercial bank for two months and has continued to review her training materials and other documents outlining official loan policies. Her review of materials has provided her with additional declarative knowledge about the domain of making loans. Similarly, her everyday work experiences also act as sources of new declarative knowledge. Perhaps more importantly, however, those experiences have provided her with repeated encounters of similar sets of information and corresponding required actions. For instance, suppose that she has been responsible for originating and monitoring five loans—one short-term single payment consumer loan, one fixed-rate 30-year mortgage, one adjustable-rate home equity loan, and two small business "line of credit" loans.

Clearly her work and her independent study are increasing her declarative knowledge about loans. She may have a mental classification of loan types, terms, and rates. Similarly, she probably knows the application forms by heart. She also probably has a mental representation of the loan department itself and its administrative structure, as well as the structure of the entire bank. In short, her knowledge about the bank-lending domain is undergoing growth, reorganization, and refinement. If she were asked some questions, she would perform as well as a true expert loan officer. However, it would not be difficult to set up complex situations where she would still perform poorly.

At the same time, the repeated encounters with similar situations are providing opportunities for her to build simple domain-specific procedures. For instance, as a result of handling the five loans, she has probably learned a procedure for originating a loan and a separate one for monitoring its status. Additionally, she has probably developed other procedures for other aspects of her job (e.g., how to match prospective borrowers with appropriate loan types, how to obtain supplies, how to request leave).

Her procedural knowledge of the loan domain will initially be comprised of a small number of relatively simple production sets and the productions within each set will themselves be simple (i.e., they will have small numbers of very specific conditions and actions). With repeated use, the individual productions will combine to form larger, more powerful productions and consequently the production set will become more powerful. As an example, our loan officer's procedural knowledge of setting up a spreadsheet may eventually develop to the point that she bypasses the available tables and actually uses her computer spreadsheet program to generate the necessary table on the spot.

In sum, the associative stage produces the rather dramatic transformation from simply knowing a little about a domain to actually being able to perform "intelligently" within it. However, one's performance capabilities are still limited. Because the declarative-knowledge base is still undergoing some growth and because it is being constantly reorganized and refined, it lacks the rich interconnectedness and elaboration that characterizes true expert knowledge. As will be seen in the section describing a research study of fledgling credit administrators, this "incomplete" knowledge state has interesting performance consequences. In addition, because domain-specific procedural knowledge is being built and modified, the learner cannot perform as efficiently or as capably as an expert. Rather, the learner will approach expert performance for some simple domain-specific tasks, and appear novicelike for more complicated tasks. In the final stage of skill acquisition, the continued refinement and smoothing occurs. Let us turn now to a discussion of the last stage.

Autonomous Stage. Although Anderson (1990a) adopts a stage conceptualization of the skill-acquisition process, the reality is that skill acquisition occurs along a continuum. One consequence of this reality is that learners move through and across the stages in an almost continuous fashion rather than in some discontinuous way. The use of "stages" simply provides some benchmarks along the continuum. With this assumption in mind, Anderson describes the autonomous stage as one in which "fine-tuning" of the cognitive skill occurs.

Fine-tuning of declarative knowledge about a domain refers to increasing the elaboratedness and interconnectedness of the network. Put simply, the declarative-knowledge base becomes enriched to the point that the person knows a lot about the domain and knows how most things are related to each other. Take a hypothetical "expert" loan officer who specializes in mortgage lending. Being an expert probably entails having a complete understanding of the bank's mortgage loan portfolio and how that particular portfolio "fits" within the complete loan portfolio of the bank (i.e., mortgage, consumer, and commercial loans). So, for example, an expert loan officer could accurately evaluate the effect of a defaulted mortgage loan on both the bank's mortgage portfolio and the full portfolio.

That type of evaluation ability would contrast sharply with our new loan officer who has had experience with five loans. While our loan officer would know that her loan portfolio is a part of a larger portfolio, she may not have the enriched knowledge that would permit her to make an evaluation. If asked about the effect of a defaulted loan, she might simply say something like, "Yeah,

I know it's a problem, but I don't know how much impact it will have."

Fine-tuning of procedural knowledge refers to two related aspects of change in the knowledge state. First, generalization and discrimination processes tune the productions for the appropriate degree of generality or specificity. For instance, the procedure for originating loans will be tuned so that a generalization will be included when all loans are affected (e.g., all loan applicants must undergo a credit check), and discriminations will be included to handle separate cases (e.g., loans of less than $5,000 need only my supervisor's approval, loans for more than $5,000 must be approved by the head of the loan department).

The second change that occurs with procedural knowledge is that the domain-specific procedures that are algorithmic in character become automated, hence the term *autonomous*. In information-processing terms (e.g., Schneider & Shiffrin, 1977), automated means that the procedures execute without awareness and use few or no cognitive resources. One of the most often cited examples of this phenomenon is driving a car. Many of the low-level motor skills associated with driving (e.g., shifting) are performed automatically. The fact that those behaviors occur contemporaneously with other behaviors, such as talking and monitoring other drivers, indicates that the low-level skills require no cognitive resources. Further, the fact that someone who owns a manual transmission car inadvertently depresses a ghost clutch in an automatic transmission car is an indicator that automated procedures operate without awareness and are difficult to control.

Once our new loan officer has enough experience with setting up a spreadsheet for a loan, this skill is a good candidate for becoming automated. It is likely to be an algorithmic task and one that will be performed frequently. As she becomes more expert at her job, other invariant tasks, even ones fairly complicated, will also become automated. Note that this automation will make our loan officer fast and efficient; she will appear to be dealing with large amounts of information in a moderately effortless manner.

The fine-tuning that occurs during the autonomous stage may be thought of as the endpoint in the evolution of one's knowledge about a domain. As the reader can tell from the foregoing discussion, this endpoint is reached only after many encounters with domain-related information. So our new loan officer has a way to go to develop true expertise, and the story does not stop there. Being a competent loan officer is only one of a number of prerequisites for being an expert credit administrator. In the next section, I describe a study that explored how expert credit administrators and inexperienced credit administrators (who happened to be very competent lending officers) reason about a case study involving a fictitious bank. In some sense, it is a study of how individuals in the associative stage of skill acquisition both approximate and differ from those in the final, autonomous stage.

A STUDY OF EXPERT AND TRAINED NONEXPERT (TNE) CREDIT ADMINISTRATORS

For the past five years, Carol Walker Yekovich and I, along with several of our students, have been studying two aspects of the effects of domain knowledge. One part of our work has dealt with how domain knowledge can compensate for deficiencies in verbal aptitude when dealing with domain-related information (see Walker, 1987; Yekovich et al., 1990). A second part of our work has been concerned more directly with the acquisition of domain knowledge and its relation to the development of expertise (e.g., Yekovich et al., 1991). In this latter vein, the recently completed study by Yekovich, Thompson, and Walker focused on the reasoning capabilities of expert credit administrators and trained but not yet expert credit administrators (referred to as TNEs). Credit administrators function in a capacity similar to school administrators and upper-level business managers. That is to say, the three types of administrators are all responsible for managing budgets, personnel, setting policy, and controlling the daily operation of a complex unit. Thus, understanding the development of expertise in credit administrators should shed light on expertise in educational administration. In the remainder of the chapter, I summarize our study of expert and TNE credit administrators, and point out how the research supports the claims of the theory of skill acquisition presented earlier.

Rationale for the Study

The study grew out of a number of concerns. At one level, we wanted to address the question of why formal education often fails to prepare individuals to function competently when they first report to work. At another level, we were interested in uncovering some of the similarities and differences in knowledge states that exist between experts and nonexperts. Because of our first concern, we wanted to study a group of individuals who by definition had been educationally prepared to assume a particular job, but by a theoretical definition lacked the experiences to qualify as "experts." Additionally, since the development of expertise falls along a continuum and since most studies of experts contrast the endpoints (i.e., experts versus novices), we were concerned with other points along the continuum, especially those closer to the expert endpoint. Finally, we were interested in exploring the degree to which formal training prepares individuals to draw complex inferences and use those inferences to reason about a domain-specific problem.

The crux of the study hinged on our assumptions about the knowledge characteristics of the experts and the TNEs. Consider what the knowledge state would be like for an individual who has received formal training for a position, and who also has some prerequisite experience in the domain, but has never functioned in the new job role (i.e., a TNE). According to the conceptualization developed in the previous section, one might suppose that such an individual would fall somewhere in the associative stage of skill acquisition. The individual would have developed a declarative knowledge base of the domain as a result of the training program and the previous related experiences in the domain. The network would be moderate to large, would probably be undergoing reorganization and refinement, and would not be very richly interconnected because of a lack of exposure to the situations that give rise to the development of associative relations.

In addition, the individual's domain-specific procedural knowledge would probably be incomplete, partially proceduralized, and possibly lacking coherent goal–subgoal structures for the production sets. Again, this state can be attributed to the fact that the individual would not have had the practice opportunities necessary to build domain-specific procedural knowledge. One consequence would be that TNEs would not be able to rely solely on domain-specific procedural knowledge when faced with credit administration problems. Rather, they would have to resort to weak methods some proportion of the time in order to solve domain-specific problems.

The primary differences between a TNE's knowledge state and an expert's would be twofold. First, the expert's declarative-knowledge base would be more tightly organized and more richly interconnected. Second, the expert would have well-developed and finely tuned domain-specific procedural knowledge and some of this knowledge would be automated.

We reasoned that the similarities and the differences in the knowledge states would lead to corresponding performance similarities and differences between the two groups. So, for instance, since TNEs possess a moderately large declarative-knowledge base about the credit administration domain, we predicted that they would perform like experts on tasks that required simple memory operations such as the encoding and retrieval of facts about a credit administration situation. Thus, if the two groups were asked to read a case study about the credit administration function of a fictitious bank, they would be equally good at recalling and recognizing the specific facts of the case. It is important to note that this prediction differs from the result that occurs when experts are contrasted with novices (see the section on characteristics of expert performance and superior short-term and long-term memory).

On the other hand, since the knowledge characteristics of TNEs and experts presumably differ in predictable ways, we reasoned that those differences would surface in performance. For instance, tasks that require the integration and synthesis of facts for the purpose of drawing inferences about the case might prove very difficult. We proposed two reasons why inferencing tasks would be difficult. The first reason stems from the lack of interconnectedness of declarative knowledge. While TNEs have a moderate amount of domain knowledge, the network has not been fully interrelated. Thus, while TNEs may have access to domain-specific facts, they may not have access to many of the relations between and among those facts. In other words, given a problem situation, a TNE might be able to list or recognize a series of facts, but fail to realize that the combination can be integrated to produce inferences about the problem. The second reason stems from the procedural knowledge deficits of TNEs. Experts sometimes solve domain-specific problems using well-developed pattern recognition procedures (Anderson, 1983, 1987). In contrast, TNEs often resort to more effort-intensive weak methods to solve those same problems because they lack the requisite domain-specific procedural knowledge. The lack of pattern recognition procedures in TNEs may result in the failure to recognize some meaningful patterns of information that are critical to the overall problem situation.

Method

The participants were seven lending officers and seven functioning credit administrators who recently completed a six-week bank management course (for a more complete description see Yekovich, Thompson, & Walker, 1991). The credit administrators (i.e., the experts) were the heads of the credit administration functions in their respective banks and had an average of nine years of experience as head. The seven lending officers (i.e., the TNEs) had an average of about three years of banking experience. They had varying degrees of responsibility for making loans, but none had ever had responsibility for setting or enforcing credit administration policy or procedures.

The management training course was comprised of three separate two-week sessions. In the six weeks of training, all 14 bankers received 100 hours of classroom instruction on topics related to credit administration. The major topics were financial management (e.g., loan portfolio management, loan quality monitoring, and advanced financial statement analysis) and personnel management (e.g., staffing, performance appraisal, conflict management, and business ethics).

According to the stated goals and objectives of the management school, individuals who complete the entire course successfully are considered adequately trained to manage the credit administration function of a bank. Thus, the training, coupled with the experience of being a senior lending officer, produced a picture of a TNE who has considerable classroom knowledge about credit administration, limited practice opportunities in that domain, and extensive knowledge and experience about one aspect of credit administration, namely, making loans.

We used a case study that described a fictitious suburban bank that was growing rapidly but had neglected to develop appropriate quality-control measures in its credit administration area. On the surface, the bank appears quite healthy, but expert credit administrators can detect (through inference) symptoms of trouble. Each banker was tested individually. First the banker read the case aloud and assumed the perspective of the newly hired head of the credit administration function of the bank. Immediately after reading, the banker retold the case and conveyed concerns, if any, about the bank. Subsequently, he or she completed a recognition test by first marking a series of printed statements for their veracity and then marking the true statements either as being explicitly mentioned in the case or as inferences. Finally, the banker listened to a series of statements from the case and responded to each as to whether it represented a problem. For each perceived problem, the banker provided a justification.

The tasks were devised so that each one provided measures about the explicit content of the case and separate measures of inferencing/reasoning about the case. For example, the retelling task was scored for explicit content recalled and for the inferences that were generated. The measures focusing on the explicit content were predicted to reveal similarities in the experts' and TNEs' knowledge states while the inferencing/reasoning measures were predicted to reveal the subtle differences.

Results and Conclusions

Table 9.2 provides a summary of the results of the study. The top portion of the table presents the measures associated with the explicit facts from the case study, and is labeled *Similarities* of the capabilities of Experts and TNEs. The bottom portion of the table presents measures that required inferencing and reasoning and is termed *Differences* in the capabilities of the two groups.

As can be seen from the upper portion of the table, each similarity measure showed the same pattern—the performance of experts and TNEs was virtually indistinguishable when the memory tasks required the encoding and retrieval of facts. Apparently, the declarative-knowledge bases of the TNEs approximated those of the experts to the degree that factual information was equally accessible to both groups.

The equivalence of the two groups also provides evidence that the development of expertise falls on a continuum. One need only contrast the present results with the general finding that experts' long-term memory for domain-related information is superior to that of novices. The clear implication is that as domain knowledge increases, the "apparent" memory superiority effects decrease.

The bottom portion of the table displays performance differences we observed. Basically, TNEs did not perform like experts when the tasks required the integration and synthesis of facts, and the use of that new information for

Table 9.2 A Summary of the Results of the Experiment Reported in Yekovich, Thompson, and Walker, 1991

Measures of the Similarities and Differences	Group	
	Experts	TNEs
Similarities		
Explicit Ideas Recalled	.10 (.06)	.11 (.06)
Recognition of Explicit Statements	.89 (.06)	.86 (.09)
Recognition of Changed Details	.96 (.09)	.89 (.13)
Correct Indication of Non-problems	1.00 (-)	1.00 (-)
Differences		
Total Inferences Generated	.20 (.07)	.13 (.07)
Simple (n=33)	.19	.14
Complex (n=4)	.29	.07
Recognition of True Inferences	.84 (.17)	.63 (.14)
Correct Identification and Justification of a Problem	.66 (.28)	.39 (.26)

Numbers are proportions of responses.
Standard Deviations are in parentheses.

reasoning about the problem facing the bank. Although the TNEs did in fact draw some of the correct inferences, most were either simple in nature (see row four in the lower panel) or were enabled by the relatively simple recognition task (see row six). As the inferencing requirements of the task increased, the performance of the TNEs decreased. This trend was particularly clear in two instances. First, the inference generation data for simple versus complex inferences showed that while experts tended to generate more complex than simple inferences, the TNEs did just the opposite. Second, when the groups were required to justify and explain why certain case statements were problems, the TNEs were not very successful (see the last row of the table).

The study has two important implications. First, it demonstrates that distinguishing between expert and nonexpert administrators is possible. This result is in keeping with the findings of others who have studied the problem-solving abilities of managers and school administrators (e.g., Leithwood & Steinbach, in press). Second, the study provides evidence in keeping with Anderson's (1982) theory of the acquisition of cognitive skill.

SUMMARY

In this chapter I have tried to accomplish two goals. First, I presented an outline of a theory that describes the development of expertise as a process of acquiring a cognitive skill. The fundamental underpinnings of skill acquisition rest on the successful accumulation and use of domain-specific knowledge. In presenting this model, I attempted to show that it is applicable to domains such as credit administration and, presumably, school administration. Second, I attempted to show that the fundamental tenets of the theory are correct by summarizing a study that tested some of the theory's assumptions about the evolution of knowledge. The basic idea underlying the study was that formal training leads to the development of declarative knowledge that has a limited resemblance to that of an expert. However, the lack of practice and experience in the domain results in an inability to use the acquired knowledge for thinking and reasoning purposes. The results clearly confirmed the theory's assumptions. TNE credit administrators were able to encode and retrieve facts about a case study as effectively as expert credit administrators, but were inferior in their inferencing and reasoning capabilities. Apparently, practice and experience in credit administration are fundamental components in the development of expertise. If our goal is to use formal education to prepare administrators who are functionally ready to perform their duties, our conceptions of formal education will have to be expanded to include the experiences that are now available only on the job.

REFERENCES

Anderson, J. R. (1982). Acquisition of cognitive skill. *Psychological Review, 89,* 369–406.

Anderson, J. R. (1983). *The architecture of cognition.* Cambridge: Harvard University Press.

Anderson, J. R. (1987). Skill acquisition: Compilation of weak-method problem solutions. *Psychological Review, 94,* 192–210.

Anderson, J. R. (1990a). *Cognitive psychology and its implications* (3rd ed.). New York: Freeman.

Anderson, J. R. (1990b). *The adaptive character of thought.* Hillsdale, NJ: Lawrence Erlbaum Associates.

Anzai, Y., & Simon, H. A. (1979). The theory of learning by doing. *Psychological Review, 86,* 124–140.

Fitts, P. M. (1964). Perceptual-motor skill learning. In A. W. Melton (Ed.), *Categories of human learning* (pp. 243–285). New York: Academic Press.

Gagné, E. D., Yekovich, C. W., & Yekovich, F. R. (in press). *The cognitive psychology of school learning* (2nd ed.). New York: Harper Collins.

Glaser, R., & Chi, M. T. H. (1988). Overview. In M. T. H. Chi, R. Glaser, and M. J. Farr (Eds.), *The nature of expertise* (pp. xv–xxviii). Hillsdale, NJ: Lawrence Erlbaum Associates.

Just, M. A., & Carpenter, P. A. (1987). *The psychology of reading and language comprehension.* Newton, MA: Allyn & Bacon.

Leithwood, K., & Steinbach, R. (in press). Improving the problem-solving expertise of school administrators: Theory and practice. *Education and Urban Society.*

Newell, A., & Simon, H. A. (1972). *Human problem solving.* Englewood Cliffs, NJ: Prentice-Hall.

Schneider, W., & Shiffrin, R. M. (1977). Controlled and automatic human information processing: Detection, search, and attention. *Psychological Review, 84,* 1–66.

Wagner, R. K. (1991). Managerial problem solving. In R. J. Sternberg & P. A. Frensch (Eds.), *Complex problem solving: Principles and mechanism* (pp. 159–183). Hillsdale, NJ: Lawrence Erlbaum Associates.

Walker, C. H. (1987). Relative importance of domain knowledge and overall aptitude on acquisition of domain-related information. *Cognition and Instruction, 4,* 24–42.

Yekovich, F. R., Thompson, M. A., & Walker, C. H. (1991). Generation and verification of inferences by experts and trained nonexperts. *American Educational Research Journal, 28,* 189–209.

Yekovich, F. R., Walker, C. H., Ogle, L. T., & Thompson, M. A. (1990). The influence of domain knowledge on inferencing in low aptitude individuals. In A. C. Graesser & G. H. Bower (Eds.), *The psychology of learning and motivation: Advances in research and theory* (Vol. 25, pp. 259–278). New York: Academic Press.

PART III

Applying Cognitive Perspectives to the Preparation of Administrators

The final section of this volume uses many of the concepts and findings developed in the first two sections as a foundation for thinking about the development of expertise in educational leadership. These authors start with the assumption that a cognitive perspective provides useful information for understanding the nature of expertise in school leadership. They further assume that there is value in focusing on the thinking processes of school leaders as part of an effort to understand how expertise in educational leadership develops. Thus, these chapters draw on a cognitive orientation to inform the design of leadership-development programs. At the same time, these chapters also draw on findings from the cognitive science literature to speculate on the instructional conditions under which leaders might learn their craft more effectively.

John D. Bransford opens this section by examining the implications of cognitive research for the teaching of thinking and problem-solving. Bransford focuses his discussion on a core issue discussed in several prior chapters: whether the appropriate focus for instruction aimed at the development of expertise in problem-solving within the professions should be "problem-relevant knowledge" or "general problem-solving skills." That is, will programs interested in the development of usable knowledge be better off focusing on the content knowledge that characterizes the domain (e.g., organizational psychology, educational law) or the general problem-solving needed to put the knowledge into action? After reviewing the state of current knowledge in the field, Bransford concludes that neither approach finds strong empirical support. He goes on to outline specific implications for instructional design that are supported by recent work in this field. His recommendations echo several ideas suggested in previous chapters (e.g., Wagner, Leithwood & Steinbach).

Nona A. Prestine shifts the focus of discussion from the broad perspective of our prior chapters to the problems entailed in using our knowledge about expert practice to inform the design of administrator preparation programs. She asserts that the goal of preparation programs for school leaders should be to "promote knowledge acquisition for later accessibility and use in practitioner problem-solving situations." Given this goal, Prestine discusses the instructional design considerations that could create an "apprenticeship approach to problem-solving" acquisition. She concludes that a more holistic approach to administrator preparation is needed—"one that recognizes the student consists not merely of intellect but also of social and affective processes; that students will not practice in a vacuum, but in a social context with others."

Ann Weaver Hart's chapter addresses a similar challenge of creating conditions that cognitive research suggests are likely to result in the formation of usable knowledge in the context of an administrator preparation program. She presents both conceptual and practical considerations involved in creating a "design studio" in educational administration, an instructional model intended to develop students' skills in reflective practice through problem-focused cases and systematic extensive coaching. Hart presents data suggesting that "systematic seminars," "studios," and "courses that focus on the processes and skills of problem-solving hold potential for refocusing graduate education in educational administration from subject-based courses to the problems of practice."

J. G. T. Kelsey maintains a focus on the development of administrators' problem-solving expertise in the context of a course taught in a university's preparation program for school administrators. He describes and analyzes his own attempts to teach problem formulation to experienced administrators in a graduate course. Kelsey's account is both personal and theoretically grounded. He discusses what seems to happen as students learn about problem formulation, how they appear to approach problems, and the types of activities that seem to help them become better problem-solvers. Although some similar goals and techniques are discussed, the chapter offers an interesting contrast with the approaches offered by Prestine and Hart.

Edwin M. Bridges and Philip Hallinger conclude the topical chapters in this volume. They examine the research on problem-based learning as it has been implemented in medical education and then discuss their own attempts to adapt this model of instruction for the preparation and training of educational leaders. Problem-based learning is a form of student-centered instruction that is explicitly grounded in the cognitive science literature. This chapter reviews research on the effectiveness of problem-based learning in medical education and discusses design considerations for those interested in incorporating a similar model into the education of school administrators.

The book closes with a chapter written by the editors that summarizes the answers to four key questions about expertise. The first two questions: What is a problem? and What is the meaning of expertise? are critical to a grasp of cognitive approaches and warrant more explicit attention than they were given in this book. Our answers to the remaining questions—How do cognitive approaches explain problem-solving? and How does problem-solving expertise develop?—seek to elaborate and extend the discussion of issues previously raised by the authors. Finally, we attempt to further the work on cognitive approaches by setting out a limited agenda for further research.

10 Who Ya Gonna Call?
Thoughts About Teaching
Problem-Solving

John D. Bransford

My goal in this chapter is to explore what I believe are some important implications of cognitive research for the issue of teaching thinking and problem-solving. In other publications, my colleagues and I discuss some of the major changes in thinking about thinking that have taken place during the past decade (Bransford, Goldman, & Vye, 1991). In particular, we note that people's beliefs about the need to teach thinking have increased during the past decade, and we discuss research findings that have changed the way theorists are thinking about issues of intelligence, human development, expertise, instruction, and assessment. In this chapter I focus more explicitly on what I believe are some major instructional implications of recent cognitive research.

I begin my discussion by exploring data suggesting that everyday problem-solving depends strongly on specialized knowledge. The question "Who ya gonna call?," borrowed from the movie *Ghostbusters* and used in the title of this article, is relevant to discussions of specialized knowledge. In the movie, the ghostbusters are a pretty strange group of individuals who would presumably fall short on normative assessments of aptitude and common sense. Nevertheless, if you had ghost problems, it seems clear that the answer to "Who ya gonna call?" is "them." They alone seemed to have the specialized knowledge needed to solve problems of ghostbusting, and it is doubtful that the ghost problems could have been solved without this knowledge.

The issue I discuss is as follows: Given the importance of specific knowledge, should not programs that attempt to teach thinking and problem-solving focus primarily on relevant knowledge rather than on general skills of problem-solving? I consider a number of problems with knowledge-oriented approaches to instruction and explore some new possibilities for helping students acquire relevant knowledge in conjunction with general problem-solving skills.

SPECIFIC KNOWLEDGE AND PROBLEM-SOLVING

Early research on problem-solving, and early instruction in it, often dealt with "toy problems" or "intellectual puzzles" rather than authentic, everyday problems (see Mayer, 1991, for an overview). For example, some of the early research involved puzzle tasks such as the games "Missionaries and Cannibals" or "Tower of Hanoi." A great deal was learned from work on intellectual puzzles and there was good reason to begin by using them. Intellectual puzzles do not presuppose specialized knowledge of specific disciplines and hence are "fair game" for almost anyone to solve. In addition, it seemed reasonable to assume that, by stripping away the discipline-specific content necessary to understand and solve problems, one could get at the essence of the problem-solving processes per se.

As researchers have moved from the study of "toy" puzzles to everyday problems, most have come to believe that an important component of effective problem-solving involves access to a great deal of well-organized, domain-specific knowledge (e.g., Bransford, Sherwood, Vye, & Rieser, 1986; Chase & Simon, 1973; Chi, Glaser, & Farr, 1991). The research literature suggests that effective problem-solving is not simply equivalent to a set of general problem-solving skills such as "break problems into parts," "monitor the distance between current states and goal states," and so forth. A brain surgeon may be brilliant in the operating room but unable to solve a plumbing problem. Similarly, a person may be able to solve intellectual puzzles yet unable to solve problems of clinical diagnosis, and vice versa. In everyday life, specialized knowledge plays a pivotal role in people's abilities to adapt.

Specialized Knowledge in Problem-Solving: An Example

A problem-solving column that appears in the magazine *Dogfancy* (McLennan, 1991) illustrates the role of specific knowledge in problem-solving. In one issue of the magazine, a dog owner wrote that he installed a dog door for his two dogs. One used it all the time. The younger one (five years old) used it to go out but would never use it to come back in. What could the owner do to make the younger dog use the door? The dog expert began her reply by asking whether the door offers the dog the same angle of entrance from each side. She then stated: "One of my dogs alerted me to this one. When I placed a large flat stone as a step outside the door, he was able to go through in both directions in same body posture" (p. 68). Note that the pet owner's problem reminded the expert of a similar problem that she herself had encountered and solved. These "remindings" of similar problems often occur to experts and hence make their problem-solving relatively routine (e.g., see Schank, 1990).

The expert realized that the "angle of the entrance" might not be the feature that was responsible for the dog owner's problem. Therefore, she also discussed other possible causes of the problem such as (1) sunlight might be reflected off the door from the outside and this might keep the dog from entering; (2) the flap of the door might have hit the younger dog in the face when it was following the older dog from the outside, hence making it wary of the entrance; and so forth.

Overall, the expert's discussion of the possible causes of the problem, plus her suggested solutions, seemed to come from a great deal of specific knowledge that she had accumulated over her career. Since she had considerable experience, it is a good bet that most problems that people ask her to solve are relatively routine to her. Many theorists argue that specific experiences are represented in memory as "cases" that are indexed and searched so that they can be applied analogically to new problems that occur (see Ferguson, Bareiss, Birnbaum, & Osgood, in press; Kolodner, in press; Riesbeck & Schank, 1989; Schank, 1991). This is very different from the idea that expertise is derived from the "top-down" application of a general set of problem-solving rules (see Dreyfus, Dreyfus, & Athanasiou, 1986).

The Specificity of Knowledge

Of course, at one level it seems obvious that experts in an area have acquired a great deal of knowledge. Nevertheless, it is still easy to overlook the need to emphasize *specific* knowledge rather than look only at general expertise. A series of articles by Rock and his colleagues (Rock & Bransford, in press; Rock, Bransford, Maisto, & Morey, 1987) is relevant to this issue. Rock et al. reviewed the literature on "clinical judgment" in psychology and found that many researchers were arguing that experienced clinicians were very poor at diagnosing patients. They were often so poor, in fact, that there was little evidence they were indeed experts in anything. However, "expertise" was defined in very general terms, such as "number of years of experience" rather than "amount of specific experience with particular types of patient problems and procedures of diagnosis." Rock and Bransford argued that this was too general a definition of expertise.

In one study, Rock and Bransford (in press) found no relationship between expertise and ability to diagnose patients when expertise was defined very generally (e.g., number of years of experience). These data paralleled the results that are so often reported in the clinical judgment literature. In contrast, when Rock and Bransford analyzed the same data by taking into account the specific nature of the clinicians' experiences that were relevant to the diagnostic categories and tasks used in the experiment, there was clear evidence of expertise. The data suggest that it is important to consider the specificity of experts' experiences and the resulting knowledge that is acquired.

Applications of the "Who ya gonna call?" test suggest that, as a society, we intuitively recognize the importance of specific knowledge. If we have a misbehaving canine we are much more likely to call a dog expert than the 150 IQ brain surgeon who lives next door who has never had a pet. If we have a plumbing problem, we call a plumber rather than our dog expert or our brain surgeon neighbor. So once again, the following question becomes relevant: If we assume that relevant knowledge plays a powerful role in problem-solving, why not simply teach students relevant knowledge rather than also attempt to teach general principles of problem-solving? This question is addressed in the discussion below.

THE "WISDOM CAN'T BE TOLD" PROBLEM

One answer to the question "why not simply teach domain specific knowledge" is that many methods of teaching facilitate fact retrieval but not problem-solving. In particular, a number of theorists argue that typical approaches to instruction are based on antiquated "transmission models" in which teachers and textbook authors attempt to directly "transmit" (tell) their expertise (wisdom) to students (Bransford, Franks, Vye, & Sherwood, 1989; Brown, Collins, & Duguid, 1989; Brown & Palincsar, 1989; Clement, 1987; Minstrell, 1989; Resnick & Klopfer, 1989; Scardamalia & Bereiter, 1991; Schoenfeld, 1989). A corollary of the transmission model is that instruction is usually decontextualized and complex skills are generally decomposed into basic components in order to make it easier for the transmission to "go through."

Researchers have identified a number of problems with approaches to instruction that are based on transmission models. The basic problem is that the ability to remember and execute individual sets of concepts and skills provides no guarantee that people can orchestrate these components to produce important, complex performances such as those involved in thinking, writing, and problem-solving. Many years ago, Whitehead (1929) referred to the problem of acquiring specific facts and skills but being unable to use them to solve problems as the "inert knowledge problem." His ideas were rediscovered, explored, and amplified during the 1980s. For example, my colleagues and I (Bransford et al., 1989) have explored the inert knowledge problem in the context of the warning that "wisdom can't be told."

An Example of Inert Knowledge

A story relayed by Michael (1991) illustrates the inert knowledge problem. She served for several years as a clinical supervisor for college students who were beginning a practicum in which they learned to engage in language therapy for children who were language-delayed. The students with whom Michael worked had all passed the required college course on theories of language and their implications for therapy, but there was almost no evidence that the students ever attempted to use this knowledge in the clinical therapy sessions. Michael concluded that the college course must have been very poorly taught.

Soon thereafter, Michael was asked to teach the college course on theories of language and their implications. She did what she considered to be a highly competent job and was pleased with the general performance of the students on her tests. A year later, she reencountered a number of her college students in the clinical practicum on language therapy. Much to her surprise and dismay, these students also showed almost no evidence of using anything they had learned in their language course. Many could remember facts when explicitly asked about them, but they did not spontaneously use the knowledge to help them solve problems in the clinic.

Michael notes that she was reluctant to conclude that her college students performed poorly because they had a poor instructor. The experience motivated her to explore problems with traditional approaches to instruction and to design a series of studies to attempt to overcome these problems. I discuss her studies later. For present purposes it is sufficient to note that Michael's experiences fit well with Whitehead's (1929) observations that much of the information acquired in school tends to remain inert.

Misconceptions That Often Arise from Ignoring the Assumption That Wisdom Can't Be Told

In addition to producing inert knowledge, traditional approaches to instruction also tend to deprive students of opportunities to explore their own abilities to think and solve problems. As a result, students often develop misconceptions about thinking, including misconceptions about their own abilities to think.

Schoenfeld (1989) notes that many college students who enter his mathematics course at Berkeley seem to have serious misconceptions about the nature of everyday problem-solving. Many assume that if they cannot solve a problem in five minutes it is basically unsolvable by them. They appear to have little idea that many everyday problems are solved only because of sustained effort that may take place over the course of days, weeks, and often months. Students need opportunities for sustained thinking about complex problems in order to experience the fact that positive changes in their thinking (the appearance of "mini-insights" into the problem) do in fact occur over time. A major goal of Schoenfeld's approach to teaching is to help students discover their own abilities to solve mathematics problems on their own (Schoenfeld, 1989).

Beliefs about one's abilities to think, learn, and solve problems seem to have important effects on behavior. Research by Dweck (1989) suggests that the effects of these beliefs become most apparent in situations where people initially experience failure or difficulty. Those who believe that intelligence is a fixed entity that someone either has or does not have tend to avoid tasks where they initially experience failure. In contrast, those who believe that intelligence is malleable as a function of learning and experience are much more likely to confront challenging tasks.

Duffy (1992) notes that many teachers do not believe in their abilities to think and invent when it comes to instruction. Many cannot imagine that they can have better ideas about instruction than the "experts" who write the curriculum guides. As a result, they tend to rely on what Duffy calls the "absentee prescriptions of master curriculum developers," and often miss opportunities to adapt instruction to fit their students' particular needs and goals. Most likely, the teachers Duffy worked with had taken courses in which they were told about "good instruction" rather than helped to invent, evaluate, and modify their own approaches to instruction. Exclusive reliance on transmission approaches to instruction has the potential to undermine students' beliefs in their abilities to identify and define problems and invent solutions on their own.

USES OF "APPLICATIONS PROBLEMS" TO TEACH PROBLEM-SOLVING

Clearly, the goal of helping people develop usable (noninert) knowledge, and helping them develop confidence in their own abilities to solve problems, is not new. A time-honored approach for achieving both of these goals is to present students with "applications problems" such as those that appear at the end of chapters in textbooks (see Stanic & Kilpatrick, 1988, for an excellent historical review of applications problems in the field of mathematics). The general approach is to first teach students relevant skills and knowledge and then let them see how this knowledge can be applied. If one is teaching about the concept of density, for example, one might first present facts and formulas relevant to the concept (Density equals mass divided by volume) and then present applications problems to be solved (An object weighs 4 grams and has a volume of 8 cubic centimeters. What is its density?).

In his paper "Problem Solving and Education," Simon (1980) provides an insightful analysis of the role of applications problems. He argues that the knowledge representation underlying competent performance in any domain is not based on simple facts or verbal propositions but is instead based on productions. Productions involve "condition–action pairs that specify that if a certain state occurs in working memory, then particular mental (and possibly physical) actions should take place" (Anderson, 1987, p. 193). Productions thus provide information about the critical attributes of problem situations that match specific actions with relevant goals.

Simon echoes Whitehead (1929) and Gragg (1940) in noting that many forms of instruction do not help students conditionalize their knowledge. For example, he argues that "textbooks are much more explicit in enunciating the laws of mathematics or of nature than in saying anything about when these laws may be useful in solving problems" (p. 92). It is left largely to the student to generate the condition–action pairs required for solving novel problems. Franks and colleagues (Franks, Bransford, Brailey, & Purdon, 1991) note that one of their favorite examples of the lack of explicit emphasis on conditionalizing one's knowledge comes from a textbook on experimental design. On page 195 of the book was a section entitled "Which Test Do I Use?" It stated: "How to choose a statistical test was postponed until now so that various aspects of data analysis could be presented." The text then included a discussion of the uses of various statistics. The entire discussion totaled 13 sentences.

Simon argues that effective learners acquire the conditionalized knowledge necessary for effective problem-solving by working through examples and sample problems. In mathematics classes, for example, word problems found at the end of each chapter can help students move from knowing "that" something is true ($5 + 5 = 10$; $A^2 + B^2 = C^2$) to knowing "when," "why," and "how" particular concepts and procedures are applicable. Lesgold (1988) also emphasizes the role of applications problems in helping students learn to solve problems rather than simply retrieve previously "told" facts.

Problems with Traditional Uses of Applications Problems

It seems clear that didactic instruction about facts, concepts, and skills is enhanced by the use of applications problems. Nevertheless, there are also severe shortcomings of traditional uses of applications problems. Several are discussed by the Cognition and Technology Group at Vanderbilt (CTGV) (in press).

First, traditional applications problems often fail to help students think about realistic situations. Instead of bringing real-world standards to their work, students seem to treat word problems mechanically and often fail to think about constraints imposed by real-world experiences (Charles & Silver, 1988; Silver, 1986; Van Haneghan & Baker, 1989). Silver (1986) provides an excellent example of relatively mechanical approaches to word problems. Students were asked to determine the number of buses needed to take a specific number of people on a field trip. Many of them divided the total number of students by the number that each bus would hold and came up with answers like 2 1/3. The students failed to consider the fact that one cannot have a functioning 1/3 bus.

A second problem with applications problems is that most of them assume only a single "correct" answer. This leads to misconceptions about the nature of problem-solving and it inadvertently teaches students to look to others for the answers rather than to seek them for themselves. In addition, because typical word problems are difficult for many students to understand (due to reading problems) and often seem arbitrary, it becomes especially difficult to present students with problems that reflect the levels of complexity characteristic of many real-world problems (CTGV, 1990). This limitation of the word-problem format becomes increasingly noteworthy in the context of recommendations from many researchers (Baron, 1987; Frederiksen & Collins, 1989; Resnick & Resnick, 1991) that instruction and assessment must focus on students' abilities to perform holistic, authentic tasks rather than on their ability to demonstrate that they have acquired the piecemeal skills and facts that make up complex performance. For example, we know from research at Vanderbilt that the ability to solve sets of simple (i.e., one- and two-step) well-defined problems is by no means equivalent to students' ability to solve realistic, complex problems that are ultimately decomposable into the same set of simple problems (Goldman, Vye, Williams, Rewey, & Pellegrino, 1991; Van Haneghan, Barron, Young, Williams, Vye, & Bransford, 1992).

A third limitation of traditional applications problems involves the "habits of mind" that they develop. Generally, applications problems can be solved by thinking back to the information in the chapter or chapters that one has been studying. This means that the goal of one's search is to retrieve previously presented information rather than to rely on one's own intuitions. This may limit the development of people's abilities to think for themselves.

A fourth limitation of traditional applications problems is also important: They explicitly define the problems to be solved rather than help students learn to generate and pose their own problems. Outside of school, one must often rely more on generative skills than on computational skills in order to solve problems. For example, imagine the task of going from one's house to a breakfast meeting at 8:30 in a new restaurant across town. First, one needs to identify the existence of a problem to be solved—namely, the need to determine the time one should leave in order to make the breakfast meeting. To solve this general problem one has to generate subproblems such as "How far away is the meeting?," "How fast will I be able to drive?," and so forth. The ability to identify the general problem and generate the subproblems to be solved is crucial for real-world problem solving. Typical uses of applications problems do not develop such generative problem-finding and problem-formulation skills (Bransford & Stein, 1984; Brown & Walters, 1990; Charles & Silver, 1988; Porter, 1989; Sternberg, 1986).

Challenges That Accompany Fast-Paced Change

The need to go beyond instruction that presents students with specific problems to solve becomes increasingly urgent in light of arguments for the need to teach problem-solving. The major argument is that increasingly rapid changes in society are becoming the rule rather than the exception; hence we need people who can continually adapt to new circumstances by being able to think and learn on their own. An important component of the argument is that the need for powerful skills of thinking and learning applies to all members of society rather than to only a select few (Resnick, 1987).

One illustration of the need to adapt to changing circumstances can be seen by the plight of many local television stations that are having to redefine their goals and methods of operation in order to compete in a world of cable, fiber optics, and other new technologies. If they are unsuccessful in doing so, they will soon be extinct. And, of course, TV stations are not alone in their need to adapt to changing conditions. Businesses, schools, universities, and even families are going to face a world in which increasing change—especially technology-driven change—requires the ability to find new opportunities and to solve problems that arise.

The effects of rapid change can also be seen in an area such as auto mechanics. It used to be the case that the skills necessary for success in this area stayed relatively stable; a youngster could learn at his or her father's knee and be relatively secure that the skills would last a lifetime. Today's auto mechanics, however, need to be retrained almost yearly.

Many instructors attempt to anticipate the major problems that their students will encounter once they leave school and teach them explicit strategies for solving them. This type of instruction can clearly be beneficial, but it should probably be called "problem-elimination" instruction rather than problem-solving instruction. It seeks to ensure that the problems a person will confront after schooling will not really be problems since a ready solution will be available. Today's students need more than a list of ready-made solutions because, in areas of rapid change, it is impossible to anticipate all the problems to be encountered. Our students need to be able to identify new problems and opportunities and generate the subproblems needed to solve them. And they need to know how to generate learning goals and strategies that will let them acquire new knowledge necessary to solve new problems. Most probably, they will also need to know how to work collaboratively rather than alone.

Novelty and the Value of General Problem-Solving Strategies

It is in the context of dealing with novel problems that general strategies for problem-solving become useful. For example, in teaching the "IDEAL" problem-solving framework (Bransford & Stein, 1984), Stein and I have found that most people skip the "define" part of problem-solving. They jump directly from a general understanding of a problem (the "identify" phase in IDEAL) to an exploration of particular strategies for solving the problem (the "explore strategies" phase of IDEAL). We try to help them learn to consider the intermediate step of defining possible sets of goals.

An example from Adams (1979) provides a powerful illustration of ways in which the definition of goals affects subsequent considerations of possible strategies. He describes a group of engineers who were trying to solve the problem of creating mechanical devices for picking tomatoes that were less likely to bruise the tomatoes. Over the course of several months, the engineers made some progress but not a great deal. Eventually some biologists joined the group and redefined the goals of the problem. Instead of the goal of trying to invent a mechanical picking device that was less likely to bruise tomatoes, they formulated the goal of creating a tomato that was less likely to be bruised. This redefinition of the goal led to a consideration of very different sets of strategies, and their efforts eventually led to success.

The moral of this story is that problem-solvers always have goals, but that they are often implicit. Limited definitions of goals often limit the kinds of strategies that are considered as possible solutions to a problem that one confronts. In the second edition of the *IDEAL Problem Solver* (forthcoming), Stein and I encourage readers to explicitly define at least two alternate goals before jumping into the "explore strategies" phase of problem-solving. Our experience is that this increases the creativity of the solutions that people eventually generate.

SITUATED COGNITION AND ANCHORED INSTRUCTION

Although programs such as IDEAL (Bransford & Stein, 1984) can be valuable for developing general approaches to problem-solving, we have seen that effective problem-solving also requires domain-specific content knowledge. In recent years, a number of investigators have begun to develop some approaches to instruction that provide opportunities for students to acquire relevant content knowledge while also having the opportunity to collaboratively explore, invent, and think deeply about issues. The framework for the approaches that I shall explore comes from researchers who are beginning to emphasize the importance of situating instruction in meaningful problem-solving contexts analogous to apprenticeship environments (Brown et al., 1989). The approach is very different from the typical decontextualized approach that begins with general facts and procedures and ends with application problems for students to solve.

My colleague Otto Bassler sent me an article written almost 50 years ago

(Corey, 1944) that provides an informative contrast between learning in formal, decontextualized settings versus learning in meaningful apprenticeship contexts. Entitled "Poor Scholar's Soliloquy," the article provides a personal account of a student (we can call him Bob) who is not very good in school and had to repeat the seventh grade. Many would write Bob off as having "low aptitude for learning," but when you look at the kinds of learning that Bob is capable of achieving outside of school, you get a very different impression of his abilities.

One part of Bob's soliloquy discusses the fact that the teachers do not like him because he does not read the kind of books that the teachers value. His favorite reading materials include *Popular Science,* the *Mechanical Encyclopedia,* and the Sear's and Ward's catalogs. Bob uses his books in the context of pursuing meaningful goals. He says of his books: "But I don't just sit down and read them through like they make us do in school. I use my books when I want to find something out, like whenever Mom buys anything second hand I look it up in Sear's or Ward's first and tell her if she's getting stung or not" (p. 219).

A little later, Bob explains the trouble he had memorizing the names of the presidents. He knew some of them like Washington and Jefferson but there were 30 altogether and he never did get them all straight. He seems to have a poor memory. Then he talks about the three trucks his uncle owns and the fact that he knows the horsepower and number of forward and backward gears of 26 different American trucks—many of them diesels. Then he states: "It's funny how that Diesel works. I started to tell my teacher about it last Wednesday in science class when the pump we were using to make a vacuum in a bell jar got hot, but she said she didn't see what a Diesel engine had to do with our experiment on air pressure so I just kept still. The kids seemed interested, though" (p. 219).

Bob discusses other areas of his schooling like his inability to do the kinds of (arbitrary) word problems found in the textbooks. Yet he helps his uncle solve all kinds of complex trip-planning problems when they travel together. Bob also discusses the bills and letters he sends to the farmers whose livestock is hauled by his uncle and notes that, according to his aunt, he made only three mistakes in his last 17 letters—all of them commas. Then he says: "I wish I could write school themes that way. The last one I had to write was on 'What a Daffodil Thinks of Spring,' and I just couldn't get going" (p. 220).

Bob ends his soliloquy by noting that, according to his Dad, he can quit school at the age of 15 and he feels he should. After all, he is not getting any younger and there is a lot of stuff for him to learn.

Bob's soliloquy is as relevant to the 1990s as it was to the 1940s. It highlights the fact that many students seem to learn effectively in the context of authentic, real-life activities yet have great difficulty learning in the decontextualized, arbitrary-task atmosphere of schools. Luckily for Bob's children, the emphasis on situated cognition is raising serious questions about typical school curricula and tasks (Brown et al., 1989; Collins, Hawkins, & Carver, 1991; CTGV, 1990).

Uses of Technology to Create Meaningful Contexts for Learning

Unfortunately, it is not feasible to place every student in real-world contexts with one or more mentors. In an attempt to overcome this problem, members of our Cognition and Technology Group at Vanderbilt have been exploring ways to use integrated media technology to "anchor" or "situate" instruction in the context of meaningful problem-solving environments that allow teachers to simulate in the classroom some of the advantages of "in-context" apprenticeship training (Brown et al., 1989). We refer to our anchored environments as "macrocontexts" because they involve complex situations that require students to formulate and solve a set of interconnected subproblems (Bransford, Sherwood, & Hasselbring, 1988). In addition, each of the anchors can be viewed from multiple perspectives. In contrast, applications problems that occur at the end of chapters in textbooks typically involve a series of disconnected "microcontexts"—one for each problem in the problem set. Our "anchored instruction" approach shares a strong family resemblance to many instructional programs that are case-based and problem-based (Barrow, 1985; Gragg, 1940; Spiro, Feltovich, Jacobson, & Coulson, 1991; Williams, 1991).

Our macrocontexts are not designed to function as applications problems that follow didactic instruction. Instead, they function as environments that are to be explored and that allow students to see the need to acquire new concepts and skills (CTGV, 1992a). Our approach is to first have students use their available knowledge to attempt to understand the problems and phenomena depicted in an anchor (macrocontext) and to set learning goals. We then attempt to structure the situation so that students can experience the changes in their own noticing and understanding that occur as they generate and learn about new ideas that are relevant to the anchors. We especially emphasize the importance of helping students learn to find and define new (1) opportunities for further exploration and (2) problems that need to be solved (Bransford & Stein, 1984).

An Example of Anchored Instruction

Several publications by the CTGV (1990, 1991, 1992a, 1992b, in press) explore theory and data relevant to anchored instruction projects. For present purposes I concentrate on a study conducted by Michael and colleagues (Michael, Klee, Bransford & Warren, in press). As noted in earlier discussion of the inert knowledge problem, Michael's college students showed little evidence of being able to use their classroom-based knowledge in a clinical practicum on language therapy, and this motivated Michael to find alternatives to traditional approaches to instruction. She did so and put her ideas to an initial empirical test.

Michael defined her goal as helping students in her college course approach language therapy from three different, but equally valuable, theoretical perspectives: behavioral, social-linguistic, and Vygotskian.

One group of college students was taught in a traditional manner. Students read about the three different theories of language (behavioral, social-linguistic, Vygotskian) and then worked through examples of how these theories might be applied to problems of language therapy. The textbook and lectures were the major sources of information that the students used.

A second group of students received instruction that was situated in the context of a video-based anchor of an actual language therapy session involving a child and a speech-and-language therapist. Students first watched the video and wrote down what they noticed about it. They were then introduced to each theoretical perspective, one by one, and encouraged to notice the changes in their noticing and understanding that resulted from an introduction to these theoretical ideas. In order to facilitate this process, Michael created videotapes of three expert language therapists, each of whom represented one of the three theoretical perspectives. Each therapist commented on the video anchor of language therapy that the students in the classroom saw. Comments by the experts included statements about the kinds of therapist–child interactions on the video anchor that they thought were important, plus interpretations of these interactions from their particular theoretical framework. In addition, the experts commented on "missed opportunities." These were instances in which the experts thought the therapist on the video could have engaged in specific types of activities that they believed would have been beneficial for the child.

Michael tested the experimental and control groups in two different manners. First, they received a factual test about the different theories. Second, the students were exposed to new instances of language therapy and asked to comment on them from the three theoretical perspectives. One of the instances of therapy was in a video format, the other was a written transcript of a therapy session.

Both groups did equally well on the factual test. This was expected, since traditional approaches to instruction tend to do a good job of helping students acquire specific knowledge. But how usable is this knowledge—how non-inert is it? This was the purpose of Michael's tests that asked students to comment on new therapy sessions. For both the verbal and video measures, there were strong differences in performance in favor of the anchored instruction group.

Michael and colleagues note that their results are preliminary and that more studies need to be conducted to establish the clear "active ingredients" in the anchored instruction. For example, they assume that it is very important for people to first view an anchor and articulate their own understanding of it, and to then have the opportunity to experience the changes in noticing and understanding that occur when new information is introduced. Nevertheless, these aspects of the students' experiences were not directly manipulated and put to experimental test. In addition, Michael and colleagues emphasize that there are important differences between the ability to comment on and interpret someone else's therapy and the ability to do therapy oneself. In order to achieve the latter goal, there appears to be no substitute for actually doing the task. The hope is that the anchored instruction approach will accelerate the development of expertise and help people become reflective practitioners.

Beyond Anchors or Cases

Attempts to teach students to become experts at language therapy provide a good illustration of the potential benefits and shortcomings of problem-based, case-based, and anchored instruction. Data suggest that these approaches have definite promise (CTGV, 1992b), but no one assumes that they will eliminate the need for the "real thing." In our center's work with anchored instruction projects, we view the work with video-based anchors as an important yet initial step in the development of problem-solving expertise. Our teachers and students are encouraged to learn from the problems on the anchors and apply their knowledge to actual, community-based projects. Many of our classes have done this with considerable success (CTGV, in press).

The importance of eventually moving beyond instructor-presented problems became clear to Stein and me in the context of working with our IDEAL problem-solving framework (Bransford & Stein, 1984). In our early work with this model, we had students use IDEAL to solve problems that we presented and they did quite well. But we also noticed that, in many aspects of their own lives (finding a topic for a paper, settling a conflict with a friend), our students consistently missed many opportunities to use a systematic approach to problem-solving. In short, our instruction remained "semi-inert."

Stein and I continue to use the IDEAL model with problems that we present to students, but we also use it in conjunction with students' own life experiences. We ask them to find (identify) their own problems and opportunities and, as noted earlier, we also ask them to define their problems from at least two different perspectives. This approach has resulted in much more general uses of the IDEAL model and much more creative approaches. We find that our students spontaneously use IDEAL to identify and define interesting perspectives on topics for papers; identify, define, and find solutions to poor study strategies and organizational skills; find and solve problems relevant to life in the dormitories, and so forth. In general, the IDEAL model provides a framework that helps students gain access to aspects of their knowledge that they otherwise would probably not access spontaneously. I am convinced that many models of problem-solving other than IDEAL would be equally effective. The important point, I think, is to help students develop a systematic approach to problem-solving so that they learn to identify and define potentially solvable problems and learn to gain access to more aspects of their knowledge than they otherwise might consider on their own.

Problem-Finding and Problem-Solving in Authentic Contexts

The importance of helping people systematically find problems and define alternate goals was made especially clear to me by an opportunity to work with a company that wanted to increase its productivity. I was very reluctant to grant the company representatives' request to hold a problem-solving seminar because I do not feel skilled working in this type of setting. Nevertheless, the company officials helped work out a situation that I found too interesting to ignore.

The problem-solving session that I chaired was an *introduction* to several months of work by the company. At the session, we first explored the fact that problem-solving requires specialized knowledge. Part of this time was spent analyzing videos of experts and novices attempting to perform a variety of problem-solving tasks. The videos showed a person who was an expert in domain A but a novice in domain B, another person who was a novice in A but an expert in B—so the videos showed the same people looking competent or awkward depending on the domain of the problems to be solved. This helped me establish the importance of knowledge, plus the fact that only they (the people in the company) had the knowledge necessary to find and solve problems relevant to their company. I as the "problem-solving expert" could not possibly solve their problems for them. I could only help them develop strategies to find problems and opportunities and gain access to aspects of their knowledge that they otherwise might not consider on their own.

After exploring the role of knowledge in problem-solving, we divided into small groups and worked on a complex "case" (anchor) from our center's Jasper Woodbury Problem Solving Series (CTGV, 1991). The solution to Jasper adventures is complex and hence is excellent for collaborative problem-solving. The important part of the experience was the nature of the teams that collaborated. Each was composed of secretaries, people from management and customer support, and company engineers. Many of them rarely had the chance to collaborate within their company. But in this setting they did.

The last part of the workshop involved a discussion of the range of expertise needed to make a company productive. Customer-support people have a great deal of information that can be of value to product engineers and vice versa. Secretaries know what it is like to attempt to learn to use some of the products that come out of the company's laboratories, so they can help both the engineers and people in customer support. They also know a great deal about aspects of a company that affect efficiency and hence can inform management, and vice versa. My goal was to help the members of the company (1) appreciate the specialized knowledge and expertise of their fellow workers who had different jobs in the company and (2) understand the value of different perspectives for problems that they wanted to solve.

Following the workshop, the company had committed to working for several months in the following manner. First, everyone would spend a week identifying potentially solvable problems that could improve the company's efficiency. This was highly successful. Many employees remarked that their ideas about problems would normally be seen as trouble making, whining, and so forth. However, when the goal became problem-finding, the same ideas were seen in a different light.

Second, the company agreed to create problem-solving teams to work on subsets of these problems. Each team would include secretaries, engineers, and people in customer support and management—people who had a chance to work together at the problem-solving workshop but rarely worked together at any other time. In addition, the teams met multiple times and met during working hours, so they had the time and the incentive to reflect and work.

I am not sure how useful my ideas were to the company, but the experience of working with them was very valuable to me. I elaborate on this point in my concluding remarks.

CONCLUDING REMARKS

At the beginning of this chapter, I noted that problem-solving was heavily knowledge dependent and then asked the following question: "Given the importance of specific knowledge, should programs that attempt to teach thinking and problem-solving focus primarily on relevant knowledge rather than on general skills of problem-solving?" My work with college students on the IDEAL model, and my work with the company that wanted to improve productivity, helped me clarify how general strategies for problem-solving can be helpful. They help people notice problems and gain access to knowledge and beliefs that they otherwise may have overlooked. This greater access helps people activate knowledge that allows them to be more creative and that impacts their attitudes and beliefs about problem-solving. Two important beliefs are that problem-solving is an ongoing process that requires continual learning, and that it can be beneficial to identify potentially solvable problems. If problems are not identified, it is unlikely that they will be solved.

My experiences with the company also helped me question some approaches to problem-solving workshops that I had never before questioned. In particular, it made me aware of the need to ask about the composition of the groups involved in workshops. My work with the company could have included only the engineers, or only the managers, and so forth. I suspect that this would have reduced many of the benefits of creating working teams that included people with a variety of relevant perspectives. With this thought in mind, it is interesting to note that we often have principals' workshops, superintendents' workshops, and so forth. Are we limiting the effectiveness of our instruction by selecting limited groups of participants? If our goal is to help an organization improve, our leaders need to gain a respect for the varieties of knowledge and experience that exist in their settings, and they need to learn strategies for bringing these different resources together to find problems and opportunities and solutions. And since "wisdom can't be told" (Gragg, 1940), potential leaders need to experience the benefits of these collaborations rather than simply be told that they are good.

My experiences working with the company that wanted to improve productivity also prompt me to raise questions about the nature of the content knowledge that we attempt to teach our future educational leaders. What should it include? Based on my experiences, it should include a heavy dose of information about the nature of learning and change—not only with respect to organizations but with respect to individuals. For example, it seems important to help our future educational leaders understand that the *development of expertise* is always a rocky road that involves periods of feeling clumsy, and that this applies to students, teachers, and themselves. And it seems important to help our future educational leaders understand why people with different types of life experiences can be valuable to consult—they will often have unique perspectives on problems that will escape the attention of others.

I would very much like to see the results of research projects that attempt to compare the effects of typical "similar persons" problem-solving training with training that involves people from many different facets of the community, and that either do or do not help people understand the personal strife involved in attempts to develop expertise in new domains. My guess is that particular types of understandings and experiences can help future leaders learn to value and create the kinds of collaborative groups and networks that provide multiple perspectives on problems and supply ongoing feedback and energy for change.

REFERENCES

Adams, J. L. (1979). *Conceptual blockbusting: A guide to better ideas.* New York: Norton.

Anderson, P. A. (1987). What do decision makers do when they make a foreign policy decision?: The implications for the comparative study of foreign policy. In C. F. Hermann, C. N. Kegley, Jr., & J. N. Fosenau (Eds.), *New directions in the study of foreign policy* (pp. 285–308). Boston: Allen & Unwin.

Baron, J. (1987). Evaluating thinking skills in the classroom. In J. Baron & R. J. Sternberg (Eds.), *Teaching thinking skills: Theory and practice* (pp. 221–248). New York: Freeman.

Barrow, H. S. (1985). *How to design a problem-based curriculum for the preclinical years.* New York: Springer.

Bransford, J. D., Franks, J. J., Vye, N. J., & Sherwood, R. D. (1989). New approaches to instruction: Because wisdom can't be told. In S. Vosniadou & A. Ortony (Eds.), *Similarity and analogical reasoning* (pp. 470–497). New York: Cambridge University Press.

Bransford, J. D., Goldman, S. R., & Vye, N. J. (1991). Making a difference in peoples' abilities to think: Reflections on a decade of work and some hopes for the future. In L. Okagaki & R. J. Sternberg (Eds.), *Directors of development: Influences on children* (pp. 147–180). Hillsdale, NJ: Lawrence Erlbaum Associates.

Bransford, J. D., Sherwood, R., & Hasselbring, T. (1988). The video revolution and its effects on development: Some initial thoughts. In G. Foreman & P. Pufall (Eds.), *Constructivism in the computer age* (pp. 173–201). Hillsdale, NJ: Lawrence Erlbaum Associates.

Bransford, J. D., Sherwood, R. S., Vye, N. J., & Rieser, J. (1986). Teaching thinking and problem solving: Research foundations. *American Psychologist, 41,* 1078–1089.

Bransford, J. D., & Stein, B. S. (1984). *The IDEAL problem solver.* New York: Freeman.

Brown, A., & Palincsar, A. (1989, March). *Coherence and causality in science readings.* Paper presented at the annual meeting of the American Educational Research Association, San Francisco.

Brown, J. S., Collins, A., & Duguid, P. (1989). Situated cognition and the culture of learning. *Educational Researcher, 18*(1), 32–41.

Brown, S. I., & Walters, M. I. (1990). *The art of problem posing* (2nd ed.). Hillsdale, NJ: Lawrence Erlbaum Associates.

Charles, R., & Silver, E. A. (Eds.). (1988). *The teaching and assessing of mathematical problem solving.* Hillsdale, NJ: Lawrence Erlbaum Associates & National Council for Teachers of Mathematics.

Chase, W. G., & Simon, H. A. (1973). Perception in chess. *Cognitive Psychology, 1,* 33–81.

Chi, M. T. H., Glaser, R., & Farr, M. (1991). *The nature of expertise.* Hillsdale, NJ: Lawrence Erlbaum Associates.

Clement, J. (1987). Overcoming students' misconceptions in physics: The role of anchoring intuitions and analogical validity. In J. Novak (Ed.), *Proceedings of the second international seminar on misconceptions on educational strategies in science and mathematics* (Vol. III, pp. 84–96).

Cognition and Technology Group at Vanderbilt. (1990). Anchored instruction and its relationship to situated cognition. *Educational Researcher, 19*(6), 2–10.

Cognition and Technology Group at Vanderbilt. (1991). Technology and the design of generative learning environments. *Educational Technology, 31*(5), 34–40.

Cognition and Technology Group at Vanderbilt. (1992a). The Jasper experiment: An exploration of issues in learning and instructional design. *Educational Technology Research and Development, 40*(1), 65–80.

Cognition and Technology Group at Vanderbilt. (1992b). The Jasper experiment series as an example of anchored instruction: Theory, program description, and assessment data. *Educational Psychologist, 27*(3), 291–315.

Cognition and Technology Group at Vanderbilt. (in press). The Jasper series: A generative approach to improving mathematical thinking. In *This year in school science*. Washington, DC: American Association for the Advancement of Science.

Collins, A., Hawkins, J., & Carver, S. M. (1991). A cognitive apprenticeship for disadvantaged students. In B. Means, C. Chelemer, & M. S. Knapp (Eds.), *Teaching advanced skills to at-risk students* (pp. 216–243). San Francisco: Jossey-Bass.

Corey, S. M. (1944). Poor scholar's soliloquy. *Childhood Education, 33,* 219–220.

Dreyfus, H. L., Dreyfus, S. E., & Athanasiou, T. (1986). *Mind over machine: The power of human intuition and expertise in the era of the computer.* New York: The Free Press.

Duffy, G. G. (1992, April). *Learning from the study of practice: Where we must go with strategy instruction.* Paper presented at the American Educational Research Association, San Francisco.

Dweck, C. S. (1989). Motivation. In A. Lesgold & R. Glaser (Eds.), *Foundations for a psychology of education* (pp. 87–136). Hillsdale, NJ: Lawrence Erlbaum Associates.

Ferguson, W., Bareiss, R., Birnbaum, L., & Osgood, R. (in press). ASK systems: An approach to the realization of story-based teachers. *The Journal of the Learning Sciences.*

Franks, J., Bransford, J., Brailey, K., & Purdon, S. (1991). Understanding memory access. In R. Hoffman & D. Palermo (Eds.), *Cognition and the symbolic processes: Applied and ecological perspectives* (pp. 281–299). Hillsdale, NJ: Lawrence Erlbaum Associates.

Frederiksen, J. R., & Collins, A. (1989). A systems approach to educational testing. *Educational Researcher, 18*(9), 27–32.

Goldman, S. R., Vye, N. J., Williams, S. M., Rewey, K., & Pellegrino, J. W. (1991, April). *Problem space analyses of the Jasper problems and students' attempts to solve them.* Paper presented at the American Educational Research Association, Chicago.

Gragg, C. I. (1940, October 19). Because wisdom can't be told. *Harvard Alumni Bulletin,* pp. 78–84.

Kolodner, J. L. (in press). Improving human decision making through case-based decision aiding. *Artificial Intelligence Magazine.*

Lesgold, A. (1988). Problem solving. In R. J. Sternberg & E. E. Smith (Eds.), *The psychology of human thought* (pp. 188–213). New York: Cambridge University Press.

Mayer, R. E. (1991). *Thinking, problem solving, cognition.* New York: Freeman.

McLennan, B. (1991, August). Prevent problems by considering the dog's viewpoint. *Dogfancy,* p. 68.

Michael, A. L. (1991, April 18). Personal communication.

Michael, A. L., Klee, T., Bransford, J. D., & Warren, S. (in press). The transition from theory to therapy: Test of two instructional methods. *Applied Cognitive Psychology.*

Minstrell, J. A. (1989). Teaching science for understanding. In L. B. Resnick & L. E. Klopfer (Eds.), *Toward the thinking curriculum: Current cognitive research* (pp. 129–149). Alexandria, VA: ASCD.

Porter, A. (1989). A curriculum out of balance: The case of elementary school mathematics. *Educational Researcher, 18*(5), 9–15.

Resnick, L. (1987). *Education and learning to think.* Washington, DC: National Academy Press.

Resnick, L. B., & Klopfer, L. E. (Eds.). (1989). *Toward the thinking curriculum: Current cognitive research.* Alexandria, VA: ASCD.

Resnick, L. B., & Resnick, D. P. (1991). Assessing the thinking curriculum: New tools for educational reform. In B. Gifford & C. O'Connor (Eds.), *New approaches to testing: Rethinking aptitude, achievement and assessment.* New York: National Committee on Testing and Public Policy.

Riesbeck, C. K., & Schank, R. C. (1989). *Inside case-based reasoning.* Hillsdale, NJ: Lawrence Erlbaum Associates.

Rock, D. L., & Bransford, J. D. (in press). An empirical evaluation of three components of the tetrahedron model of clinical judgment. *Journal of Nervous and Mental Disease.*

Rock, D. L., Bransford, J. D., Maisto, S. A., & Morey, L. C. (1987). The study of clinical judgement: Ecological approach. *Clinical Psychology Review, 7,* 645–661.

Scardamalia, M., & Bereiter, C. (1991). Higher levels of agency for children in knowledge building: A challenge for the design of new knowledge media. *Journal of the Learning Sciences, 1*(1), 37–68.

Schank, R. C. (1990). Case-based teaching: Four experiences in educational software design. *Interactive Learning Environments, 1*(4), 231–253.

Schoenfeld, A. H. (1989). Teaching mathematical thinking and problem solving. In L. B. Resnick & L. E. Klopfer (Eds.), *Toward the thinking curriculum: Current cognitive research* (pp. 83–103). Alexandria, VA: ASCD.

Schoenfeld, A. H. (1985). *Mathematical problem solving.* Orlando, FL: Academic Press.

Silver, E. A. (1986). Using conceptual and procedural knowledge: A focus on relationships. In J. Hiebert (Ed.), *Conceptual and procedural knowledge: The case of mathematics* (pp. 181–189). Hillsdale, NJ: Lawrence Erlbaum Associates.

Simon, H. A. (1980). Problem solving and education. In D. T. Tuma & R. Reif (Eds.), *Problem solving and education: Issues in teaching and research* (pp. 81–96). Hillsdale, NJ: Lawrence Erlbaum Associates.

Spiro, R. J., Feltovich, P. L., Jacobson, M. J., & Coulson, R. L. (1991). Cognitive flexibility, constructivism, and hypertext: Random access instruction for advanced knowledge acquisition in ill-structured domains. *Educational Technology, 31*(5), 24–33.

Stanic, G. M. A., & Kilpatrick, J. (1988). Historical perspectives on problem solving in the mathematics curriculum. In R. I. Charles & E. A. Silver (Eds.), *The teaching and assessing of mathematical problem solving* (pp. 1–22). Hillsdale, NJ: Lawrence Erlbaum Associates and National Council for Teachers of Mathematics.

Sternberg, R. J. (1986). *Intelligence applied.* San Diego: Harcourt Brace Jovanovich.

Van Haneghan, J. P., & Baker, L. (1989). Cognitive monitoring in mathematics. In C. B. McCormick, G. Miller, & M. Pressley (Eds.), *Cognitive strategy research: From basic research to educational applications* (pp. 215–238). New York: Springer Verlag.

Van Haneghan, J. P., Barron, L., Young, M. F., Williams, S. M., Vye, N. J., & Bransford, J. D. (1992). The Jasper series: An experiment with new ways to enhance mathematical thinking. In D. F. Halpern (Ed.), *Enhancing thinking skills in the sciences and mathematics* (pp. 15–38). Hillsdale, NJ: Lawrence Erlbaum Associates.

Whitehead, A. N. (1929). *The aims of education.* New York: Macmillan.

Williams, S. M. (1991). *Putting case-based instruction into context: Examples from legal, business, and medical education* (Technical report). Nashville, TN: Learning Technology Center, Vanderbilt University.

11 Apprenticeship in Problem-Solving: Extending the Cognitive Apprenticeship Model

Nona A. Prestine

One of the primary tenets of recent research on cognitive learning theories has been the emphasis on the inextricable link between knowledge and the context of use. In essence, it is this interconnectedness, expressed by the term "situated cognition," that undergirds understandings of the teaching–learning process and recommendations for instructional design and delivery. "We now recognize that skills and knowledge are not independent of the context—mental, physical, and social—in which they are used. Instead they are attuned to, even part of, the environments in which they are practiced. A new challenge for instruction is to develop ways of organizing learning that permit skills to be practiced in the environments in which they will be used" (Resnick, 1989, p. 3).

A variety of instructional models have developed from this basic social constructivist tenet of situated cognition, including cognitive apprenticeship (Collins, Brown, & Newman, 1989), anchored instruction (Cognition and Technology Group at Vanderbilt [CTGV], 1990), reciprocal teaching (Palincsar & Brown, 1984, 1989), and guided, cooperative learning (Brown & Palincsar, 1989). Precepts underlying these approaches have been applied in teacher education (Fosnot, 1989; Shulman, 1987), continuing professional education (Cervero, 1989) and, most recently, educational administration preparation (Prestine & LeGrand, 1991). Specifically, in the latter, it has been argued that an application of the cognitive apprenticeship model holds much promise for redesigning and reconstituting administrator preparation programs in congruence with cognitive learning ideas. At the individual course or instructional level, cognitive learning precepts argue for teaching the processes experts use to handle complex tasks by externalizing the cognitive and metacognitive processes usually carried out internally and using instructional methods that emphasize active, social, and authentic learning experiences. This type of instructional delivery allows students to incorporate and internalize new knowledge into prior knowledge structures (schemata) and promotes knowledge accessibility for future problem-solving in novel contexts. At the programmatic level, cognitive apprenticeship implications include the formation of practitioner cohort groups, flexible time schedules, differentiation in residency and course requirements, and coherence of progression in the sequence and content of coursework (for a more detailed discussion of these implications, see Prestine & LeGrand, 1991).

While there appears to be some validity in applying cognitive apprenticeship ideas in professional preparation, other concerns have remained problematic or at least unexplored. For the most part these concerns center around the largely ambiguous, uncertain, and uncharted nature of administrative practice. For the practicing administrator these are the all-too-familiar "unfamiliar situations where the problem is not clear and there is no obvious fit between the characteristics of the situation and the available body of theories and techniques" (Schön, 1987, p. 34). Prescriptive, formulistic, and preemptive organizations of knowledge have little applicability in such ambiguous and complex contexts. Moreover, the generalizability of knowledge structures is usually insufficient for transfer across differing problem contexts. Thus, the lack of well-defined problems witnessed in the practitioner context precludes the a priori identification of relevant knowledge structures that can be readily transferred across the possible representations of problems as they occur in the contexts of practice. Rather, practitioner knowledge must have "significant context-dependent variations" that will allow for flexible use in " 'messy' application situations" (Spiro, Coulson, Feltovich, & Anderson, 1988, p. 375). In other words, if set structures of knowledge needed in practice cannot be predetermined across possible applications, then it becomes imperative to focus on *how* knowledge is used in practice, rather than on *what* the knowledge structures are.

Framed in this manner, the question for preparation programs becomes one of how the acquisition of knowledge structures amenable to flexible use in practice can be facilitated. What basic assumptions undergird a cognitive-based view of practitioner preparation? How can the interaction between and interdependence of knowledge, process, and context in the problem-solving activities that characterizes administrative practice be better understood? What instructional designs and methods will facilitate knowledge accessibility and transfer in novel problem situations? In a field of study characterized by ill-defined and constantly shifting problems of practice, how does a conception of expert practice as knowledge-in-use affect preparation programs? What implications does a constructivist view of knowledge creation hold for redefining the relationship between educational administration programs and the practitioners' world?

ASSUMPTIONS ABOUT PROBLEM-SOLVING, APPRENTICESHIP, AND EXPERTISE

The reconceptualization of educational administration preparation programs presented in this chapter is framed around three basic assumptions: *on thinking* as a functional effort to solve problems; *on development* as an apprenticeship in which intellectual tools are used in active, social, and enculturated contexts with peers and experts; and *on expertise* as a flexible reconstruction and use of knowledge schemata in novel, context-specific problem situations. These assumptions warrant further discussion.

Thinking as Problem-Solving

The conceptualization of thinking as problem-solving is both consistent with and an extension of the basic tenets of cognitive learning theory. The consistency is grounded in a view of thinking as an active, social, contextualized, and meaningful action, not as a passive, isolated, and barren possession of mental objects or precepts.

> The purpose of cognition is not to produce thoughts but to guide intelligent interpersonal and practical action. A problem-solving approach places primacy on people's attempts to negotiate the stream of life, to work around or to transform problems that emerge on the route to attaining diverse goals of life (Rogoff, 1990, p. 9).

This conceptualization of thinking as problem-solving emphasizes the critical element of context of use or action and is congruent with cognitive understandings of the situated nature of learning, problem-solving, and understanding (Resnick, 1987).

Yet, conceptualizing problem-solving simply as situated cognition is limiting. Situated cognition is often presented as basically a one-directional, linear approach to the teaching/learning process that views meaningful, hence usable, knowledge acquisition (and, by inference, later knowledge accessibility) as an end product of cognition in context. This would seem to characterize and be quite appropriate for school learning, where problems are reasonably well defined (or at least definable) and finite; where the context is bounded, knowable, stable, and supportive; and where achievement of levels of mastery is verifiable with progressive and identifiable benchmarks of success. This would also seem to characterize and be appropriate for certain well-defined problems of administrative practice.

Recognition of the limitations of this use of situated cognition is made only to point out that the circumstances and stakes of problem-solving activities vary across contexts. School learning experiences, even those deliberately constructed in accordance with situated cognition principles, as well as experiences with well-defined problems of administrative practice, simply are not reflective of the majority of the ambiguous, complex, and context-specific problematic situations of practice (Schön, 1987).

In a focus on practitioner experience, the level of complexity and the relationship of the context to the problem and individual become significantly different from the more prevalent school-related uses of situated cognition. From a practitioner perspective, context "refers to a relationship rather than to a single entity. For on the one hand, context connotes an identifiable, durable framework for activity, with properties that transcend the experience of individuals, exist prior to them, and are entirely beyond their control. On the other hand, context is experienced differently by different individuals" (Lave, Murtaugh, & de la Rocha, 1984, p. 71). It is the latter point that is crucial to this discussion because the context experienced is constituted by the mind. "Meaning and context are not elements that can be handled separately or derived from adding elements together. Context is not so much a set of stimuli that impinge upon a person as it is a web of relations interwoven to form the fabric of meaning" (Rogoff, 1982, p. 149). This suggests that the practitioner's problem-solving activity itself is an active construction of the "mind in society" (Vygotsky, 1978). It is dialectically constituted in that the mind, problem, and context mutually create, interact, and change or restructure each other. What this suggests is that not only is "all knowledge . . . a joint construction of the mind and the situation in which the mind finds itself confronted with a problem" (Lampert & Clark, 1990, p. 22), but that the problem is also a joint construction of the mind (knowledge structures and processes) and the context; and, the context a joint construction of the mind and the problem.

In well-structured domains such a dialectic is minimized and the problem-solving activity follows a relatively prescriptive and straightforward path. The problems are recognized as definable, bounded, and solvable units; there is a direct and identified correspondence between a codified knowledge base and the problem-solution process; and the context is stable, uniform, and not of significant importance. Achievement of expertise (consummate skill in problem-solving) in such domains is determined by relatively clear-cut, unambiguous, and readily verifiable criteria. Such well-structured problem-solving domains include physics, mathematics, and chess. Not coincidentally, these domains also represent the areas in which much of the primary research on expertise has taken place (see, for example, Chi, Glaser, & Rees, 1981). As Glaser (1987) has noted, "this picture of expertise is probably biased by the high structured domains in which it has been studied, and the demands of situations in which cognitive expertise has been analyzed" (p. 92).

Ill-structured domains present a much different characterization of the problem-solving activity as little is certain or constant. In ill-structured domains, "surity about right action does not exist, [and] the choice of a sensible solution strategy for a problem is a more complex task than is solving a problem in well-structured domains" (Berliner, 1986, p. 13). The dialectic is maximized as problems remain stubbornly ill-defined and messy; solutions are elusive and uncertain; routinized or a priori identified knowledge structures and processes are either lacking or insufficient for the problem-solving activity; and the context is complex, ambiguous, and in constant flux. Achievement of expertise in ill-structured domains is difficult to ascertain as its development remains relatively uncharted and examination of the route to success in one problem-solving activity will not necessarily provide reliable markers applicable to attaining success in the next (Kliegl & Baltes, 1987). Berliner (1986) identifies teaching as one example of an ill-structured domain; another likely candidate would appear to be educational administration.

Development as Apprenticeship

As discussed here, development focuses on the transitions that allow an individual to more effectively define and solve problems characterized by active situations (constantly changing and shifting circumstances), a social milieu (other people who constrain or forward progress), and authentic contexts (enculturated practices and ideas). As a guiding metaphor for this development, the apprenticeship provides a model that is consistent with this conceptualization; a model that features active learners involved with a community of people who support, challenge, and guide the novices as they increasingly participate in skilled, valued, context-specific problem-solving activity. These apprenticeship characteristics require further clarification and explanation.

To a large extent, using the apprenticeship metaphor rests heavily on Vygotskian theories of cognition and learning, aptly and succinctly portrayed by the phrase "mind in society." Brown and Palincsar (1989) provide a cogent summary of this concept: "Vygotsky argued that thinking is a social activity, initially shared between people but gradually internalized to reappear again as an individual achievement. For Vygotsky, individual thinking is essentially the re-enactment by the individual of cognitive processes that were originally experienced in society" (pp. 396–397). Cognitive development, then, is characterized by the learner's active involvement in a social process of appropriating the necessary intellectual tools, social skills, and cultural understandings that will later become internalized. Such appropriations occur in problem-solving activities because problem-solving occurs in what Vygotsky (1978) terms the learner's zone of proximal development.

> The zone of proximal development is the distance between the actual developmental level as determined by independent *problem solving* and the level

of potential development as determined through problem solving under adult [or expert] guidance, or in collaboration with more capable peers. (Vygotsky, 1978, p. 86, emphasis added)

From this perspective, problem-solving is a profoundly social learning process encapsulated within and inseparable from the larger cultural context in which it is experienced and practiced.

The apprenticeship metaphor also provides an appropriate connection to ideas of expertise. Traditionally and historically, apprenticeship was seen as the model for professional development of novices that culminated in "master" or expert status. Interest in studying the idea of expert practice and the development of expertise in a variety of human activities has gained momentum (see Chi, Glaser, & Farr, 1988; Chi et al., 1981; Lesgold, 1984; Lesgold, Rubinson, Feltovich, Glaser, Klopfer, & Wang, 1988; Schooler & Schaie, 1987; Scribner, 1984). Only recently, though, have researchers turned their attention to the study of the development of professional expertise. In a comprehensive review of research of this area, Kennedy (1987) identified four conceptions of expertise:

1. As technical skill
2. As the application of theory or general principles
3. As critical analysis
4. As deliberate action.

While all four have some basis in empirical research, the first two views of expertise as technical skill or application of general principles are rather limiting. Both assume (1) that expertise entails possession of a rather narrow and prescriptive body of how-to knowledge developed by others and transmitted intact as directives for achieving expert practice; (2) that relatively narrow parameters of variability in problem-solving context exist. This type of expertise has been termed routine (or conventional) expertise (Glaser, 1987, citing Hatano & Inagaki, 1983). "Routine experts are outstanding in terms of speed, accuracy, and automaticity of performance, and construct mental models convenient for performing their tasks, but they lack adaptability when faced with new kinds of problems. Repeated application of a procedure, with little variation, probably leads to routine expertise" (p. 92).

This technical-rational interpretation of expertise is valid only if one holds that expertise is singularly constituted by possession of a body of specialized, invariant declarative knowledge (Shuell, 1986) that can be directly applied to well-defined problems in relatively stable contexts. (For an exemplary instance of this interpretation and its application to teaching, see Welker, 1991.) Yet, as Kennedy (1987) noted, this conceptualization does "not address the complicated judgments involved when practitioners adjust general principles to specific circumstances, select the most appropriate principles from several that apply, or merge multiple applicable principles into a single integrated formulation" (p. 143). While an adequate explanation of expertise in solving well-defined problems, such limited conceptions of expertise cannot address the complex and interactive realities of problem-solving activities involved in much of the authentic administrative context and culture. This type of expertise, calling for critical analysis and deliberate action, has been termed "adaptive." "Adaptive expertise requires variation and is encouraged by playful [and problematic] situations and in cultures where *understanding is valued along with efficient performance*" (Glaser, 1987, p. 92, emphasis added).

Administrative expertise would seem to involve an amalgamation of all four conceptions with special emphasis on critical analysis and deliberate action. Expertise then becomes the process of critically analyzing and acting on problem situations by actively and flexibly reconstructing propositional and procedural knowledge structures within a context of use. Using this conception of expertise allows that the expert practitioner does develop an automaticity in responding to well-defined or frequently encountered problems and to those that evolve and accumulate over time into a body of routine problems of practice (Leithwood, 1989, 1991). However, this automaticity is not to be confused with a mere rote application of prescribed directives for practice. A deeper level of cognition and understanding is implicit in this conceptualization and is consistent with Schön's (1987) idea of reflection-in-action, Shulman's (1986) use of wisdom of practice, and Soltis' (1990) conception of knowledge-in-use. In this enhanced and expanded interpretation, professional expertise becomes "making sense of what is going on and critically seeking its improvement rather than [a singular] knowledge of how to do something in particular" (Soltis, 1990, p. 320).

Given this conceptualization of professional expertise, it becomes clear that it can be acquired only by engaging in apprenticelike approaches, involving problem-solving activities (or at least problem-solving simulations) that are situated in time and context and oriented toward action. The cognitive apprenticeship (Collins et al., 1989) is designed to give novices this opportunity to observe, engage in, and discover the kind of knowledge-in-use that characterizes expert performance. Even the typology of methods (modeling, coaching, scaffolding, articulation, reflection, and exploration) presented in the cognitive apprenticeship model suggests a progression that corresponds with the four conceptions of expertise discussed earlier.

The first three apprenticeship methods include modeling, coaching, and scaffolding. These provide the learner with the most support and guided participation in knowledge areas with which they are unfamiliar. The methods of modeling, coaching, and scaffolding seem most viable and appropriate for acquisition of the technical or procedural knowledge and the basic principles or abstract theories of the knowledge domain. These methods provide organizational schemata or temporary models to be used as scaffolds while new knowledge gained from the social interaction is internalized. The next two methods, articulation and reflection, are designed to help learners gain conscious access to and control of their own knowledge structures, reasoning processes, and problem-solving strategies. The growing independence of the learner means that a priori external structures need no longer dictate paths or provide direction through problem-solving activities. The learner now is gaining independence and reflective mastery in problem-solving activities that allow him or her to engage in more independent critical analysis and decision making. What has been learned through collaborative social interaction and social construction of knowledge, hallmarks of the first three methods, has now been internalized and individual ownership established. The last method (exploration) is action-oriented and looks for complete learner independence and autonomy in flexibly reconstituting and reconstructing existing knowledge to define and formulate problems to be solved as well as engage in expert problem-solving processes. At this stage, problem-solving activities are marked by the self-regulation of cognitive processes "manifested by proficiency in techniques of solution monitoring, by the allocation of attention and by sensitivity to informational feedback" (Glaser, 1987, p. 91).

Expertise as the Flexible Reconstruction of Prior Knowledge

In examining the diagnostic practices of physicians, Shulman (1988) noted that evidence of expertise appeared to be definable only in a context of use. The implication of the situated nature of expertise is, then, that the question of importance concerns not "what" structures of knowledge might be said to constitute expert knowledge, but "how" prior knowledge structures are used in expert practice. To this Lampert and Clark (1990) add that "knowing how experts structure their thinking about a problem tells us little about how they use those knowledge structures in practice . . . [this] cautions us to pay attention to how experts *acquire* whatever knowledge might be said to characterize their thinking about the problems of practice" (p. 22). What this suggests is that how knowledge is acquired will affect its later accessibility and transferability or applicability to novel and context-specific problem-solving activities. While the use of prior knowledge is very much evident in expert performance, the ability to access and apply it remains "very much a matter of how the knowledge and skill [were] acquired" (Perkins & Salomon, 1989, p. 22).

The cognitive apprenticeship model addresses this transferability concern by suggesting that through externalizing expert cognitive processes that are normally performed internally and situating learning in a variety of contexts of use, the new knowledge is more meaningfully incorporated into the learner's existing schemata and that this then promotes accessibility for future problem-solving in novel contexts (Collins et al., 1989). Yet this process of externalizing expert cognitive processes, even as they occur in the context of practice, is difficult to achieve. It would seem more likely that such a process could be accomplished in discrete, well-structured knowledge domains where such cognitive problem-solving paths are relatively straightforward and identifiable (e.g., teaching multiplication) and would be less likely to occur in more complex and ill-structured knowledge domains (e.g., interpreting literature).

Studies of problem-solving by both novices and experts have consistently shown that "problem representation is constructed by the solver on the basis of domain-related knowledge and the organization of this knowledge. The nature of this organization determines the quality, completeness, and coherence of the internal representation, which in turn determines the efficiency of further thinking" (Glaser, 1987, p. 84). While I agree in part with this representation, the assumptions about problem-solving, apprenticeship, and expertise constructed in this chapter suggest that this representation is too limited, too linear, too passive, too simplified. Such a conceptualization may well characterize research focused on expert problem-solving in well-structured knowledge domains and conducted under laboratory conditions. It would seem less useful for knowledge acquisition in ill-structured domains and problem-solving in the context of professional practice. While the relationship between prior knowledge and the problem representation is significant, the interrelatedness and the dialectical nature of the mix of problem, context, prior knowledge, and cognitive processes, including affective and social components, are of equal importance.

Based on the assumption presented in this chapter, the role of prior knowledge structures in a problem-solving activity is more aptly represented as a part of the dialectic of the problem-solving activity rather than the sole determiner of its course. "We recognize, actively select and subjectively interpret only part of the vast array of information to which we are exposed. Acquired knowledge determines *in part* the selection of items and elements for inclusion within the problem space" (Hoyer, 1987, p. 132, emphasis added). Prior knowledge not only influences perception of the problem-solving activity but is itself affected and changed by the problem context. Soltis (1990) suggests this interactive process in his conceptualization of professional knowledge-in-use. Using knowledge in a problem-solving activity becomes "an occasion for the reconstruction, reorganization, and transformation of one's fund of knowledge. . . . There is a dynamic, creative, transactive, and continuous quality to the growth of personal knowledge and our ability to act effectively in the world in the pursuit of our purposes. This kind of knowledge-in-use is cumulative not in some simple additive way, but organically and transformationally" (pp. 320–321).

In ill-structured domains where ambiguity and complexity abound, where routine and formulistic prescriptions for practice are minimally effective, and where the contexts of the problem-solving activities are uncertain, constantly shifting, and yet of paramount importance, expertise will in part be a function of the complexity of the network of relationships among existing knowledge structures (Leithwood, 1991) and the ability to control the process of flexibly reconstructing and reconstituting the relationships between schema representations. "Monolithic representations of knowledge too often leave their holders facing situations for which their rigid 'plaster-casts' simply do not fit. The result is the often heard complaint of students: 'We weren't taught that.' By which they mean that they weren't taught exactly that. They lack the ability to use their knowledge in new ways, the ability to think for themselves" (Spiro, Vispoel, Schmitz, Samarapungavan, & Boerger, 1987, p. 180). Such knowledge then becomes knowledge that is built for use, not for imitative reproduction in artificial and inauthentic school settings (Resnick, 1987). It is the inherent meaningfulness and accessibility of such a complex network of relationships among knowledge schemata that provide a necessary first step toward the development of expertise. As Brown and Palincsar (1989) point out, if the learner "has not established ownership of that knowledge that would afford him or her flexible access" (p. 394) to modify or reconstruct it at will, then such knowledge is neither accessible nor usable.

IMPLICATIONS FOR EDUCATIONAL ADMINISTRATION PROGRAMS

The conceptual framework presented has been developed around assumptions directly tied to situated cognition precepts and the cognitive apprenticeship model: of thinking as a functional and goal-directed effort to solve problems and of development as an apprenticeship in which intellectual tools are used in an active social and enculturated context with peers and experts. Through the integration of recent cognitive research on expertise and advanced knowledge acquisition and use in ill-structured domains, the boundaries of the cognitive apprenticeship model are expanded to more adequately address understandings of advanced knowledge acquisition and, especially, the development of professional expertise. Professional expertise emerges as an amalgamation of both routine and adaptive expertise, incorporating the use of procedural, how-to knowledge for routine (well-defined) tasks, but emphasizing the ability to critically access and flexibly reconstruct and use prior knowledge in novel, context-specific, and action-oriented (ill-defined) problem situations.

What is proposed here is a framework for reconceptualizing educational administration programs guided by the assumptions developed for problem-solving, apprenticeship, and professional expertise. Although the implications are discussed separately under the three concept headings, it should be understood that this is done only for heuristic purposes. All three conceptions are intertwined, interdependent, and interactive.

Problem-Solving

One of the difficulties in using problem-solving as part of a framework for discussing the educational administration program is that it sounds so grim. A certain stigma has been attached to "problems" that implies a difficulty or issue in a situation that should not, under more efficient and effective management, be present. Yet, problem-solving activities are in fact opportunities and need to be viewed as such. Only in problem situations are we challenged, our minds engaged, knowledge restructured, creativity evidenced, artistry shown, and growth enhanced.

Educational administration, as a field of study, fits the description of an ill-structured knowledge domain. Unilateral, routinized directives for practice are, at best, of limited utility for a practitioner context characterized by ill-defined problems that often do not have clear-cut solutions, or present multiple solution paths with minor changes in the problem requiring major changes in the solution. Formalized, didactic approaches that emphasize one best way or one perspective are inappropriate in most cases. What is needed are multidimensional, multifaceted perspectives emphasizing the interconnectedness between different aspects of domain knowledge. "Instead of using a single knowledge structure ... multiple knowledge precedents will need to be applied to new situations. Under conditions of ill-structured complexity, single approaches provide insufficient coverage" (Spiro et al., 1987, p. 184).

At the individual course level there already exists some encouraging evidence of uses of this approach. Most notably, Haller and Strike's (1986) introductory text for educational administration examines administrative problems from social, legal, and ethical perspectives using a case-presentation format. As well, Bolman and Deal's (1984, 1991) use of "reframing" and Morgan's (1986) more expansive and inclusive "images of organizations" are ways of approaching and understanding organizations from multiple perspectives. These examples of the use of a multidimensional approach allow students to gain a diversified repertoire of ways of thinking about an abstract conceptual topic. This same approach can be expanded to other courses as well. In fact, multiple-perspective approaches may be enhanced when instructor-designed, rather than text-dependent. For example, an introductory research course was designed around a multiparadigmatic approach. Using the functionalist, interpretivist, and critical-theory paradigms, research design and methodology were explored emphasizing the multiple beliefs about and means and methods of systematic inquiry. Following the precepts of the cognitive apprenticeship model, instruction was designed to attend first to a holistic understanding of the paradigms before exploring the particulars of each.

Case-based instruction is particularly amenable to this multiple-perspective approach and "encourages students to articulate their own practice-based knowledge and problem-solving efforts to generate a dialogue between theory and practice" (Prestine & LeGrand, 1991, p. 76). A case-study approach facilitates the integration of practical and abstract knowledge. The intent is not to arrive at a "right" answer, but to allow students to flexibly reconstruct theoretical and practical knowledge and to reflectively experience knowledge-in-use in safe simulations of practice. The use of an instructor-designed case-study guide is most helpful as an initial scaffold for students in becoming familiar with a reflective and critical analysis of cases. An important and distinguishing feature of the case method in this model, as with the cognitive apprenticeship model, is that the instructor first overtly models the case-analysis process, articulating and externalizing internal tacit knowledge structures through use of the guide.

The use of case-based instruction is not new and is even considered foundational in professional preparation fields such as business administration. In educational administration, as well, instruction in the use of case studies has been widely and enthusiastically advocated (see McConnell, 1991; Silver, 1986) and several anthologies of case studies in educational administration have recently been published (see Ashbaugh & Kasten, 1991; Kowalski, 1991). Yet, what is advocated here for case-based instruction is somewhat different. Traditional case-study methods certainly can be used, although an instructor-developed guide based on cognitive precepts is probably preferable to the recent introduction of "instructor's manuals" appended to such texts.

What is advocated here is the use of student-generated case studies from experienced "critical incidents." These are beneficial for a number of reasons. First, the importance and the reality of the practitioner's world is firmly established within the classroom context. As Friedson (1986) noted, "To assume . . . that textbooks and other publications of academics and researchers reflect in consistent and predictable ways the knowledge that is actually exercised in concrete human settings is either wishful or naive" (p. 229). In essence, such an exercise communicates to the student, "What you do and experience is important and valued in this setting." Case-study writing also forces students to critically assess and reflect on an incident experienced from practice and to take note of the important particulars of the case. By sharing these case studies in a small group, students become aware of insights and perceptions that may not have been part of their original framing of the problem. A communal sharing of each group's efforts serves as a forum in which ideas may be critiqued and/or challenged. Students might also be asked to "reframe" their cases through the multiple theoretical perspectives developed within the class. This reframing exercise allows the instructor to assess the student's knowledge-in-use (evidence of the restructuring and reconstituting of prior knowledge structures) as well as the student's zone of proximal development (that which the student can completely do only with the aid of those more skilled).

Another strength of this type of case method is that it can encourage the reflective exploration of ethical considerations and moral orientations not only in the simulated practice situations of the case itself but also within the dynamics of the group. To encourage this kind of reflection within what are set up as collaborative decision-making groups, the group and its deliberation processes themselves become the raw material from which a further case is crafted. (Wineburg [1991] has described a somewhat similar tactic he uses for reflective examination of pedagogical issues in a teacher education course.) In other words, analysis takes place at two levels. First there is a level of analysis of the assigned case itself, whether student-generated or otherwise. In addition, the level of analysis is extended to an examination of the group collaborative decision-making processes. Was everyone given a voice? Were there nonparticipants? If so, why? Did one person seem to have preference in addressing the group? Was leadership deferred because of power positions? Were disagreements glossed over in the interest of completing the task or were they aired? This type of analysis seems especially important if we truly seek to develop administrators who will promote a professional climate in schools through collaborative decision-making and shared leadership. As one student, who had completed an advanced graduate course in administrative leadership that used this technique, commented in a written evaluation:

> This whole class has been a struggle because putting leadership-oriented people in a situation where they have to reach consensus is difficult. I am confident in my abilities to get consensus with my faculty and yet feel ineffectual in this class. Is this because I am able to dominate my faculty? I never thought so before but now doubt exists. Now I have a better sense of how they [the faculty] feel. I guess I always had my own agenda and that's what came through to them.

The stuff of case-study work is best when actually experienced.

Apprenticeship

Most educational administration preparation programs are designed around a profoundly misleading idea: that one first acquires administrative knowledge and later applies it in practice. In fact, as this chapter has argued, knowledge acquisition should not be separated from the context of its intended use. The apprenticeship model offers a promising vehicle for linking knowledge acquisition with the context of use by emphasizing the active, social, and enculturated nature of learning in the design of individual course instruction and overall preparation program. Through emphasis on the social nature of problem-solving, guided cooperative learning techniques, the formation of cohort groups, and the deliberate valuing and integrating of students' practitioner knowledge and experience, apprenticelike experiences are specifically fashioned for students to tie knowledge to context of use.

The basic precepts of the cognitive apprenticeship model (content, method, sequence, and sociology) are used as a scaffold for building a problem-solving approach to instruction and program design. *Content* considerations must be inclusive of the different types of knowledge needed for expertise. This includes the explicit factual and conceptual or theoretical knowledge that is consensually agreed on and identified with the field of study. This type of knowledge has dominated preparation programs and, while necessary, is not sufficient for the development of expert practice "as it tends to remain inert and untapped in problem solving in the context of practice" (Prestine & LeGrand, 1991, p. 69). Various typologies of strategic knowledge are also needed, including problem-solving strategies and heuristics, control strategies for the flexible reconstruction of knowledge in the context of the problem-solving situation, and strategies used by experts for knowledge acquisition. A problem-solving orientation uses teaching *methods* that offer the opportunity to observe, engage in, and discover the flexible use of knowledge and appropriate control strategies for reconstruction in novel problem-solving situations. The methods of modeling, coaching, scaffolding, articulation, reflection, and exploration, as used progressively and developmentally in the span of both individual courses and program progression, follow a developmental *sequence* leading toward expertise. At the crux of the cognitive assumptions discussed is the Vygotskian concept that learning is product of *social* interaction that is later internalized for individual use. "The knowledge that will guide expert practice is to be learned in the context of its application to realistic problems within the culture of actual practice. This means that learning is not done in isolation. Other people, including experts and novices, are present when tasks are carried out and knowledge is incorporated" (Prestine & LeGrand, 1991, p. 70).

The apprenticeship model also offers a means of bridging the rift between professor and practitioner, between theory and practice, by allowing students to remain in the context of their practice while completing the preparation program. Removing students from the context of practice, as programmatic residency policies require, impedes the development of knowledge-in-use. While problem-solving activity in the preparation program may be reflective and theory-driven, problem-solving in the practitioner context is under far less control. Quite simply, the use of theoretical ideas and concepts in intellectual classroom work does not ensure use in an isolated practitioner context without further intellectual effort and support from peers and experts. The demands of the academic and practitioner contexts are different and determine the manner in which knowledge is used. In the preparation program, possession of knowledge is the goal, demonstration is at a private and individual level, and evaluation is nonnegotiable. In the practitioner context, however, the primary aim is not knowledge itself but action, knowledge use takes place in an intensely social and often conflictual context, and validity of knowledge use can be a matter of public debate. The stakes are higher, the pressure for action is immediate, and reflective questioning may be taken as a sign of weakness.

For the practitioner, incorporating significant new knowledge into administrative practice involves stress, risk, and time. It requires challenging and modifying fundamental beliefs and established routines that may leave practitioners feeling especially vulnerable, confused, and isolated. The collegial support of the cohort group and the guidance of experts become critical at this time. The apprenticeship period must be a time in which the practitioner is encouraged to take these risks and make substantive changes in ways of thinking with a safety net of support, encouragement, and counsel provided by peers and more skilled others. For new knowledge to be integrated with existing schemata in the context of use, the support offered by the apprenticeship model may be invaluable.

Expertise

If one accepts the proposition that expertise develops within the context of the practitioner's world, then this suggests important and far-reaching implications for educational administration programs. First, and most critical, educational administration programs must strive to extend and continue linkages to the practitioner far beyond the completion of a degree program or awarding of certification. It seems both misguided and self-defeating to assume that the conferring of a terminal degree or certification signifies total mastery or competence beyond which further development toward expertise is not necessary or of importance. Worse yet, it betrays a callous indifference to practitioners once they are beyond the walls of the academy. Yet the current system encourages this rigid separation of professional preparation from continuing professional development. At best, tenuous and limited linkages between professor and practitioner are maintained primarily through consultancy services and research activities.

What is needed is a deliberate, continued linkage between departments of educational administration and the professional practice community. In essence, educational administration departments must expand their horizons to assume an active and vital role inclusive of both initial preparation and career-long professional development concerns. A continuing and collaborative dialogue needs to be developed between the two, specifically addressing professional development concerns and working toward the understanding and development of expertise during the post–degree/certification period.

To a large extent it must be the responsibility of the educational administration program to establish and nurture new connections and linkages to the practitioner. In addition, participation in continuing professional development must mean more than just developing new courses for post-degree students or one-shot in-service programs for administrators. One vision of this future may be in an extended apprenticeship model, where educational administration programs work to enhance the knowledge creation capabilities of practitioners in the professional community. Options could include traditional, though rarely used, approaches to joint ventures, like collaborative action-research projects and problem-oriented seminars. Collaboratively planned "reflective opportunities" or retreats can be designed explicitly for professionals to share, interpret, and learn from practice experiences. Through careful guidance and support from professors and peers, these reflective opportunities can also allow practitioners to escape from their experience, leading them to challenge traditional assumptions and acquire new perspectives.

The collaborative nature of these linkages between the practitioner community and the university suggest a relationship that is not only beneficial to both parties but also a relationship between equals. Educational administration departments must recognize that a component part of expertise is what Shulman (1988) calls the "wisdom of practice." Yet, little is known about what knowledge constitutes administrative thinking, how professionals learn and use such knowledge, or how the development of administrative professional expertise is fostered.

A small but growing body of research on expertise and teacher thinking (Clark, 1988; Clark & Peterson, 1986; Eisner, 1985; Feiman-Nemser & Floden, 1986; Grimmett & Erickson, 1988) already exists. It is perhaps time to extend this work to a more serious, systematic, and concentrated look at administrative thinking and evidence of the development of administrative expertise and expert practice. Lampert and Clark (1990) point directly to studies focusing on the work of personnel managers as significant for informing studies of how expertise is acquired and used in professional practice: "These studies have found that managing the actions and purposes of other people involves learning to think in ways that are highly responsive to the social details of particular problem situations and integrated with action" (p. 22). It would seem reasonable that with an extended relationship between professor and professional, new avenues of inquiry into administrative knowledge-in-use and the development of professional expertise could be accelerated. The field of educational administration would seem ripe for such research efforts.

Finally, educational administration research agendas in general will be affected by practitioner linkages. With professors spending more time listening to and working with practitioners, their research will very likely be more reflective of practitioner concerns and perspectives. While this may lead to significant redirection of research agendas, the knowledge development potential of practitioners, a largely untapped resource, should also be exploited in this extended collaborative model. Knowledge-in-use created by expert practitioners in practice contexts exists, but is rarely transmitted to others. This knowledge-in-use created by practitioners involved in problem-solving activities within their own context contributes to their own personal store of knowledge, experience, and expertise but is rarely disseminated to a wider audience.

Of course, the intellectual problems of attempting to describe, share, and develop expert knowledge and expert practice so that it becomes more widely available are formidable indeed. Expert practice, especially in ill-structured domains, is never tidy and will be difficult at best to codify. Even appropriate language for describing much of it has yet to be developed. Prolonged interaction, acute and sensitive observation, and open, analytic dialogue between researchers and practitioners will doubtless be necessary. Yet, a beginning must be made.

CONCLUSIONS

If one agrees that the goal of learning and instruction in educational administration preparation programs should be acquisition of generative knowledge with wide application in novel but partially related contexts, then the framework presented here may hold some promise for redesigning preparation programs. In the most basic sense, the focus of an apprenticeship-in-problem-solving approach for preparation programs is to promote knowledge acquisition for later accessibility and use in practitioner problem-solving situations. Such knowledge cannot be thought of as being rigidly structured but must be considered as intricate networks of relationships among schema representations that are accessible as needed within the infinite permutations of the practitioner problem context. At present, the possession of such an adaptability (expert practice) comes only with accumulation of actual field experience over a considerable period of time, if at all. The apprenticeship-in-problem-solving approach argues that the development of administrative expertise needs to be taken out of the realm of haphazard acquisition and made a significant component of and focus for program redesign.

Emphasis on an apprenticeship in a problem-solving approach removes the dominant role of isolated, passive, and sterile knowledge acquisition as the primary activity of preparation programs. The analogy of the medical specialization versus holistic medicine is apt. The medical specialist focuses narrowly on that which he or she specializes in, for example, surgery. Specialized treatment is administered to a passive patient who receives it. The surgeon-specialist has little interest that the condition being treated exists in the larger context of the patient, including affective, social, and cultural processes. For the specialist, once the surgery is over, interest and involvement are finished. The outcome is now up to the patient and blind luck—the surgeon washes his or her hands of all responsibility. This clinical-specialist model is not dissimilar from the traditional approach of educational administration preparation programs. What is suggested here is that a more holistic approach is needed—one that recognizes that the student consists not merely of intellect but also of social and affective processes; that students will not practice in vacuum, but in a social context with others. There is a need to recognize that professors of educational administration are connected to and a part of the larger profession and the practitioner community. This holistic perspective suggests that linkages need to be forged beyond an annual meeting with alumni groups or the occasional consultive work with, or in-service presentation for, a given district's administrators.

Conceptualizing educational administration programs as an apprenticeship in problem-solving may also suggest the beginnings of a paradigmatic shift from the traditional systems of thought and organization that have served to separate administrative practice from professional preparation and have hindered the development of more educationally constructive ways of thinking about all aspects of educational administration. One path such a shift might follow involves reconceptualizing educational administration in light of cognitive learning theory precepts. This is not as radical a thought as it might appear at first blush. Educational administration and indeed the educational system in general have long been dominated by thought and theory from the functionalist paradigm. Included in this functionalist paradigm are fundamental behavioral psychology perspectives and orientations about the teaching/learning process. Like conceptions of routine expertise, this perspective may help to define and explain only the most formalized, routinized, and observable elements of administrative practice, while ignoring the novel and interesting, but more complex and problematic. An apprenticeship-in-problem-solving approach suggests that a phenomenological or interpretivist approach (inclusive of cognitive learning theories) merits further examination and consideration as a guiding paradigm for educational administration and education in general. While the apprenticeship-in-problem-solving approach is far from a fully explicated model, it may be at least a beginning, perhaps a first thread of a design that will weave together in a rich pattern the elements of cognitive learning theories, professional expertise, and educational administration.

REFERENCES

Ashbaugh, C. R., & Kasten, K. L. (1991). *Educational leadership: Case studies for reflective practice*. New York: Longman.

Berliner, D. C. (1986). In pursuit of the expert pedagogue. *Educational Researcher,* *15*(7), 5–13.

Bolman, L. G., & Deal, T. E. (1984). *Modern approaches to understanding and managing organizations.* San Francisco: Jossey-Bass.

Bolman, L. G., & Deal, T. E. (1991). *Reframing organizations: Artistry, choice, and leadership.* San Francisco: Jossey-Bass.

Brown, A. L., & Palincsar, A. S. (1989). Guided, cooperative learning and individual knowledge acquisition. In L. B. Resnick (Ed.), *Knowing, learning and instruction: Essays in honor of Robert Glaser* (pp. 393–452). Hillsdale, NJ: Lawrence Erlbaum Associates.

Cervero, R. M. (1989, March). *Professional practice, learning and continuing education: An integrated perspective.* Invited address presented at the Annual Meeting of the American Educational Research Association, San Francisco.

Chi, M. T. H., Glaser, R., & Farr, M. J. (1988). *The nature of expertise.* Hillsdale, NJ: Lawrence Erlbaum Associates.

Chi, M. T. H., Glaser, R., & Rees, E. (1981). Expertise in problem solving. In R. J. Sternberg (Ed.), *Advances in the psychology of human intelligence* (Vol. 1, pp. 7–75). Hillsdale, NJ: Lawrence Erlbaum Associates.

Clark, C. M. (1988). Asking the right questions about teacher preparation: Contribution of research on teacher thinking. *Educational Researcher, 17,* 5–12.

Clark, C. M., & Peterson, P. L. (1986). Teachers' thought processes. In M. C. Wittrock (Ed.), *Handbook of research on teaching* (3rd ed.) (pp. 255–296). New York: Macmillan.

Cognition and Technology Group at Vanderbilt. (1990). Anchored instruction and its relationship to situated cognition. *Educational Researcher, 19*(5), 2–10.

Collins, A., Brown, J. S., & Newman, S. E. (1989). Cognitive apprenticeship: Teaching the craft of reading, writing, and mathematics. In L. B. Resnick (Ed.), *Knowing, learning, and instruction: Essays in honor of Robert Glaser* (pp. 453–494). Hillsdale, NJ: Lawrence Erlbaum Associates.

Eisner, E. (Ed.). (1985). *Learning and teaching the ways of knowing: Eighty-fourth yearbook of the national society for the study of education.* Chicago: University of Chicago Press.

Feiman-Nemser, S., & Floden, R. E. (1986). The cultures of teaching. In M. C. Wittrock (Ed.), *Handbook of research on teaching* (3rd ed.) (pp. 505–526). New York: Macmillan.

Fosnot, C. T. (1989). *Empowering teachers, empowering learners: A constructivist approach for teaching.* New York: Teachers College Press.

Friedson, E. (1986). *Professional powers.* Chicago: University of Chicago Press.

Glaser, R. (1987). Thoughts on expertise. In C. Schooler & K. W. Schaie (Eds.), *Cognitive functioning and social structure over the life course* (pp. 81–94). Norwood, NJ: Ablex.

Grimmett, P. P., & Erickson, G. L. (Eds.). (1988). *Reflection in teacher education.* New York: Teachers College Press.

Haller, E. J., & Strike, K. A. (1986). *An introduction to educational administration: Social, legal, and ethical perspectives.* New York: Longman.

Hatano, G., & Inagaki, K. (1983, April). *Two courses of expertise.* Paper presented at the Conference on Child Development in Japan and the United States, Stanford, CA.

Hoyer, W. (1987). Acquisition of knowledge and the decentralization of g in adult intellectual development. In C. Schooler & K. W. Schaie (Eds.), *Cognitive functioning and social structure over the life course.* Norwood, NJ: Ablex.

Kennedy, M. M. (1987). Inexact science: Professional education and the development of expertise. In E. Z. Rothkopf (Ed.), *Review of research in education, 14* (pp. 133–167). Washington, DC: American Educational Research Association.

Kliegl, R., & Baltes, P. (1987). Theory-guided analysis of mechanisms of development and aging through testing-the-limits and research on expertise. In C. Schooler & K. W. Schaie (Eds.), *Cognitive functioning and social structure over the life course.* Norwood, NJ: Ablex.

Kowalski, T. J. (1991). *Case studies on educational administration.* New York: Longman.

Lampert, M., & Clark, C. M. (1990). Expert knowledge and expert thinking in teaching: A response to Floden and Klinzing. *Educational Researcher, 19*(5), 21–23.

Lave, J., Murtaugh, M., & de la Rocha, O. (1984). The dialectic of arithmetic in grocery shopping. In B. Rogoff & J. Lave (Eds.), *Everyday cognition: Its development in social context* (pp. 67–94). Cambridge: Harvard University Press.

Leithwood, K. (1991, November). Personal communication.

Leithwood, K. A., & Stager, M. (1989). Expertise in principals' problem solving. *Educational Administration Quarterly, 25*(2), 126–161.

Lesgold, A., Rubinson, H., Feltovich, P., Glaser, R., Klopfer, D., & Wang, Y. (1988). Expertise in a complex skill: Diagnosing X-ray pictures. In M. T. H. Chi, R. Glaser, & M. J. Farr (Eds.), *The nature of expertise* (pp. 311–342). Hillsdale, NJ: Lawrence Erlbaum Associates.

Lesgold, A. M. (1984). Acquiring expertise. In J. R. Anderson & S. M. Kosslyn (Eds.), *Tutorials in learning and memory: Essays in honor of Gordon Bower* (pp. 31–60). San Francisco: Freeman.

McConnell, D. M. (1991). The emergence of a case study professor. *Praxis, 3*(2), 3–4, 9.

Morgan, G. (1986). *Images of organizations.* Beverly Hills, CA: Sage.

Palincsar, A. S., & Brown, A. L. (1984). Reciprocal teaching of comprehension-fostering and comprehension-monitoring activities. *Cognition and Instruction, 1*(2), 117–175.

Palincsar, A. S., & Brown, A. L. (1989). Instruction for self-regulated reading. In L. B. Resnick & L. E. Klopfer (Eds.), *Toward the thinking curriculum: Current cognitive research. 1989 Yearbook of the Association for Supervision and Curriculum Development* (pp. 19–39). Alexandria, VA: Association for Supervision and Curriculum Development.

Perkins, D. N., & Salomon, G. (1989). Are cognitive skills context-bound? *Educational Researcher, 18*(1), 16–25.

Prestine, N. A., & LeGrand, B. (1991). Cognitive learning theory and the preparation of educational administrators: Implications for practice and policy. *Educational Administration Quarterly, 27*(1), 61–89.

Resnick, L. B. (1987). Learning in school and out. *Educational Researcher, 16*(9), 13–20.

Resnick, L. B. (1989). Introduction. In L. B. Resnick (Ed.), *Knowing, learning and in-*

struction: Essays in honor of Robert Glaser (pp. 1–24). Hillsdale, NJ: Lawrence Erlbaum Associates.

Rogoff, B. (1982). Integrating context and cognitive development. In M. E. Lamb & A. L. Brown (Eds.), *Advances in developmental psychology* (Vol. 2) (pp. 125–170). Hillsdale, NJ: Lawrence Erlbaum Associates.

Rogoff, B. (1990). *Apprenticeship in thinking: Cognitive development in social context.* New York: Oxford University Press.

Schön, D. A. (1987). *Educating the reflective practitioner.* San Francisco: Jossey-Bass.

Schooler, C., & Schaie, K. W. (1987). *Cognitive functioning and social structure over the life course.* Norwood, NJ: Ablex.

Scribner, S. (1984). Studying working intelligence. In B. Rogoff & J. Lave (Eds.), *Everyday cognition: Its development in social context* (pp. 9–40). Cambridge: Cambridge University Press.

Shuell, T. J. (1986). Cognitive conceptions of learning. *Review of Educational Research, 56*(4), 411–436.

Shulman, L. S. (1986). Those who understand: A conception of teacher knowledge. *American Educator, 10*(1), 9–15.

Shulman, L. S. (1987). Knowledge and teaching: Foundations of the new reform. *Harvard Educational Review, 57*(1), 1–22.

Shulman, L. S. (1988). The wisdom of practice: Managing complexity in medicine and teaching. In D. Berliner & B. Rosenshine (Eds.), *Talks to teachers* (pp. 369–386). New York: Random House.

Silver, P. F. (1986). Case records: A reflective practice approach to administrator development. *Theory into Practice, 25*(3), 161–167.

Soltis, J. F. (1990). A reconceptualization of educational foundations. *Teachers College Record, 91*(3), 311–321.

Spiro, R. J., Coulson, R. L., Feltovich, P. J., & Anderson, D. K. (1988). Cognitive flexibility theory: Advanced knowledge acquisition in ill-structured domains. In *Tenth Annual Conference of the Cognitive Science Society* (pp. 375–383). Hillsdale, NJ: Lawrence Erlbaum Associates.

Spiro, R. J., Vispoel, W. P., Schmitz, J. G., Samarapungavan, A., & Boerger, A. E. (1987). Knowledge acquisition for application: Cognitive flexibility and transfer in complex content domains. In B. C. Britton (Ed.), *Executive control processes* (pp. 177–199). Hillsdale, NJ: Lawrence Erlbaum Associates.

Vygotsky, L. S. (1978). *Mind in society: The development of higher psychological processes.* Cambridge, MA: Harvard University Press.

Welker, R. (1991). Expertise and the teacher as expert: Rethinking a questionable metaphor. *American Educational Research Journal, 28*(1), 19–35.

Wineburg, S. S. (1991, April). *A case of pedagogical failure—My own.* Paper presented at the Annual Meeting of the American Educational Research Association, Chicago.

12   A Design Studio for Reflective Practice

Ann Weaver Hart

Students describe a ubiquitous and jarring disjunction when they move from formal academic study into the practice of administration in schools. Most find that they have no strategies or skills for applying what they know to what they do. New instructional methods for professional preparation in educational administration being designed often attempt to respond to these complaints. Cognitive psychology and traditions of experiential learning based on systematic reflection form the bases for many of these innovative instructional techniques (Kelsey, this volume; Wagner, this volume).

The need for these new approaches to defining and solving problems increases as society becomes more complex and the problems of schools multiply. Concurrently, the confidence society places in professionals appears to be waning as professionals come increasingly under scrutiny and criticism (Metzger, 1987; Schön, 1983). In order to improve student learning, accomplish school goals, and win the confidence of those who no longer trust the educated professional, administrators need problem-solving skills that enable them to apply knowledge from many sources to the actions they take in schools. One approach to improving the problem-solving and actions of professionals during pre-service education has come to be known as "reflective practice." Interest in the application of reflective practice to educational administration is growing, but specific programs in universities for nurturing the necessary skills during the formal education process are rare (Hart, 1990; Kerchner & King, this volume; Murphy, 1990; Ramsey & Whitman, 1989).

This chapter reports the ongoing systematic study of one such program that attempts to develop students' skills in reflective practice. The power and potential of reflection as the principle around which a pre-service seminar in educational administration could be organized is examined, along with the relative success of different elements of the seminar in producing desired outcomes. Modeled after the design studio proposed by Schön (1987), problem-based teaching in other professional fields (Ramsey & Whitman, 1989), and principles of experiential learning (Boud, Keogh, & Walker, 1985a), the seminar calls on expert practitioners to coach students through the process of thinking through, developing, and defending an action plan—from problem definition to action recommendations—as they confront a group of situations in a hypothetical school. This coaching process focuses on the problems of practice (problem-based) rather than on the traditional subjects around which educational administration programs customarily are built (subject-based). It differs from most case-study methods because it involves multiple cases or problems engaging the same actors in a single setting, adding a level of complexity and a need for integration to case-study problem-solving. The goal of the seminar is to nurture reflective practice in students as part of their formal course of study and move them toward accepting accountability for their actions as administrators as they move into the field.

PROBLEM-BASED REFLECTION

The use of research, theory, and experience to make professional decisions is difficult to teach, yet it substantially affects the quality of professional work (Hart, 1990; Ramsey & Whitman, 1989; Townsend, 1989). The idea that reflection can be used to turn experience into learning is not new (Boud et al., 1985b; Grundy, 1982; Jenks & Murphy, 1979). It draws on extensive work in cognitive psychology (Wagner, this volume; Yekovich, this volume), classical traditions of philosophy and thought about the thinking human being, learning and inquiry, and progressive philosophies of education (Dewey, 1933). A number of exploratory approaches to integrating reflection into the pre-service education of professionals recently have emerged. Problem-based, student-centered learning draws on these traditions to improve problem identification and enhance the creativity and appropriateness of actions. A focus on problem sets in complex professional settings rather than on traditional subject matter changes graduate professional preparation substantially. It transfers emphasis from subject-matter learning to constructions of knowledge tied to practice.

Educational administration is not alone or even a pioneer in this change of focus. Architecture, psychotherapy, medicine, counseling, engineering, dentistry, management, musical performance, business, and other professional training programs have applied the methods of reflection to preparation. Schön (1983, 1987) outlined numerous examples in which reflective practical experiences enhance professional skills or in which professional problems form the organizing foundation of study. Early results of these programs are promising. Researchers find that methods based on reflection about problems aimed at problem-solving produce content mastery equivalent to that achieved in rigorous subject-based instruction. They also produce superior application, transfer, and problem-solving in the field (Barrows, 1988; Bransford, 1979, 1984; Ramsey & Whitman, 1989; Shaw & Bransford, 1977).

The term *reflection* sometimes presents a barrier to understanding the nature of these educational programs because of its commonly accepted meanings. In systematic application to problem-solving, reflection is much more than quiet thinking over past events. It aims toward a goal—a set of solutions to dilemmas or problems or the redefining and understanding of "the problem," and it often takes place while actions are being taken. In pursuit of this goal, a person creates a sequence of ideas that project the possible consequences of a series of events (Dewey, 1933; Kolb, Rubin, & McIntyre, 1971). Schön (1983) went further, distinguishing between the reflection-in-action in which skilled professionals engage as simultaneous processes and the reflection-on-action that complements and solidifies professional learning.

Because a knowledge base is required in order to form accurate projections of the possible outcomes of a course of action, knowledge is a critical component of this process. Theory, research, and experience provide valuable sources of knowledge and include critical values and beliefs (Hart, 1990; Leithwood, Begley, & Cousins, 1992). The linkage between knowledge and potential outcomes—the progression of thought that links complex parts of the whole toward possible outcomes—can lead to increased complexity, creativity, and surprise as new ideas emerge and actions lead to desired and productive conclusions. What has been tacit becomes increasingly explicit and, therefore, more deliberate and amenable to modification. At the same time, reflection toward action is a complex process that requires practice and involves skills different from those required for knowledge acquisition alone. The major benefits appear to be increased creativity and imagination and the ability to move from theory to practice and back again with ease. As Mills asserted:

> Every self-conscious thinker must at all times be aware of—and hence be able to control—the levels of abstraction on which he is working. The capacity to shuttle between levels of abstraction, with ease and with clarity, is a signal mark of the imaginative and systematic thinker (Mills, 1959, p. 34).

Reflection also provides a model for learning based solely on experience. Boud et al. (1985a) proposed a staged model of experiential learning based on reflection. They concentrated on the sort of reflection Schön would label reflection-on-action. Three major stages in this model include:

1. Returning to experience
2. Attending to feelings
3. Reevaluating the experience.

The advantages of these stages apply to structured reflection on case studies and vicarious experience as well as personal experience. First, by systematically noting or telling the essential features of the experience (returning to the experience), the learner can focus on what is happening, tell the experience to others, and try to remain nonjudgmental. Second, attending to feelings provides the opportunity to prevent vicarious or projected emotions from becoming barriers to learning. Third, reevaluating the circumstances of a problem situation prevents quickly reached conclusions from obscuring important issues:

> It is easy to jump from the initial experience to evaluation, and judgments are often a part of the original experience. [By doing this we] can potentially lose a great deal of value. We may find ourselves operating on false assumptions or reflecting on information which we have not comprehended sufficiently. (Boud et al., 1985a, p. 30)

Four processes are critical to quality reflection in this model:

> *Association* (relating new information to what is already known)
> *Integration* (seeking relationships among the data)
> *Validation* (determining the authenticity of values, ideas, and feelings)
> *Appropriation* (acquisition and integration of the new knowledge).

This notion of reflective practice to enhance experiential learning capitalizes on the logic of deliberate, conscious thought as a way to improve the quality and quantity of learning that results.

Experiential learning offers one view of reflection as a tool for improving professional education for administration in schools. Cognition theory provides another—explaining how reflection improves application, transfer, and problem-solving by hypothesizing that, through the use of mental advanced organizers or schemata, people form initial perceptions and judgments of new events (Prestine, in press). Patterns of concepts and associations held within the mind as a framework for the formation of expectations shape initial responses. People use these schemata to interpret new, related information (Thorndyke & Hayes-Roth, 1979). They also help people process and transfer knowledge from one situation to another (Luiten, Ames, & Ackerson, 1980), and deliberately structured reflection expands skill in systematically recognizing similar patterns in unique events (Bransford, 1979, 1984; Shaw & Bransford, 1977; Simon, in press).

BACKGROUND

These bodies of theory and research affirm the usefulness of reflective processes as tools for improving the transfer and application of knowledge. By integrating reflective processes in professional education, universities can affect not only the present abilities of students to apply their newly acquired knowledge but the quality of future reflection and action as skill and knowledge increase. This occurs in three ways. First, as learning is assisted and inappropriate inferences and judgments are reduced, skill improves. Second, as knowledge increases and a person learns to draw associations between past problems and common features in newly encountered situations, the ability to draw appropriate inferences improves (Nickolson & Imlack, 1981; Pearson, Hansen, & Gordon, 1979). Difficult problems even accelerate the learning process when successfully dealt with. This occurs because relevant deviations from habitual behavior create vivid memories (Bower, Black, & Turner, 1979), which then become resources for future reflection and action. A strong relationship between action and memory then is established. Practical problems become the focus of the process and evaluative judgments part of the process of problem-solving, for "To detect practical problems is to make evaluations" (Mills, 1959, p. 90). Intransigent problems and surprises that challenge existing schemata bring with them an important addition to the quality of reflection. As Schön pointed out:

> When the phenomenon at hand eludes the ordinary categories of knowledge-in-practice, presenting itself as unique or unstable, the practitioner may surface and criticize his initial understanding of the phenomenon, construct a new description of it, and test the new description by an on-the-spot experiment. (1983, pp. 62–63)

Each new set of observed outcomes results in some adjustments in a schema that will, in turn, be applied the next time an event with similar (and some unique) characteristics occurs.

Another positive impact on professional practice of the skill and knowledge acquired during reflection is an increase in awareness and sensitivity to one's own thinking and values. This awareness makes self-consciousness and improved thinking more likely. At a more conscious level, reflective thinking replicates the processes Mead (1934) proposed to explain the interactions between people using symbols of word and gesture. It requires self-awareness, a way of processing information from the environment *and* about oneself—in a sense, observing oneself respond. Using the analogy of an experimenter studying the psychology of stimulus-response while conditioning a rat, Morris (in Mead, 1934) argues that, by understanding reflection in this way, we are able to explain both the conditioning of the rat and the behavior of the scientist conducting the experiment. By extending this analogy, one can see how the scientist comes also to understand his or her own behavior. In a professional school setting, educators can provide students with a way of analyzing and understanding not only the responses and events they observe in their professional practice, but also their own experiences, responses, and adjustments in behavior, knowledge, and understanding.

Action and altered understanding are the desired outcomes of skilled reflection. Action follows after reflection occurs; adjustments to existing conceptions, knowledge, and beliefs are made; and inferences are drawn. When these steps are taken, the act is integrated with knowledge and thought. Outcomes of action may lead to further adjustments in existing cognitive and value structures. Continuous repetitions of this process throughout a professional career lead to development as a reflective practitioner. As each new cycle of reflective practice occurs, the habit and orientation of reflection become more firmly established, and speed of reflection under the press for immediate action increases. Schön (1987) asserted that expert professionals become so adept at this process that they have difficulty retracing their own cognitive processes to explain their reasoning to students. During pre-service education, however, students need deliberate practice with reflection; speed and quality of reflection under pressure for action take time and practice to develop. In summary, the logic supporting efforts to improve proficiency in using reflective processes in professional education is supported by theory and research. Experiential learning theory provides a model for structuring a return to practice and reconceptualization through reflection. Cognition theory and social psychology provide explanations for its utility. Research comparing the application of professional knowledge by practitioners who have been educated using traditional subject-based methods that focus on the instructor with those who have been educated using more problem-based, student-focused methods provide evidence of its success. In educational administration, it remains to be seen how these principles play out in practice. The remainder of this chapter reports some outcomes of two years of work on a seminar designed to build the habit, orientation, and skills of reflection in educational administration students. In the following sections the components of the seminar, its operation, and emerging outcomes are discussed.

COMPONENTS OF THE DESIGN STUDIO (REFLECTION SEMINAR)

A seminar applying knowledge to action in the principalship was developed at the University of Utah to attempt an application of the principles of problem-based learning discussed above. Components of the seminar include:

1. Problem-based stimulus materials for students
2. Professional coaches
3. Theoretical and empirical resources (a common knowledge base)

4. Student action plans (written)
5. A panel of professors, superintendents, and principals who review written plans and oral arguments, question students, and prepare systematic feedback and assessment.

Stimulus Materials

Stimulus materials were written by a faculty member and a graduate student and are continually revised each year. The first set of materials drew on a core of case problems, some of which were collected and written by students over a four-year period in a seminar on the principalship, some of which were previously published cases, and some of which were faculty and graduate student experiences. Coaches for the first seminar session read and revised the materials. Subsequent revisions reflect the feedback of students and of participating administrators who identify major issues currently of interest in nearby school districts. After the second year, seminar stimulus materials were again revised. This time, the secondary school student-discipline problem included a structure for high school student control popular in the region—citizenship credit for graduation and denial of diploma for insufficient credits. Subsequent revisions as school problems evolve can be made on an ongoing basis. A major goal of these ongoing revisions is to balance the need to make the seminar manageable for students while exerting some of the diffuse pressure that characterizes administrative work.

Each group of stimulus materials creates a hypothetical set of issues occurring concurrently within a single school and provides the students with background information about the school. Two sets of materials are used—one for elementary school and one for secondary school. Students choose to work from either the elementary or secondary school materials. The dilemmas raise issues that can be analyzed using the knowledge base provided by courses and seminars in administration and leadership, philosophy and foundations, policy, personnel, finance, law, curriculum, and instruction. While drawn from real field experiences, the cases are fictionalized in order to better represent the range and depth of the problems associated with schools and to refer students to the subject-based administration curriculum they have studied during their preparation (Ramsey & Whitman, 1989).

Professional Coaches

Coaches are selected from adjunct and clinical faculty of the department of educational administration who are practicing school administrators and respected school leaders. At present, the choice of coaches is largely based on convenience. They are professionals whose quality of teaching and presentation is known, and who are willing to coach as a service to the university, since no funds are available to pay them. The number of coaches varies, depending on the number of students. Every attempt is made to retain a ratio of no more than two students per coach in each session. The seminar instructor also coaches.

In the first year of the seminar, the six coaches included one male and two female elementary principals, one female junior high assistant principal, one male junior high principal, and one male high school principal. All were Anglo-American. In the second year, eleven coaches participated—seven women and four men. While the coaches again represented all levels of administration, all but one, a Native American woman, were Anglos. Coaches meet prior to the sessions for orientation and training in reflective questioning, coaching, and problem-solving techniques.

Resources

The selection of a knowledge base for which participants (students and coaches) are accountable presents some challenge at this stage in the development of the seminar. A full problem-based course of study would move systematically through problems designed to send students to a curriculum and resource materials assuring subject mastery. At this stage, this careful control is not possible. Because students are enrolled in the seminar in place of a course on the principalship, no prerequisites were in place at the time of the studies, nor was the seminar well integrated into the subject-based curriculum of the masters and certification programs. While most of the students had completed most of their course work for a masters degree in educational administration or a post-masters administrative certificate, a substantial minority (about 40 percent) in each of the two years had taken only a few courses in administration. Two basic texts thus were assigned for the first two seminar sessions (Bolman & Deal, 1984; Duke, 1987). These books are presented as neither the only nor the primary sources on which students should depend as they develop rationales for their action plans. This situation has since been rectified. The department requires that the students take the seminar at the end of their administrative preparation programs.

The readings and the course of study in place at the university influence the structural and intellectual resources available to students. The University of Utah presents a course-driven certification and masters degree program in educational administration. But educational administration courses are by no means the only sources of professional knowledge on which students draw. At the university, students confront alternative and critical perspectives on schools and schooling through the history, philosophy, and foundations courses they take, and several students in each seminar have chosen to apply critical paradigms to their action plans and analyses. Students also bring with them varied experiences, perspectives, and academic backgrounds on which they draw (e.g., a high school art teacher, a fundamentalist religious school educator, an elementary teacher, a retired military officer, an administrative intern, a private school principal).

The format of the seminar allows for considerable flexibility in the application of paradigms and guiding philosophies to problem-solving and professional action. The goal is to confront the effects of reflection on frames of reality, interpretations of social life, and power. Kemmis provides a powerful rationale for this goal: "Reflection is a political act, which either hastens or defers the realization of a more rational, just and fulfilling society" (1985, p. 140). He bases this contention on the action-oriented and historically embedded nature of reflection; its use of language and roots in social processes; the embedded human interests it reveals; the ideologies people apply during reflection; the reframing of social life through communication, decision-making, and social action that reflection represents; the interactive nature of the "double dialectic of thought and action, the individual and society"; and the necessity to critique ideology during reflection (Kemmis, 1985, p. 140).

Process

Because the design studio occurs at a university that is on the quarter system, seminar activities cover a 10-week period. During the first 4 weeks of the seminar, students systematize their notes and readings from previous courses, preparing a personal knowledge base of sorts, and complete the core assigned readings. Students keep a weekly reflection journal in which they record and respond to ideas as they confront them and project possible relationships these ideas have with their work in schools. During the next 4 weeks students meet for one and a half hours with coaches in reflective questioning sessions designed to help them make plans for action on the stimulus materials. Coaches rotate among students during the coaching sessions so that each coach and each student will interact. During the first year of the seminar, rotations were held one-on-one while students not paired with a coach during interim periods gathered their notes, thoughts, and questions for subsequent rotations. The six coaches each attended two sessions, while the instructor/coach attended all four sessions. Due to the coaches' time constraints, it was not possible for all the coaches to attend every session. The rotation did, however, provide each student with multiple coaching experiences. In the second year, coaches again rotated. Students also requested a modification of the one-on-one format that matched coaches with two students at a time and in small groups. During the second year, students chose to hold some of the coaching sessions in groups of three—two students and one coach.

Following the one and a half hours of coaching, the instructor(s) meets with the students for one and a half hours of debriefing. During these sessions, the students reflect on their ideas, values, and new knowledge sources—a student version of reflection-on-action (Schön, 1983). The purpose of this activity is to have the students describe their experience and how they thought about their action plans during the coaching sessions. They engage in the four deliberate processes of association, integration, validation, and appropriation that assist them in using the experience for learning. The goal is to make them more skillful at asking questions, seeking relevant information, defining problems, and selecting alternatives for action. The functions of debriefing in structured reflection experiences are fourfold:

1. To articulate what is being learned
2. To evaluate the experience
3. To contribute to group cohesion and identity
4. To summarize what has been achieved to that point. (Pearson & Smith, 1985)

The merits of this activity become apparent as students begin to connect what they are doing with different understandings of the problems or invent better solutions for them. During the debriefing sessions, students also talk about process issues and address general questions about the reflective process, such as:

1. What are the most helpful forms of questions from coaches?
2. How do you feel about the session?
3. What are possible formats for the action plans?
4. What might you expect during the presentations and final evaluations?

These debriefing sessions help the students and the coaches. Students solidify and grasp the process more fully, and information about the most useful questioning techniques being used is fed back to the coaches prior to the next session. During the first year, students formed study groups to work together on action options. During the second year, students asked for a practice session in which they could present their action plans prior to their presentations to the review panel, as well as group coaching sessions for some of the time.

Action Plans

Each student prepares a written action plan. The students participated in the design of the action-plan format and evaluation criteria. The plans included:

1. A philosophy or vision statement that includes a description of the hypothetical school under their leadership

2. Specific action recommendations for each of the five dilemmas in the stimulus materials
3. An overall plan for the school that unifies the action plan for the school.

Written plans include specific references to empirical and theoretical knowledge acquired during formal studies (in this or any other course), individual experiences and coaches' feedback, and exemplary practice. Action plans are submitted to a panel of two professors, one superintendent, and one principal. Panel members independently read and evaluate these plans. The rationale for requiring an action plan is simple:

> [The] benefits of reflection may be lost if they are not linked to action. Although some of the outcomes are long term and often intangible . . . others are more prosaic and can be consolidated by application. Application and action need not necessarily involve acts which can be observed by others. What is important is that the learner *makes a commitment of some kind on the basis of his or her learning.* What has been rehearsed must face the test of reality. Action ends the reflective process for the time being. (Boud et al., 1985a, p. 35, emphasis added)

After reading and evaluating the plans, the panel sits as a review board for oral presentations. Panel members question students about their recommendations, rationale, and supporting evidence during these presentations, which are made at the end of the academic quarter. The second year the design studio operated, the students used part of a coaching session to practice for their presentations. (This activity improved neither the reasoning and rationales for their chosen actions nor the quality of their presentations. This outcome may be related to the increased pressure students were able to exert on coaches to give solutions in answer to their questions and suggests that the coaches need much more training and practice in questioning and coaching techniques. The coaches affirmed this conclusion in the second-year exit interviews.) The panel members and instructor provide written feedback to students in addition to the feedback provided during the oral presentation and defense.

REFLECTIONS ON THE DESIGN STUDIO

Coaches

In exit interviews, coaches were asked a series of questions:

- Could you give me a general reaction to your experience with the seminar as part of an educational administration program?

- What direction did your questioning seem to take most comfortably?
- What kind of questions yielded the best responses from students in your assessment?
- What would you say might be the major advantages and disadvantages of an approach such as the seminar in educational administration programs?
- What changes would you recommend?
- What did you like most and least about the stimulus materials? Would you recommend any changes?

Students were asked parallel questions with minor wording adjustments that referred to student experiences. With reassuring frequency, they identified the same advantages and disadvantages to the reflective, problem-based approach as did the coaches.

Overall, coaches reacted positively to the seminar experience, calling it a "unique approach to training." They were "very enthusiastic" and "very positive," and saw it as "very practical" and a "great opportunity to blend theory with the practical." Coaches agreed that its major advantage might be in the way the process "challenges preconceived ideas." Coaches also identified a number of problems. They pointed out that the stimulus materials combined with initial readings presented students with an "overwhelming amount of material," that "students seemed overwhelmed." They also cautioned that practice changes (if only the "hot" topics) and stimulus materials need to change accordingly. Early on, coaches asserted, the students learn that "I don't even know what I don't know."

Coaches who were most effective (according to student reports) argued that they took their cues for questioning from the students and "always had to come back to looking at the full picture," asking "how does this fit into the plan of the school—the holistic approach." They "tried to get students to see implications," to "look at what they would need to check out." Others reported that they felt "pressure from students to answer questions." These coaches also tended to ask more cryptic questions like "Why?" or "Where would you look for that information?" It was hard for coaches to refrain from elaborating, providing insight they had gained from their experience, giving answers by describing others' solutions to similar problems before students had even properly or creatively "defined" the problem.

When asked what kinds of questions yielded the "best" responses, coaches identified questions that directed students toward problem solving. They said: "What if?" "Have you thought about . . . ?" "Where would you find this information?" "How would you feel if . . . ?" They also referred to the need to look at the "whole perspective" and force students "to look at their own philosophies and beliefs." They felt that they needed to remind students to "look at facts." Coaches argued persuasively that their own thinking about practice was changed by these questions. They said, "I believe that [we] are really on to something here . . . something that can change the way we think about practice." They also pressed students to defend their searches for information and project possible outcomes. "Why do you really want to know that?" "If you were to select that [option], what might be a negative outcome?"

Coaches concentrated on high-quality outcomes and high costs when talking about the advantages and disadvantages of the seminar. For both students and coaches, they argued, the format places new time pressures; cognitive overload sometimes results from the complexity of its demands. The advantages coaches saw centered in "the mix of theory and textbook with the practical" under the guidance of the coaches, its "hands-on, experiential" nature, the variety of "mentors" the coaches represented and their varied perspectives, and the personal interaction between coaches and students and among the coaches. One coach said he thought that the exchanges among coaches during their conferences and debriefings were as beneficial to them as the interactions among coaches and students were to the students. Many coaches agreed that the structure "allows the opportunity to practice decisions and justify them without getting into trouble." While some coaches criticized the "overwhelming" complexity of the materials and time restrictions, they said that the seminar failed to simulate the press of administration—the time frame under which decisions must be made in administrative work and multiple actions taken under pressure. One contended that "students don't feel the time pressure" and the seminar is "not real life."

Students

Students also held strong opinions about the studio experience. They said that coaches helped students most "when they tried to get me away from my tunnel vision," when the students made the effort to bring more ideas with them to sessions, and when they searched for knowledge. One said, "The more ideas I had, the more they gave me," while another pointed out, "Questioning was more helpful as I did more reading." Students thought that questions that forced them to "go broader" in early sessions and "narrow down" in the last sessions helped them the most. They also admitted that "at first, questioning was hard to deal with." They liked "what if" and "what about" questions and praised coaches who responded to their conclusions by asking, "If you did this, can you see that this might be a problem?" in later sessions.

Students most liked the realism, high interest, and challenge of confronting school issues. They least liked the complexity of overlapping problems and the pressure to produce and defend an action plan. They felt they lacked skills for linking research and theory to their action plans. The changes recommended by students illustrate the tension between the need to create a manageable problem and the need for enough complexity to convey some semblance of real pressure. Students wanted some time to work (perhaps a two-week break in the middle) without interacting with coaches so they could have more plans to present. They also would have liked a more lengthy presentation and defense time for the action plans. All these requests place additional pressure on the time frame of an academic schedule. Like the coaches, students generally agreed that the design studio should follow the completion of the majority of course work and precede the internship. Students made such statements as "I liked the intuition"; "I like it because we sort of participated in creating the class"; "The administrators and students together offer a lot."

Some general observations can be drawn from field notes of the coaches and students interacting. First, a small proportion of the talk between coaches and students was casual—getting acquainted, sharing job information—or directed toward the process. While too much small talk or storytelling by coaches was dysfunctional, stories also served an interpretive role. They helped established a personal tone but could deteriorate into directives. Most students failed to recognize the difference, and the students who were most likely to initiate or sustain casual talk during sessions also received less positive feedback from the review panel and lower ratings on their action plans at the conclusion of the studios. These students were less focused on problem identification and action-plan development throughout the weeks of coaching, and the quality of their action plans reflected their lack of focus.

Second, task interactions illustrate important features of studio learning. Coaches found it easier to avoid giving one answer to students' direct questions in one-on-one interactions than in group sessions. When coaches told students what to do, interaction sometimes ground to a halt. Coaches challenged students to defend their decisions, to seek information, to question whether a stimulus dilemma really was a problem, to project. By their own account, coaches found questioning toward problem analysis and knowledge application more difficult to do than offering direct suggestions. They recognized a need for training in the coaching process itself.

Students' problem-solving errors were most apparent in their action plans. Pseudodiagnosticity appeared as digressions from parsimonious solutions and elaborate action recommendations only tangentially related to core issues. Incorrect synthesis appeared as simplification, often as students announced an intended action in the first coaching session and retained it through to the final plan. The failure to adequately synthesize or reach warranted conclusions often emerged in verbose explanations and justifications, in tentative conclusions, or in plans that tied totally unrelated issues (e.g., children's safety and teachers' conditions of work contracts) tightly together. Finally, premature closure and selective inattending or anchoring were the most common problem-solving errors and often went hand-in-hand. One student said in the first session, "I don't see what the problem is," and she never did. Once students formed "theories" about what was going on, they ignored contradictory information.

SUMMARY AND CONCLUSIONS

Following the conclusion of two design studio experiences, some general conclusions and projections for the future are possible. First, all coaches require training and practice in reflective and inductive questioning, in the development of questions that provide options when they recognize the students are in danger of making problem-solving errors, and in problem-solving techniques in general. In order to help students define problems, assess what they know, project possible actions and probable outcomes of each, and select a course of action, coaches need to be personally adept in their profession and knowledgeable about cognitive processes on which the seminar depends. Consequently, it might be necessary for a partnership in which a group of coaches develops the knowledge and skills that facilitate the process and then rotates. Over time, a human resource comprised of knowledgeable and committed practitioner-coaches to the seminar could be developed.

This high demand on people's time might be alleviated by the use of technology as well. Programs based on interactive video disk, computer programs that require problem-solving, and other innovations that require high up-front investment but use fewer human resources hold promise. However, the personal interactions between coaches and students provided a signature feature of the seminar frequently praised by participants and should not be lost.

Second, more careful research on the gradual shift in questions and focus by coaches as the students move through the problem-solving process is needed. The data reveal that coaches whom students found most helpful changed their approach from the first to the last sessions when students were in different stages in the process. Productive questioning techniques at the beginning of problem definition differ from the most effective techniques near closure. Questions that stimulate divergent thinking and highlight that students "do not know what they do not know" stimulate quick engagement and increase search for knowledge at the early problem-solving stages. Questions that help students reach closure by eliminating options and explaining rationales lead to more singular and concrete action plans toward the end of the seminar experience. Yet much more systematic knowledge about possible question structures and diagnosis of students' readiness to move forward is needed.

A third conclusion involves the structure and stage in a preparation program of such a design studio or reflective problem-solving seminar. While students argued that they need problem-solving and problem-based instruction earlier in their formal course of study, students with little formal knowledge have difficulty finding resources other than the experiences of others. The subject-based study of the foundation readings completed in four weeks left students reeling with too much too fast and reporting significant cognitive over-load. I believe that the design studio itself should be free of an explicit subject-based curriculum and students should be free to focus on problem-solving and the application of previously acquired knowledge to that process. This may re-quire that programs in educational administration include more deliberate in-struction and structured experience in problem-solving centered around ad-ministrative action per se throughout a program. It would require a great deal more coordination among courses and planning among professors than is now the case.

Fourth, good stimulus materials require continuous revision, careful plan-ning, and deliberate thought. A simple compilation of real experiences from the field is insufficient. Depending on the stage of a program of study and the learn-ing goals of the course or field experience, a problem-based teaching case may need to be more or less complex and interactive, point students directly toward different reference materials or knowledge bases, and raise dilemmas of varying familiarity. This need could be met by systematically collecting vivid cases aris-ing from professional practice as part of the knowledge base (Osterman, 1989) and by developing cases designed to teach specific subjects as part of the formal curriculum for the professional school. Additionally, some features of the stimu-lus material need to be very current and locally salient.

Fifth, coaches and students need more systematic exposure to the skills and processes of problem-solving and priming to alert them to potential problem-solving errors. The data from the studio suggest a conclusion that, as organized, it provided insufficient time and training in the problem-solving, cognition, and thinking processes themselves. By replacing the subject-based activities with problem-solving activities, this shortcoming might be eliminated (Kelsey, this volume).

Sixth, while group interactions relieve pressure on coaches and students, they may lead to increases in student problem-solving errors and to coaches' answer-giving. If the goal of reflective seminars is to improve students' ability to reflect on knowledge and use this reflection to construct appropriate profes-sional interventions and actions, comfort may be a dysfunctional aspect of the studio. More training for coaches in productive questioning and more aware-ness on the part of students about the common problem-solving errors against which they must be on guard may alleviate this problem. More development of deliberate group and individual strategies at different stages in the seminar also would be productive.

Experience with a design studio leads to the conclusion that systematic seminars, "studios," and courses that focus on the processes and skills of problem-solving hold potential for refocusing graduate education in educational administration from subject-based courses to the problems of practice. Knowledge from many sources (much of it found in the content of subject-based courses) can be drawn on as part of the application of knowledge to action, providing a basis on which students can reflect and project possible outcomes. While much refining and reorganization lie ahead and the implications of technology for expanding the use of these techniques remain largely unexamined, these preliminary results suggest that many realistic changes can be made in professional preparation that will enhance parallel attempts to improve professional practice.

REFERENCES

Barrows, H. S. (1988). *The tutorial process.* Springfield: The Southern Illinois University School of Medicine.

Bolman, L. G., & Deal, T. E. (1984). *Modern approaches to understanding and managing organizations.* San Francisco: Jossey-Bass.

Boud, D., Keogh, R., & Walker, D. (1985a). Promoting reflection in learning: A model. In D. Boud, R. Keogh, & D. Walker (Eds.), *Reflection: Turning experience into learning* (pp. 18–40). New York: Nichols Publishing Company.

Boud, D., Keogh, R., & Walker, D. (1985b). What is reflection in learning? In D. Boud, R. Keogh, & D. Walker (Eds.), *Reflection: Turning experience into learning* (pp. 7–17). New York: Nichols Publishing Company.

Bower, G. H., Black, J. B., & Turner, T. J. (1979). Scripts in memory for text. *Cognitive Psychology, 11,* 177–220.

Bransford, J. (1979). *Human cognition: Learning, understanding, and remembering.* Belmont, CA: Wadsworth Publishing.

Bransford, J. (1984). *The ideal problem solver: A guide for improving thinking, learning, and creativity.* New York: Freeman.

Dewey, J. (1933). *How we think.* Chicago: Henry Regnery Company.

Duke, D. (1987). *School leadership and instructional improvement.* New York: Random House.

Grundy, S. (1982). Three modes of action research. *Curriculum Perspectives, 2*(3), 23–34.

Hart, A. W. (1990). Effective administration through reflective practice. *Education and Urban Society, 22,* 153–169.

Jenks, C. L., & Murphy, C. J. (1979). *Experience-based learning and the facilitative role of the teacher.* San Francisco: Far West Laboratory for Educational Research and Development.

Kemmis, S. (1985). Action research and the politics of reflection. In D. Boud, R. Keogh, & D. Walker (Eds.), *Reflection: Turning experience into learning* (pp. 139–163). New York: Nichols Publishing Company.

Kolb, D. A., Rubin, I., & McIntyre, J. (1971). *Organizational psychology: An experiential approach.* Englewood Cliffs, NJ: Prentice-Hall.

Leithwood, K. A., Begley, P., & Cousins, B. (1992). *Developing expert leadership for future schools.* New York: Falmer Press.

Luiten, J., Ames, W. S., & Ackerson, G. (1980). A meta-analysis of the effects of advance organizers on learning and retention. *American Educational Research Journal, 17,* 211–218.

Mead, G. H. (1934). *Mind, self, and society: From the standpoint of a social behaviorist.* Edited and with an introduction by Charles W. Morris. Chicago: University of Chicago Press.

Metzger, H. (1987, August-September). The spectre of "professionalism." *Educational Researcher, 16*(6), 10–19.

Mills, C. W. (1959). *The sociological imagination.* New York: Oxford University Press.

Murphy, J. (1990). Restructuring the technical core of preparation programs in educational administration. *UCEA Review, 31,* 4–5, 10–13.

Nickolson, T., & Imlack, R. (1981). Where do their answers come from? A study of the inferences which children make when answering questions about narrative stories. *Journal of Reading Behavior, 13,* 111–129.

Osterman, K. F. (1989). *Building a knowledge base from experience: An analysis of administrative problem-solving strategies.* Paper presented at the annual meeting of the University Council for Educational Administration, Phoenix, AZ.

Pearson, M., & Smith, D. (1985). Debriefing in experience-based learning. In D. Boud, R. Keogh, & D. Walker (Eds.), *Reflection: Turning experience into learning* (pp. 69–84). New York: Nichols Publishing Company.

Pearson, P. D., Hansen, J., & Gordon, C. (1979). The effect of background knowledge on young children's comprehension of explicit and implicit information. *Journal of Reading Behavior, 11,* 201–209.

Prestine, N. (in press). Cognitive learning theory and the preparation of educational administrators: Some implications. *Educational Administration Quarterly.*

Ramsey, R., & Whitman, N. (1989). *A problem-based, student-centered approach to teaching geriatrics in the classroom: Guidelines and sample cases.* Cleveland: The Western Reserve Geriatric Education Center.

Schön, D. A. (1983). *The reflective practitioner.* New York: Basic Books.

Schön, D. A. (1987). *Educating the reflective practitioner.* San Francisco: Jossey-Bass.

Shaw, R., & Bransford, J. (1977). *Perceiving, acting, and knowing: Toward an ecological perspective.* Hillsdale, NJ: Lawrence Erlbaum Associates.

Simon, H. A. (in press). Decision making: Rational, non-rational, and irrational. *Educational Administration Quarterly.*

Thorndyke, P. W., & Hayes-Roth, B. (1979). The use of schemata in the acquisition and transfer of knowledge. *Cognitive Psychology, 11,* 83–106.

Townsend, R. G. (1989). Cunning and integrity: One way to teach administrators about policy deliberation. *Journal of Educational Administration and Foundations, 4,* 19–25.

13   Learning from Teaching: Problems, Problem-Formulation, and the Enhancement of Problem-Solving Capability

J. G. T. Kelsey

This chapter is about my experience in teaching a course on problem-solving. EADM 502 ("Problem Analysis and Formulation Skills for Administrators") was created in 1987 as a core course in the M.Ed. program in educational administration at the University of British Columbia and its purpose is to help students develop competencies that will make them better problem-solvers. In this account I am drawing on my experience with 97 students (mid-career educators) in five sessions—the summers of 1988, 1989, 1990, and 1991, and the winter of 1990–1991. My data consist of my own plans, notes, and observations; entries in student journals; student ratings of success in alleviating a particular problem at the end of each course; and the results of a survey of some students after their return to work following the course.

I explain first the origins of the course and the concept of problem-formulation on which it is based. In the second section, I deal with my approach to teaching it, and in the third section I describe what seems to happen as students learn about problem-formulation. The chapter concludes with some observations on how reasonably experienced educators appear to approach problems, on what activities seem to help them become better problem-solvers, and on how my own understanding of both problem-formulation and the teaching of it has been affected by the experience of providing this account.

THE ORIGINS OF THE COURSE AND THE CONCEPTS OF PROBLEM AND PROBLEM-FORMULATION

The course has its origins in the experience of a professor in the department who returned for a year to a school principalship and was thereby led to propose changes in administrator preparation programs (Hills, 1975). One of the proposals was that heavy emphasis should be placed on the development of critical-analytical and problem-solving skills. On his return to the university, Hills continued to refine his ideas. Dissatisfaction with the term "critical-analytical skills" and a sense that "problem-solving" was dependent on a prior set of cognitive activities led him eventually to speak of the skills of problem analysis and formulation. Hills has developed the ideas in a number of papers (Hills, 1987, 1991; Hills & Gibson, 1988a, 1988b, 1990), and my exposition of them here is a simplified overview of the key arguments.

Hills challenges two assumptions of a classical, "technical-rational" view of problem-solving: (1) that the problem as initially identified is the problem to be solved, and (2) that it provides a satisfactory basis on which to begin identifying solutions. His observations (1975) of unproductive administrator behaviors led him to reject these assumptions. He argues that what is usually called our initial identification of a problem is better described as our initial *formulation* of a problem and that its analysis can lead to a *reformulation* with important consequences for the subsequent generation of possible solutions.

Problem-formulation, however, is a complex activity that usually operates below the level of awareness, and Hills argues, drawing on Bruner (1964), Vygotsky (1962), and Luhmann (1982), that unless we understand what we are doing when we perform any given activity, we are not able to think productively about, or change, that activity. In a catchy phrase, he says that it is very important to know what we do when we do what we do. Knowing what we do when we do what we do is made possible by our ability to classify phenomena in a hierarchical fashion, and hence to see any action as a special case of a more general class of actions, thereby acquiring an increased understanding of it. Hills quotes Vygotsky:

> As long as [one] operates within the decimal system without having become conscious of it as such, he has not mastered it, but is, on the contrary, bound to it. When he becomes able to view it as a particular instance of the wider concept of a scale of notation, he can operate deliberately with this or any other numerical system. (1962, p. 115)

Applying Vygotsky's illustration to the present case, we might ask, "Of what general case is problem-formulation a particular instance?" The answer to this question can best be understood in the light of two propositions (adapted from Hills & Gibson, 1988a):

1. Problems are not objective states of the world on which all observers will agree; they are discrepancies between what some observer perceives and what that same observer considers desirable. (That is to say,

we do not "find" or "encounter" problems; we create or formulate them by imposing values, norms, and desires on perceived situations.)

2. Perception is not one act, but a process in which sensory information from the environment is decoded and made meaningful through concepts learned as we develop. (Concepts, that is to say, are mechanisms for the selection, exclusion, and classification of information.)

In the light of these propositions, the answer to the question "Of what general case is problem-formulation a particular instance?" is that it is a particular instance of decoding and evaluating information received in a given situation. To speak of improving problem-formulation is, therefore, to speak of getting better at either or both of these two activities (decoding and evaluating). Consequently, we can identify four activities that should help people to improve their ability to assess their initial problem-formulations and to explore the possibility of reformulating them productively (adapted from Hills & Gibson, 1988a):

- Develop increased consciousness of the concepts we have used in decoding (giving meaning to) a particular situation
- Acquire and make conscious use of alternative concepts
- Develop increased consciousness of our conceptions of the desired and the desirable in relation to any particular situation
- Increase our capacity to examine critically our conceptions of the desired and the desirable and entertain alternatives.

Hills has argued that certain techniques help in one way or another in carrying out these four activities. They are *specification, categorization, dimensional analysis, situational analysis,* and *special case analysis* (Hills & Gibson, 1988a). Hills has recently (1991) come to use the term *special case analysis* to encompass combinations of these activities. For each technique, he suggests a particular question or form of words as an operator: to *specify,* for example, one might ask, "What basis do I have for saying that?"; to *categorize,* one asks "What kind of problem is that?"; and so on. Although Hills does not say so, there is a sense in which these are all variations on the same basic technique, that of making as explicit as possible the conceptual framework one has used in understanding any phenomenon, event, or situation. This is, in effect, his special case analysis and its most useful operator is the question "Of what general case is this a special case?"

The use of techniques, of course, is mechanical and is not liberating unless one understands what it is that one is doing in applying each technique. Thus we come full circle and need to recognize each technique as a special case of clarifying the meanings and evaluations given to particular situations and extending the range of meanings and evaluations that might be given to them. Another way of saying this is to say that the techniques need to be applied wittingly or, as Hills and Gibson (1988b, p. 163) put it, "reflexively."[1] It is this aspect of the approach that makes the teaching of EADM 502 at once challenging and rewarding.

TEACHING PROBLEM-FORMULATION

EADM 502 is by design a skill-development course, but what especially attracted me to teaching it was that it seemed like an invitation to have fun—I was easily able to interpret Hills' approach as an attempt to broaden students' thinking and to help them be creative. The nature of the course as a skill-development course and this invitation to have fun underlay my decisions about the way it should be designed and delivered. In the following pages I describe first the decisions about content and sequence and second the strategies that guided my choice of instructional activities and some of the activities themselves.

Content and Sequence

The four objectives I specified for the course are as follows:
Students who complete the course will

- Have acquired an understanding of the conceptual bases on which problem-reformulation rests
- Have become familiar with a number of techniques for the reformulation of problems and the enlargement of their thinking about any given problem
- Have acquired through practice some facility in the identification of appropriate techniques and their use
- Have had the opportunity to think through in detail at least one problem of relevance to their own work situation.

To achieve these objectives, the ideas put forward by Hills would constitute a major part of the content of the course. In 1988 they were available in the form of the 206-page manuscript by Hills and Gibson (1988a). Some of the literature in cognitive psychology as it related to problem-solving, creativity, and the differences between novices and experts also seemed relevant, and conversations with Hills confirmed that he thought so too. At his recommendation, I adopted a straightforward text by Kahney (1986). This text is particularly help-

ful for a number of ideas: the distinction between well-defined and ill-defined problems,[2] the idea that problems' underlying structures are often masked by surface features, various conceptualizations of the process of problem-solving, explorations of the role of analogy in problem-solving, and a summary of much of the work to 1986 on the differences between novices and experts.

These two kinds of content covered the ideas to be taught, but they did not provide one particular kind of content necessary for a skill-development course. Skills can be developed only in doing something. There needed to be what some have called "domain-specific content." Two possibilities for providing such content were cases and simulations. Both were available in the department, but both were used in other courses. Further, my experience in working with them (especially with cases) was that they tended to evoke a detachment in the analyst that I did not want. If improving problem-formulation was to be more than a game, I thought it should involve participants in as authentic a way as possible. For this reason I decided to ask participants to provide their own problems as the third component of the course content.

I thus had three kinds of content: the Hills-Gibson material, the cognitive psychology work on problem-solving, and the students' own problems. As to sequencing these three kinds of content, it seemed to me that we could not afford to put off dealing with students' own problems while we worked through difficult concepts and a wealth of research on problem-solving. Neither could we deal with the problems before the students had been exposed to the concepts that were to be applied to them. The three kinds of content, therefore, were used in parallel, not in series. In the schedule of class meetings, they were shown in parallel columns and labeled "Band 1" (the Hills-Gibson formulation), "Band 2" (cognitive psychology), and "Band 3" (class members' own problems). These labels have become a shorthand way of referring to each kind of content. The parallel arrangement of content had the added advantage of allowing some "modeling" of how to switch from one conceptual framework to another by enabling me to raise questions about how material in Band 1 illuminated content in Band 2 or Band 3 and vice versa.

Strategies and Instructional Activities

I have identified four strategies, each associated with a number of instructional activities.[3] In what follows I deal with each strategy in turn and describe the activities that have particular significance for the way the course runs. In a final subsection I comment on the activities as stimulation for creative thinking.

Strategy No. 1—Use a mixture of direct instruction, group activity, and individual activity in a way that encourages "reflection." Every class session in-

cludes direct instruction and group and individual activity. In every session reflection is encouraged. Three important features are the creation of groups, the
use of provocative questions, and the journal requirement.

Work in small (three- to five-person) groups occupies about half the class
time. On the first day people are invited to form groups with whomsoever they
please, provided that no two people in a group work in the same school district.
After the first day I systematically rotate people so that each day each group
has a completely (or predominantly) new membership. These group rotations
are continued until the last three or four class sessions, when I reduce the number of groups and invite people to choose which of the resulting larger groups
they would like to be in for all remaining group work. The very frequent group
rotation allows for maximum variation in the perspectives that are brought to
the discussions of each problem, a feature that is essential to the exploration of
the different meanings that can be attached to problem situations. The students
also find it of value. After about eight rotated sessions I begin to worry that
students are finding too little stability and ask them if they would prefer not to
rotate, but they always say they want the new perspectives brought by the rotation. The "permanent" groups over the last days are used for more sustained
group reflection in considering what has been learned.

My use of questions that provoke reflection on what students are doing is
not an occasional event. It happens at least once and often more than once a
day. I frequently ask groups to report not on the substance of their discussions,
but on their character ("What did we just do?" "What *really* happened in your
group?" "How is what you did with this puzzle like what you did with that problem?") and I frequently invite them to consider, for example, how a Band 2
activity can be related to a Band 3 issue. The result seems to be a heightened
level of reflexive activity in groups—at about the mid-point in the course, for
example, it is not unusual to find the members of a group beginning to talk
spontaneously about how they did the task they have just finished.

Keeping a journal is the only sustained written assignment in the course.
One of the requirements is that it include some reflection on at least one of the
class events each day and in the course outline I try to specify what I consider
to be reflection:

> The journal should contain a brief account or summary of what happens
> in each class session and some reflection upon it. . . . What I have called
> reflection may take many forms and any attempt to specify what they are
> would almost certainly omit some important ones invented by some
> people. What is necessary is that the entries should show that you have
> done some thinking about each day's work (why it did or did not turn a
> light on for you, its relation to something else you have read, or experi-

enced, or learned in another class, or . . . etc., etc.) and that the thoughts provoked are not entirely banal!

Strategy No. 2—Use students' own problems and capitalize on their expertise. The use of the students' own problems is more than a gimmick to achieve "relevance." The problems are both course content and a medium for transmitting content. As content they are primarily for their individual authors. As a medium for transmitting content, the way they are made available needs both to ensure that students are respectful of others' private problem worlds and to allow in-depth examination. The caveat of Murphy and Hallinger (1987) is important here: "New approaches to training need to ensure that the sharing of experiences among practitioners is not an end in itself, but rather a catalyst for reflection, and that exchanges of experiential information occur within a larger context or framework of knowledge" (p. 270).

The way in which I use the students' problems poses some logistical difficulties, but provides a means of undertaking a number of activities that could not be done any other way. On the first day each student is asked to describe in not more than three lines a problem that

1. Exists in the student's own organization
2. Is important
3. Is related to work
4. Has the writer as the problem-solver (or a member of the problem-solving team)
5. Is a problem the student is willing to talk about in class.

These written statements are used for discussion in groups on the first day and are then handed in. The statements are then typed out as a complete set, and copies are distributed at the start of the second class. At two or three other points in the course, students are asked to hand in any revised or reformulated versions. These again are typed and copied, and become a second (or third or fourth) set for circulation. At the beginning of the last one-third of the course, I produce a final composite listing that shows all versions of each problem.

This procedure ensures that all members of the class have the same data, it allows each member to see his or her problem in the context of all the others, and it enables me to design a number of useful exercises for the whole class. I have used the lists, for example, to comment on similarities between apparently dissimilar problems and to draw attention to different kinds of reformulation. A particularly useful exercise is one in which I first ask class members to classify all problems into a small number of categories and then display the results publicly in a blackboard matrix that allows one to see how many people classified problem 1 with problem 2 and with problem 3 and so on. The demonstration of the hitherto unrecognized variety of ways of seeing what their authors thought were straightforwardly worded problems is dramatic. The matrix then provides a data base, in conjunction with the problem lists, for further explorations of such questions as "What is it about problem 5 that leads you to see it as being like problem 22?" Eventually, the final composite list of all versions of each problem provides a useful resource for examining the changes made in various problem statements over the period of the course.

Strategy No. 3—Provide a clear structure. I try to design, for both content and activities, a structure that will facilitate the understanding of material and permit the variety of activity that accommodates different learning styles and maintains participants' interest.

The course outline document is explicit about the course objectives, the "3-Band" format of content, and the expected sequence of various topics and techniques. Each day begins with a blackboard outline of proposed topics and a request for students to say whether they want to add a topic or change the ones proposed. Activity in groups is always for a particular task, and time limits are imposed in order to ensure that there is time for reflection and reporting back. Some assigned tasks at first seem artificial but can prove useful in later analysis: For example, in an early small-group discussion of the students' problems, I will often instruct each person to let other group members ask questions about his or her problem and to take note of what the questions are, but not to answer them. Almost never is this successfully accomplished without prompting from me, but it always yields a forceful recognition by each person of the ways in which his or her own problem is hidden even from experienced others.

Strategy No. 4—Provide periodic review and feedback. Review and the provision of feedback are ongoing features of the course. Each day begins (assuming the class does not wish to change the routine, and it never has) with a review of the previous day's work. This review is usually done by a student and frequently by means of asking for a volunteer to read his or her journal entry for that day. This has proved to be an effective means of review and a popular way for people to get feedback (from both me and their colleagues) on the accuracy of their journals.

Competency in the writing of the journal is not something that can be assumed. Students need coaching in the kind of writing that expands their thinking rather than allowing it to stop with a declaration such as "I found that interesting." I offer to take journals in after the first four sessions, review them, and provide feedback without recording any mark. If students want me to review their work again a few days later, I do (and I sometimes suggest to a student that I should see his or her particular journal for a second or even a third review). Feedback from peers is constant as groups work together on problems. I also arrange occasionally for a formal kind of peer feedback by asking students to select, for example, a problem whose development they find interesting and write a note to "the author of problem X," saying why.

The Stimulation of Creative Thinking. The preceding paragraphs have not given a complete account of the variety of experiences in the course. We engage in many activities to stimulate creativity and increase the number of ways in which students look at problems. The class may be asked to spend 10 minutes describing what, if anything, is abnormal about the reality represented in an Escher drawing, or what number completes a given series and why, or what is the key to a particular crossword puzzle clue, and so on. An exercise that students first mock, and then come to find very useful, requires the members of a group to classify their own problems by assigning each to one of three complex inkblots. In an evaluation of the course, one student referred to it as being "good, if a bit eclectic" (and then went on to say that the eclecticism was "in fact one of its chief charms"—a statement intended I think as a compliment). As far as the variety of activities is concerned, the eclecticism is deliberate, because activities need to be meaningful and making an eclectic set of activities meaningful requires that one become adept both at switching conceptual frameworks and at comparing the results of the switching.

STUDENTS LEARNING PROBLEM-FORMULATION

Students say they enjoy this course. Other indicators suggest that the four objectives are usually met, and that many students do change the way they approach problems. I examine first the evidence of what happens to students' thinking during the class and, second, evidence about changes that have occurred by the end of the class.

Learning as We Go

At the beginning of the course, students usually experience difficulty with the concepts in the Hills-Gibson material and, at the same time, enjoy working through the puzzles in the Kahney text that illustrate the nature and structure of well-defined problems. There is always interest in the basic ideas of the Hills material, that problems do not have an objective reality "out there" and that they lie in our ways of perceiving and evaluating experienced reality. There is also interest in Kahney's idea that the statement of a well-defined problem includes information about both its initial and its goal states. However, merely acquiring that knowledge (which happens in the first two days) does not seem

to engage students in using it. That engagement comes largely through the
small-group discussions of their own problems as, over the first two or three
days, group members' experiences are a little surprising to them, and yet are
shown to be explainable through the theoretical frameworks provided by Hills
and Kahney.

The groups at first provide the enjoyable experience of professionals learning about each others' problems. As one student's journal noted, "Discussions
in the first group were a mixture of clarification, ways to get a solution, and
supportive gestures to the person who presented the problem." Then, over the
next two or three sessions, some of the realizations that are to become very
important emerge. The first of these is that other people often do not understand the problem one has described, or that if they do, they understand it
differently from the way it "really" is. As Mary[4] noted:

> The first time I shared my problem statement with the others in my
> group, I was anxious to hear their responses because I was sure they
> would respond by saying "Oh, Mary, that is a terrible problem" or "Yes, I
> can see how you would need a full time coordinator to resolve this one,"
> or "I understand your problem fully, I don't know what you are going to
> do, and I sure wouldn't want that problem." The responses I received
> from my group members shocked me because I could not understand
> why they had so much difficulty even *comprehending* what the problem
> was. It just was not obvious or clear to any *one* of the members.

This kind of naive shock is very common. One student wryly noted his
discovery that "what we have is [a set of] problems representing multiple perceptions, smothered with rampant subjectivity." Another wrote ruefully, "We
were to review what questions had been asked about our problem [in the previous day's group] and to predict what questions we would get in the new group
today. Few of the predicted questions were asked at all."

A second realization that many students quickly come to is that their statement of a problem does not include any description of its "goal state" (although
it is, in their view, often self-evident). This realization is helped by my asking the
class to assign each class member's problem statement to one of four categories
according to whether it has information about (1) the initial state only, (2) the
goal state only, (3) both states, (4) neither state. Two facts become evident from
the display of the results of this exercise: First, more statements are thought to
fall into the first category than into the others; second, scarcely any of the problem statements produce unanimous agreement about their classification.

The two realizations evoke different responses. For the first, the response
is to add detail to the problem statement, to "explain" it, to engage in Hills'

specification by answering the question "What basis do I have for saying that?" The response to the realization that most statements have no information about the goal state is to add some such phrase as "The goal is X." My impression of this action is that for many students at this beginning stage it is mechanical, a sort of "Oh-well-we're-supposed-to-have-a-goal-state-so-here-it-is" response. Often the "X" in the phrase "The goal is X" is no more than a statement that the initial state will cease to exist ("The goal is to ensure that this does not occur"). Frequently, when a goal statement does go beyond this I-would-like-the-problem-not-to-be-there kind of wording, it is phrased in a way that specifies not only the goal, but the means to its attainment ("We would like to change the attitudes of parents so that . . ."). Often, such goal statements are of the "how-to" kind ("How could attendance be improved?" "How can standardized procedures be implemented?"). Together, these ways of responding to the first two realizations suggest that most students come more easily to an understanding of the need to clarify their perception of the situation than of the need to clarify the way in which it falls short of what they would prefer. It is as if values are assumed to be universally understood and to require no clarification.

The clarification of values comes later and seems to result from (1) becoming frustrated that one's colleagues are not "seeing" the problem, (2) asking a different specification question ("Why is that a problem?"), (3) engaging in the more sophisticated of Hills' techniques (categorization, dimensional analysis, special case analysis). What it usually involves is one or both of two kinds of change in the problem statement: naming a less global, more easily achieved set of desiderata and removing the specification of means from the goal statement and broadening it to allow for a variety of ways of achievement. These two kinds of change are illustrated by comparing the first and final versions of the problem statements made by two students:

Peter: *Version 1:* Moving a group of successful intermediate teachers who are insular and subject-oriented, toward incorporating more cooperative and holistic approaches into their programs.
Version 4: I do not know how my staff feels about integration of curricula and cooperative learning. My goal is to find out what attitudes they have toward these two techniques.

Arnold: *Version 2:* I must place two teachers in aged portable classrooms that nobody wishes to work in. I must offer some form of incentive to encourage teachers to accept a year in the portable.
Version 3: I must place two teachers in aged portable classrooms that nobody wishes to work in. My goal is to develop some sort of equitable solution so that both I and the staff feel the room assignments are fair and equitable.

The kind of progress illustrated in these examples usually comes later in the course. The pleasure that builds up over the first days as people begin to work with the reality of multiple perceptions and clarify their problem statements is then not infrequently followed by a realization that the application of specification and categorization is not in fact helping as much as it appeared to be. Clare wrote:

> I asked the group, "Has using specification shed any light on the problem?" Their response was "Yes." So I said "How, specifically?" . . . and no one could show how it had changed their problem.

Others noted the same thing with respect to the use of categorization. Some noted also that they found it stimulating and easy to apply the techniques productively (in their view) to other people's problems, but made little progress in applying them to their own. For some, other people's problems were at this stage more interesting anyway. Noted Petra:

> I find other people's problems often more interesting and certainly more inviting to deal with than my own. Most of the skills studied to date are more easily applied to others' problems than to my own. Perhaps there is a lesson in this. We are too close to our own problem to see it clearly.

It may be this closeness to one's own problem that impedes progress at this stage, but if so it is a closeness that seems to bring with it a *closedness* that prevents any real change in the way one views one's problem. As Norman wrote, "I had a false sense that I was reformulating my problem when in actuality I was only rewording it."

Release from this bondage of the ego came in different ways for different people. A fruitful insight for one person came when he asked himself what it was that he did when he asked other people questions about their problem, found a satisfactory answer, and then asked himself questions about his own problem in the same way. For a number of people it was useful to examine data showing how many people had classified problem X in the same category as various other problems. Initially what interested most students about this was to see which problems had been deemed to be alike by a majority of the class. I pointed out that it might be interesting to look at the ones that only very few people had put in the same category. This proved to be a turning point for some class members. As one put it, "I had always been looking for people who agreed with my classification of my problem. It was only today that I realized I needed the point of view of someone who didn't." And in the words of another, "The suggestion to look at least as closely to unique categories as to those that reflect a popular classification is perhaps the most valuable suggestion I have assimilated to date."

Gradually class members began to cast their intellectual nets more broadly. Material from this class would be related to work in other classes or to work in the professional field. Analogies and examples began to be fruitfully used—as when a special education consultant reflected on the importance of a counterintuitive move in solving one of Kahney's (1986) contrived puzzles and observed (with evident pleasure), "Of course, it's a counterintuitive move when we deal with disruptive students by giving them some control—and it works!"

What we have come to call the "Aha!"—the moment when reformulation seems to have some point—comes differently and at different times for different people. For Sharon, who had generated a long list of problem conditions in her specification activity (and watched in frustration as nothing seemed to change), the breakthrough came when someone suggested that instead of applying categorization to her "problem" she should apply it to the long list of problem conditions she had specified. The result was an insightful identification of three different problems, only one of which she was in a position to tackle. For Tony and George the "Aha!" came late, and not as a result of any one activity that they could identify:

> The consolidation of ideas and questions triggered by the course materials occurred at the end of the second week of the session [it was three-week summer session]. The moment was interesting in that it was not a product of any one technique or idea. It was not linear. Instead, a number of arenas of ideas solidified and insight arose out of the transformation. (Tony)

> I have the feeling that I have been missing the point of the problem-formulation exercise until today [it is day 11 of 14] . . . I must confess that I have been evaluating my problem formulations and those of my classmates in terms of solutions and failing to see the point of the exercise—not as the search for an optimum solution, but rather the attempt to generate a wider range of problem formulations. Despite all the attempts of the instructor to keep the focus on the process instead of the product, I have been willing to stand pat with a particular formulation because I believed it led to a satisfactory solution and nothing better had come along. . . . I am only now recognizing (and accepting) that the goal is . . . to develop the ability to more quickly and with more fluency and flexibility generate a wide range of frameworks from which to choose. (George)

Learning Accomplished by the End of the Course

Three kinds of evidence show what learning has occurred by the end of the course:

- The extent to which students have reformulated their problems
- The students' views of whether their problems are easier for them to handle by the end of the course than at the start
- The results of a postcourse survey designed to assess longer term learning.

The Extent to Which Problems Are Reformulated. To assess the extent to which reformulation had occurred, I compared the first and final versions of the 68 problem statements worked on in the summer sessions of 1989 and 1991 and the winter of 1990–1991.

Seventeen statements (25 percent) showed no change—they either retained wording for the final version that was almost identical to that of the first, or had rewording that appeared to indicate no real change in the way the problem was to be interpreted. Nineteen statements (28 percent) showed minor change: The final version of 10 of them differed from the first version only by the specification of either a goal state or an initial state already implicit in the original, and 9 were changed only by the removal of wording indicating either a particular solution or a cause for the problem. Thirty two statements (47 percent) showed substantial change. These were statements whose final version pointed to different actions from those indicated by their original versions. These may be considered the most successful demonstrations of problem-reformulation. Three will serve to illustrate the kinds of change achieved. In each case, the statements are identified by the year of their creation and a serial number.

1991.19-1 My position as principal was in a full-size school with very poor facilities and serious plant/operational problems. I faced many structural problems during the course of the year which interfered with administering the educational program. Having a vocal community, a strong emphasis had to be placed on public relations and communications. This problem will continue for two more years. (Maintain staff morale, student morale, community support in an unorthodox situation = main problems?)

1991.19-3 How can an instructional program that is limited by inadequate facilities be turned into a well-rounded instructional program that is satisfying for students, staff, and parents?

1991.18-1 How do you manage the problems associated with running a computer lab with no time (or additional resources) made available to the school-based coordinator? It is a burden on the staff and must be shared, but how?

1991.18-4 I am a full-time grade 5 classroom teacher who has volunteered to assume the responsibilities of a school-based computer coordinator in addition to the grade 5 responsibilities. Some of these responsibilities include 1. management of 18 computers along with their components (modem, printer, mouse), 2. maintenance of all program and student diskettes, 3. protecting the lab from incoming computer viruses, and 4. assisting teachers and students when required. My ultimate goal is to have both teachers and students share the responsibilities for the coordination of the lab. My first sub-goal is to find out what both teachers and students know about 1. hardware, 2. diskette handling, 3. individual program use, and 4. computer viruses.

1990.11-1 Most teacher contracts require staff committees be set up and run in all district schools. But many teachers don't know what these committees were meant to do and are feeling great stress as a result.

1990.11-3 Staff committees now operating in [our] schools have not been established, and are not functioning, with a clear purpose in mind. [Those] who are writing and negotiating collective agreement language and providing staff committee training, must reach agreement on why staff committees are desirable and what their ultimate purpose is. Such changes are easy to identify as reformulation, but there are also cases in which a greatly altered approach to the problem is not reflected in the wording changes—for example, for two weeks one principal defined her problem as one of teacher supervision and then, having listened to other people's classifications of it, realized that she had a problem, not of supervision, but of ensuring that a progressively disabled teacher received proper counseling and insured benefits.

The Extent to Which Students Feel Their Problems Are Easier to Handle. In the final class session of the course I use a 5-point scale to ask students to say whether their problem seems easier to handle than it did when we began. Total results over all five sessions show that 41 percent answered "Yes, very much"; 48 percent, "Yes"; and 11 percent, "Well . . . sort of." No student used the lowest points on the scale ("Well . . . not really" and "No"). Clearly, whether or not a substantial reformulation had occurred, students felt that they had benefitted.

Many aspects of the course experience are mentioned as effective in bringing about this benefit. Several people claimed that writing the journal was important. "The journal will make a very useful future reference," noted one student, "but I believe its greatest value lies in the actual process of writing it." Others spoke of how being obliged to write a summary for the journal had helped them to clarify ideas. Several of the different ways in which classification was introduced seem to be enjoyed and for one student the effect of being asked to classify problems by relating them to inkblots was very powerful:

> [The exercise] brought an insight to my problem that was very reassuring. Before this lesson, if anyone had told me that I would find any meaning at all in an inkblot, much less find one that was useful to me . . . I would definitely have disagreed. To me, thinking about the problems of the real world required a logical, no nonsense approach, but now I think there may be more than one way to approach a situation. How can one duplicate the exercise for later use? It would seem rather odd to carry a set of inkblots in my brief case to pull out when I needed to see something in a different manner. Are there other things that could trigger that type of thinking? Perhaps thinking of the problem as a metaphor would work, comparing it to things that are completely different and then specifying why they are alike.

There is little doubt that most class members found the small-group work to be a great help. "The collaborative process of the structured group provided perspective and new ideas," wrote one. "As a result of the group processes, feedback and questions, the growth demonstrated in problem formulation has been incredible," said another. One person noted what were for him two important characteristics of the groups, their "careful structuring and empathetic ethos." It is perhaps this ethos that enables so much to happen that, without it, would be threatening and suppressing. Two comments are revealing about the strength of the influence of the groups. The first came late in the course, after some consideration of the tendency of people to lay blame:

> Authors of the problems in my group have changed from placing the problem "under the skin of the actor" . . . [they] have stopped pointing fingers and have begun to work at looking at the key features of a problem. Would we have recognized the tendency to lay blame in the beginning of the class? Probably not. Some people would become defensive and others would say "Yes—but . . . " This behavior was only revealed through the learning process.

The second comment came in the final "reflection" of the author's journal:

> For many reasons I have [before this course] been reluctant to expose my inability to resolve this situation. . . . The ideas and moral support offered by participants in this course have done much to free me from the bonds of my own self-consciousness.

The Transfer of Learning to the Workplace. In December, 1990 I surveyed the students who had taken the course in the summers of 1988, 1989, and 1990 (i.e., those who had been back at work for between three months and two years after completing the course). Mail addressed to 6 of these 62 students was returned by the post office marked "moved, address unknown." Of the remaining 56, 37 responded, a return rate of 66 percent.

I asked these former students, "Has the course EADM 502 made a difference to your working life?" and I invited them to explain their answers. Of the 37 people responding, 31 (83 percent) said "Yes" and 5 (14 percent) said "Possibly." One respondent said "No." The explanations were detailed and contained a total of 98 different comments. They can be classed in two broad groups: (1) recollections about the course and about which of the activities had been helpful (18 comments) and (2) descriptions of ways in which the respondent's way of working was different from what it had been before taking the course (80 comments).

The first group of comments referred to a broad range of course activities and confirmed what students had said at the conclusion of the course itself about the value of those activities. The second and larger group referred to the respondents' current ways of working. These comments fell into four fairly distinct clusters. First were those that acknowledged in a nonspecific way that their authors worked differently now. "It has changed my approach," wrote one person. "The way I now approach problems has enabled me to play a new role," wrote another. A second cluster made reference to the continuing use of one or more of the techniques taught in the course. The most frequently mentioned were categorizing and asking "Of what general case is this a special case?" or "Why is that a problem?" or "For what problem is that a solution?" One person wrote that he had found keeping a journal so useful during the course that he now kept a daily journal for himself. Third were comments alluding to the broadening of the concept of "problem" in the respondent's mind and many of these noted that their authors now actively worked with the idea that the concept of problem was one that obliged them to invoke consideration of values. Finally, a smaller number of comments described how their authors deliberately sought a variety of perspectives in dealing with issues and problems.

There is a clear resemblance between these comments made after the return to the workplace and those made immediately after the end of the course. What is especially striking, however, is the contrast between the value attached by these people to what was learned in the course and the lack of long-term value typically ascribed by administrators to their work in graduate programs (Pitner, 1982). In the final section of the chapter I reflect briefly on what it is that seems to make the course a good experience for most people when they take it and for me when I teach it.

OBSERVATIONS AND REFLECTIONS

My stock-taking in EADM 502 leads me to define three categories of new insights. First, I have learned something about how mid-career professionals "normally" think of problems and problem-solving. Second, I am coming closer to being able to formalize a view of what helps them to develop an understanding of problem-formulation and the ability to use it productively. Finally, I have a better sense of what it is that I do when I teach 502.

In all five sessions discussed here, the first two or three classes have been more alike than different. They reveal some basic features of the concept of problem and the approach to problems in the minds of these students. I have identified five such features:

1. Students rarely have difficulty identifying and briefly describing a work-related problem
2. Initial discussion of problems is usually oriented toward solving them rather than gaining a fuller understanding of them
3. The unproductive problem-solving behaviors identified by Hills (1975, pp. 4–6) are seen in the actions and comments of many students at the start of the course
4. When students describe problems, they more frequently describe the problematic situation than their view of the situation as they would prefer it to be
5. Students do not easily entertain the possibility that others might have a different view of either the problem situation, or the preferred situation, or both.

These features are perhaps not surprising. The first three would probably be recognized as normal by experienced observers in the everyday world of practitioners. It appears also to be normal in other fields—Whelan's (1988) description of medical students' clinical problem-solving has similar features, as does Schön's (1987) description of the student in an architecture studio. My identification of features 4 and 5 is possible only because of my awareness of Kahney's (1986, p. 20) distinction between the "initial state" of a problem and the "goal state." It is a distinction I have found useful in drawing attention to the dimension of values implicit in any designation of something as a "problem." With respect to features 4 and 5, my impression is that when students do recognize that multiple perceptions of their problem exist, they move to clarify the initial state, not the goal state. It is as if the student takes for granted the universal desirableness of the goal state he or she has in mind—an assumption that, I suspect, underlies much miscommunication about problems and their solutions. Certainly, many of the students' breakthroughs in communicating their problems to others, or in reformulating them, begin when they are asked to make explicit the goal state of their problem.

One way to see the five features is to see them as the description of the initial state of the problem of teaching problem-reformulation. The goal state is that the students will be able to engage in the kind of problem-reformulation that improves the operation of their schools. The data described in the previous section show that this goal is achieved to some extent by almost all the students and well achieved by many. Beginning to understand what helps them to this achievement is the second kind of insight I have acquired in teaching EADM 502. Overall, my sense is that three elements are important: first, the use of students' own active problems as an important part of course content; second, the existence of an ethos of interest in each others' problems, of mutual understanding and support; and third, the constant insistence on trying to know what we do when we do what we do (and, by that knowledge, being enabled to do differently what we do, to formulate differently what we have formulated).

The first two of these elements seem to be what liberates the discussions. The discussions are not contrived because the problems are not contrived; they are not threatening because "we're all in this together" and "we know how you feel" and "we've met something like that, too, and we'd like to help." It is the third element, however, that seems to result in real learning.

More and more as I have worked with the course, I have come to see what Hills (1991) calls the "technique" of categorization or classification as one that undergirds all others, the one that is instrumental in coming to understand what we do when we do what we do. It is by our capacity to categorize that we can say "this is like this" or "this is not like this." It is by being obliged to try to make explicit why "this" is like (or not like) "this" that we are forced to examine what it is that we do when we categorize. The capacity of categories to be both wholes and parts (to be what Koestler [1967] calls "holons") is what gives high potential value to the questions "Of what general case is this a specific case?" "What are some other specific cases of this general case?" and "Could this be a specific case of a different general case?" Different activities release that potential for different people—indeed it seems that almost any of the various activities can "work" for someone, provided that people are constantly asked to reflect on what it was that they did when they did it.

If it is true that three elements are important in helping students acquire the ability to make constructive reformulations and that almost any activity will be the right trigger for someone, it seems also true that the breakthrough, what we called earlier the "Aha!," does not happen with the use of this or that particular "skill" or "technique"; it happens when activities, problem content, group context, and personal reflection come together to provide the experience of what reformulating can feel like. The result is an attitude shift. Several students' journals have commented on this—those of Tony and George were quoted ear-

lier—and it is interesting that Tony's description used the word "transformation" to describe his passage from not having learned to having learned. The
idea of learning as transformation and its relation to content and instructional
activities is also found in recent work on new perspectives on learning: Marton
and Ramsden (1988) observe that what they call learning is

> a qualitative change in a person's way of seeing, experiencing, understanding,
> conceptualizing something in the real world, rather than . . . a quantitative
> change in the amount of knowledge someone possesses. It is logically impossi-
> ble for learning defined in this way to be content- and context-free. Learning
> techniques and instructional strategies are inextricably linked to subject mat-
> ter and the students' perceptions. (p. 271)

In this quotation we come close to much of what is in Schön's (1987) work
on the education of professionals who can be "reflective." That work is one I
may use as a starting point to describe the third and final kind of learning my
teaching of EADM 502 has given me: some insight into what it is that I do
when I teach 502.

The first thing I have come to recognize is that students beginning EADM
502 are faced with the paradox of the *Meno* as described by Schön: "The student
knows she needs to look for something, but does not know what that something
is" (1987, pp. 82–92). The second is that as I invent activities, questions, and
exercises for the class, I am the Socratic gadfly who, in Schön's reconciliation
of the *Meno* paradox, "serves as gadfly and midwife to others' self-discovery." I
had previously thought of myself as providing structure, content, and direction.
I now find it helpful to see doing that as a special case of the general cases of
being "gadfly" and "midwife."

Finally, I have a new understanding of what Hills calls "skills" or "techniques." As Hills (1975) described them, they are "tricks of the trade" that he
observed himself using and that he offered as useful tools for administrators
who wanted to reformulate problems. I adopted this view of the techniques as
I took on the course. In my first use of them I was, to use Vygotsky's (1962)
term, "bound" by them. I introduced them as a sequence and tried to get flu-
ency in each before going to the next, only to become aware that it could be
sometimes more productive in a given case to reverse the sequence, or skip a
technique. I now see these techniques as special cases of the general category
of means by which we can ask new questions, expand horizons, and acquire
new perspectives. When I consider this realization together with the observation that the most successful students experience a transformation to a completely new approach to viewing problems, I am no longer sure that the course
title should even include the word "skills."

I noted earlier that teaching EADM 502 promised to be fun. I have learned that "having fun" in this context is a special case of being the gadfly, watching discovery occur, and hearing students joyfully admit that they know what they do when they do reformulation—and it works!

NOTES

1. As I understand it, this kind of knowing or thinking is what others have called "metacognition" (see Leithwood and Steinbach, this volume).

2. Kahney (1986) argues that a well-defined problem is one whose statement includes all the information needed for its solution. Specifically, it includes information about the *initial state* of the problem, the *goal state,* which *operators* are legal, and what *operator restrictions* exist. This definition proved very useful as students in EADM 502 began their analysis of problems.

3. The distinction between strategies and activities is not unlike that made by Leithwood and Steinbach (this volume) between "conditions" and "strategies." What those authors call "strategies" are for me "activities." Most of the "conditions" listed by Leithwood and Steinbach are incorporated in my strategies and those that are not are encompassed by my activities.

4. Here and in all other quotations from student journals, fictitious names replace real ones to preserve the anonymity of the students.

REFERENCES

Bruner, J. S. (1964). The course of cognitive growth. *American Psychologist, 19,* 1–5.

Erickson, G. L. (1988). Explorations with field of reflection: Directions for future research agendas. In P. P. Grimmett & G. L. Erickson (Eds.), *Reflection in teacher education* (pp. 195–205). New York: Teachers College Press.

Hills, J. (1975). The preparation of administrators: Some observations from the "firing line." *Educational Administration Quarterly, 11*(3), 1–20.

Hills, J. (1987). *A conceptual framework for thinking about conceptual frameworks.* Unpublished paper. The University of British Columbia. Department of Administrative, Adult and Higher Education.

Hills, J. (1991). *Analysis and reformulation skills for problem solvers and decision makers.* Unpublished paper. The University of British Columbia. Department of Administrative, Adult and Higher Education.

Hills, J., & Gibson, C. (1988a). *Problem analysis and reformulation skills for administrators.* Unpublished instructional materials.

Hills, J., & Gibson, C. (1988b). Reflections on Schön's *The reflective practitioner.* In P. P. Grimmett & G. L. Erickson (Eds.), *Reflection in teacher education* (pp. 147–175). New York: Teachers College Press.

Hills, J., & Gibson, C. (1990). *A conceptual framework for thinking about conceptual frameworks: Bridging the theory-practice gap.* Unpublished paper. The University of British Columbia. Department of Administrative, Adult and Higher Education.

Kahney, H. (1986). *Problem solving: A cognitive approach.* Milton Keynes: Open University Press.

Koestler, A. (1967). *The ghost in the machine.* London: Hutchinson.

Luhmann, N. (1982). *The differentiation of societies.* New York: Columbia University Press.

Marton, F., & Ramsden, P. (1988). What does it take to improve learning? In P. Ramsden (Ed.), *Improving learning: New perspectives* (pp. 268–286). London: Kogan Page.

Murphy, J., & Hallinger, P. (Eds.). (1987). *Approaches to administrative training in education.* New York: State University of New York Press.

Pitner, N. J. (1982). *Training the school administrator: State of the art.* Eugene: University of Oregon, Center for Educational Policy and Management.

Schön, D. A. (1987). *Educating the reflective practitioner.* San Francisco: Jossey-Bass.

Vygotsky, L. S. (1962). *Thought and language.* Cambridge, MA: The MIT Press.

Whelan, G. (1988). Improving medical students' clinical problem solving. In P. Ramsden (Ed.), *Improving learning: New perspectives* (pp. 199–214). London: Kogan Page.

14 Problem-Based Learning in Medical and Managerial Education

Edwin M. Bridges and Philip Hallinger

The preparation of school administrators currently occupies center stage on the intellectual agenda of professors and departments of educational administration (Griffiths, Stout, & Forsyth, 1988). One manifestation of this newfound interest in preparing administrators is a proposal to increase the relevance of preparation by orienting it more explicitly to problems of practice. This proposal, like many others, lacks specificity and skirts the issue of whether it is supported by theory or research or both.

This chapter seeks to fill this gap by drawing on the problem-based-learning (PBL) literature in the field of medical education. As we shall see, medical educators throughout the world use problem-based learning to train physicians. Moreover, medical educators have studied this instructional approach extensively. Their experience offers us a unique opportunity to build on and go beyond what they have learned as we apply this promising approach to preparing educational administrators.

PROBLEM-BASED LEARNING IN MEDICAL EDUCATION

Problem-based learning is used in more than 80 percent of the medical schools in the United States (Jonas, Etzel, and Barzansky, 1989) and has five defining characteristics:

1. The starting point for learning is a problem.
2. The problem is one that students are apt to face as future physicians.
3. Subject matter is organized around problems rather than the disciplines.
4. Students assume a major responsibility for their own instruction and learning.
5. Most learning occurs within the context of small groups rather than lectures.

Apart from these five common features, problem-based learning curricula in medical schools vary along the following two dimensions: (1) the program's major goals (e.g., knowledge acquisition and use, problem-solving skills, and self-directed learning skills) and (2) the extent to which the instructors or the students choose the learning objectives, resources, and modes of student evaluation.

Rationale

Medical educators justify using problem-based learning on grounds that, in our judgment, apply with equal force to the preparation of school administrators. First, medical educators contend, and buttress their contention with empirical evidence, that medical students retain little of what they learn in the basic disciplines (Bok, 1989). Second, medical educators cite research showing that students in medicine and a host of other fields often do not appropriately use the knowledge they have learned (Schmidt, 1983). (We suspect that researchers in the field of educational administration would find similar results in both instances.) Third, since students forget much of what is learned or use their knowledge inappropriately, instructors should create conditions that optimize retrieval and appropriate use of the knowledge in future professional practice.

Fourth, PBL creates the three conditions that information theory links to subsequent retrieval and appropriate use of new information (Schmidt, 1983):

Prior knowledge is activated, that is, students apply knowledge they already possess in order to understand the new information. This prior knowledge and the kind of structure in which it is stored determine what is understood from the new experience and what is learned from it. Problems are selected and sequenced to ensure that this activation of prior knowledge occurs.

The context in which information is learned resembles the context in which it will later be applied (referred to as "encoding specificity"). Research shows that knowledge is much more likely to be remembered or recalled in the context in which it was originally learned (Godden & Baddeley, 1975). Encoding specificity in problem-based learning is achieved by having students acquire knowledge in a functional context, that is, in a context containing problems that closely resemble the problems they will encounter later in their professional career.

Information is better understood, processed, and recalled if students have an opportunity to elaborate on that information. Elaborations provide redundancy in the memory structure, which in turn reduces forgetting and abets retrieval. Elaboration occurs in problem-based learning in various ways, namely, discussing the subject matter with other students, teaching peers what they first learned themselves, exchanging views about how the information applies to the problem they are seeking to solve, and preparing essays about what they have learned while seeking to solve the problem.

Fifth, PBL explicitly forces students to adopt a problem-solving orientation when learning new information.

> The advantage of such an approach is that students become much more aware of how the knowledge they are acquiring can be put to use. Adopting a problem-solving mentality, even when it is marginally appropriate, reinforces the notion that the knowledge is useful for achieving particular goals. Students are not being asked to store information away; they see how it works in certain situations which increases the accessibility. (Prawat, 1989, p. 18)

Finally, the disciples of PBL stress the motivational value of the approach. They maintain that students enjoy the opportunity to play the role of doctor during their preclinical training and find the activity of working on simulated patient problems intrinsically rewarding.

Empirical Evidence

Although medical educators present a rather persuasive rationale for using PBL to train a physician, do they provide any evidence that the approach is a sound one? Yes, compared with traditional programs in medical education, PBL programs generally yield equal or superior results. The results are summarized below.

Students in PBL programs express substantially more positive attitudes toward their training than do students in more traditional programs. The former praise their training, especially those aspects that are unique to problem-based learning, while the latter often describe their training as boring, irrelevant, and anxiety-provoking (deVries, Schmidt, & deGraaff, 1989; Schmidt, Dauphinee, & Patel, 1987).

Besides expressing more favorable attitudes toward their education, students in PBL programs also adopt more desirable approaches to studying than their traditional program counterparts. PBL students are more likely to adopt a meaning orientation to studying, that is, to be intrinsically motivated by the subject matter and to strive to understand the material. Students in traditional programs, on the other hand, are more likely to adopt a reproducing orientation to studying; to use rote learning and seek to reproduce the factual information in the syllabus (Coles, 1985; deVolder & deGrave, 1989; Schmidt et al., 1987).

These differences in attitudes and approaches to studying also translate into differences in rates and time of completion. In countries with relatively high dropout rates among medical students, students in PBL programs are much more likely to graduate and to complete their programs of study in less time than students in traditional programs (deVries et al., 1989).

Students in PBL programs also tend to perform better than students in conventional programs on measures of problem-solving proficiency and clinical competence (deVries et al., 1989; Jones, 1986; Kaufman, 1989; Schmidt et al., 1987). However, we should note that the performance differences are small and that the outcome measures vary in quality.

When medical knowledge is considered, the pattern of differences reverses itself. Students in conventional programs score slightly higher on standardized tests of medical knowledge than do students in PBL programs (deVries et al., 1989; Kaufman et al., 1989; Schmidt et al., 1989). One explanation for this finding is that traditional programs spend more time emphasizing lower-level facts—the type of content easily addressed by multiple-choice standardized tests. Regardless, the differences are small enough that they are of little practical importance.

Limitations of the Research on PBL

The research that has been conducted on the effectiveness of problem-based learning versus the traditional approach is flawed in several respects. Let us examine the deficiencies of this research in terms of the specification of the independent variable and the measurement of dependent variables.

Independent Variable. Although researchers claim that they are contrasting problem-based learning with traditional training programs, their claims are suspect. There are virtually no attempts to define what is meant by "traditional." Moreover, when problem-based learning is compared with the traditional approach, PBL often is not the main instructional approach. In those cases where PBL appears to be the main approach and is explicitly defined, it is clear that the PBL programs belong to the same genus but different species.

Measures of the Dependent Variables. The measures of the dependent variables, like the specification of the independent variable, are suspect. Researchers rarely cite any evidence that attests to the reliability of the measures. In those rare instances where the researcher supplies data about reliability (deVolder & deGrave, 1989; Imbos et al., 1984), the coefficients are moderate at best (.26 to less than .80).

When measuring differences in medical knowledge (e.g., deVries et al., 1989; Jones et al., 1984; Kaufman et al., 1989), researchers appear to be testing recall via cued questions (i.e., alternative answers furnished), rather than recall and spontaneous use of knowledge in clinical contexts. Given the rationale for problem-based learning in medical education, it seems more appropriate to measure how well students retrieve and correctly use knowledge in clinical contexts without external prompts (Claessen & Boshuizen, 1985).

Unlike medical knowledge, problem-solving proficiency is measured in the context of patient problems. Researchers supply medical students with bits of information about patients and then ask the students to reproduce as much of this information as possible. Their proficiency in problem-solving is assessed in terms of how many items of information they correctly recall and the degree to which the information is structured or randomly reproduced. This mode of assessment represents a limited measure of problem-solving proficiency—efficiency in encoding and chunking information that is used in solving problems.

Designing Problem-Based Learning Programs for Educational Administrators

As we have indicated, there is ample though not conclusive evidence that PBL equals or is superior to traditional instructional approaches in producing desirable outcomes for medical education. In light of these promising results, we think it is important to experiment with different forms of problem-based learning in preparing administrators. To facilitate this experimentation, we have identified eight major design issues that represent possibilities for developing and studying different PBL program designs. In the discussion that follows we discuss these various issues and what we have learned about them through our reading and our own efforts at Stanford and Vanderbilt Universities to prepare aspiring and practicing administrators using PBL.

Issue One. How should PBL be incorporated into the curriculum? There are at least four different ways PBL can be incorporated into the curriculum for preparing educational administrators:

1. PBL can be used as the main instructional approach for the entire curriculum
2. The curriculum can consist of two tracks with one of these tracks using PBL as the main approach
3. One or more courses in the curriculum can be organized around problem-based learning
4. A portion of one or more courses can use PBL.

The first alternative appears to be the least desirable choice for several reasons. Although students apparently enjoy the approach, it is clear that some students prefer a more traditional learning format (Jones et al., 1986). Other students like the variety reflected in programs employing both traditional and PBL approaches. Instructors, like students, differ in their preferences for traditional and problem-based learning. These differences may lead to needless, destructive conflict within departments of educational administration. Finally, problem-based learning, though a promising alternative, remains an unproven method in preparing educational administrators. Since its effectiveness remains in doubt, trials on a more limited basis seem warranted.

Issue Two. What problems should be used, and how should they be presented? Since problems are one of the defining characteristics of the genus PBL, program designers need to devote considerable time and thought to this second issue. When choosing focal problems for the PBL curriculum, one or more of the following criteria may be used:

- Prevalence (i.e., the problem is a common one)
- Integrative value (i.e., the problem is suitable for studying concepts from a range of disciplines)
- Prototypic value (i.e., the problem, though rare, is an excellent model for study)
- High potential impact (i.e., the problem threatens large numbers of people for an extended period of time)
- Lack of structure (i.e., the problem is a "swamp" with many issues and sub-issues).

In the presentation of focal problems to students, a problem can be presented as a written case, a live role play, an interactive computer simulation, an interactive video disk, or a taped episode. Sole reliance on written cases or verbal vignettes, as Bransford, Franks, Vye, and Sherwood (1989) have noted, may have dysfunctional consequences for the learner. In order to become an expert, a great deal of perceptual learning must occur and this cannot happen unless the student learns to recognize the salient visual, auditory, and nonverbal cues. When designing a PBL curriculum, program designers should strive for a variety of modalities in presenting problems to educational administrators. If students encounter only verbal descriptions of problems, they may be unprepared to deal with real problems.

Issue Three. What should be the goals of problem-based learning for educational administrators? There are at least four major goals that may lie at the heart of problem-based learning: (1) acquisition of retrievable and usable knowledge, (2) problem-solving skills, (3) administrative skills, and (4) self-directed learning skills. Since most professors of educational administration are quite familiar with the rationale for the first three goals, we will limit our discussion to the goal of self-directed learning skills. This goal rarely surfaces in discussions of curriculum in our field; moreover, it represents the most important and problematic choice for PBL designers.

The rationale underlying the need for self-directed learning skills is straightforward. The knowledge base that undergirds professional practice is vast and continually undergoing change. If professionals are to keep abreast of this knowledge base, they need to acquire skills in learning how to learn. These self-directed learning skills include proficiency in identifying one's own learning needs and objectives; skill in locating and evaluating resources (reference material and expert advice); competence in applying the knowledge to professional problems; and skill in self-evaluation.

The decision to make self-directed learning skills a major goal is a crucial design decision. If designers decide to emphasize these skills, many of the subsequent design decisions will be made by the student, rather than by the instructional staff. These design decisions include the specific learning objectives, the relevant resources, and the modes of evaluation.

When designers turn these decisions over to students, two risks arise. First, there is limited evidence that students select learning objectives that do not always correspond to the ones envisioned by the instructional staff (who, in turn, may be responding to the program requirements of state accreditation agencies). There is some overlap, but it is less than perfect. Second, when given the opportunity to define their own learning needs and resources, students, in our experience, may transform PBL into a library research project. If this happens, students devote more time and effort to summarizing what they have learned than to applying the knowledge to the focal problem.

Issue Four. How should the small learning groups be constituted? One of the defining characteristics of PBL is that the primary learning format is a small group. These small groups may be constituted as a tutorial (Barrows, 1984), a cooperative learning group (Slavin, 1989), or a project team. Our experience, thus far, leads us to favor constituting the small group as a project team, but the other two ways remain viable choices.

Each project team consists of five to seven students; the instructor is not a member of the team but serves as a resource to it. Since administrators frequently administer projects, the small group affords students an opportunity to develop an array of skills associated with project management. Most notably, students learn skills in planning how to accomplish the project's goals in a fixed period of time with existing resources. In addition, students learn what is involved in shouldering responsibility for carrying out a plan with the members of a project team. By varying the goals, the composition of the team, the leader, and the duration of the project, PBL designers are able to expose students to the situational nature of leadership and the risk and uncertainty that are characteristic of managerial work. Project meetings also provide opportunities for students to acquire competence in running meetings, a major medium of managerial work.

Issue Five. How much should each focal problem (or problem-based learning project) be prestructured? When designing a PBL program for educational administrators, designers may elect to provide varying amounts of prestructuring for each focal problem or project. At one extreme, the designer may supply only the problem and permit students to define the rest of the structure (i.e., the learning objectives, the resources, and the mode of evaluation). At the other extreme, the designer may provide the problem and specify the learning objectives, resources, guiding questions (either to highlight certain concepts or to help the student analyze the problem), and mode of evaluation. Between these two extremes, the designer can vary the degree of prestructuring by allowing students to decide one or more of the following: learning objectives, learning resources, and mode of evaluation.

How much prestructuring occurs depends on two factors. The first factor involves the major goals of the program. If the designer wishes to emphasize self-directed learning skills, each project is likely to reflect a minimal amount of prestructuring. If, however, the designer attaches little or no importance to self-directed learning skills, each project is apt to be highly prestructured. A second factor relates to the availability of resources: The less students have easy access to a library and relevant experts, the greater the need for prestructuring the learning objectives and resources.

Even if the designer elects to emphasize self-directed learning skills, it is important to prestructure the focal problems or projects during the early stages. Students find it difficult to make the transition to a problem-based learning program, and the transition is sometimes slow. Accordingly, projects need to be prestructured at the outset with the amount of prestructuring being gradually reduced as students become more comfortable and more familiar with problem-based learning.

Issue Six. What form should evaluation take in the context of problem-based learning? When grappling with this issue, designers need to distinguish between program and student evaluation and between formative and summative evaluation. In the early stages of implementing PBL, we have found it valuable to emphasize formative evaluation. Despite our efforts to create units that are flawless from the outset, we inevitably learn from the initial field tests of these projects. Student feedback, supplemented by our own observations, leads to revision. In some cases these revisions are substantial. The second trial of the unit or project generally results in little or no revision. Once the problem-based learning projects have been field-tested and debugged, it is appropriate and desirable to conduct summative evaluations.

When conducting formative or summative evaluations of student performance, designers may use one or more methods to assess the quality of a student's performance. The most commonly used methods in medical education are self-evaluation, peer evaluation, and instructor evaluation. We have followed the practices used in medical education and have used all three methods to evaluate student performance.

Issue Seven. How should students be prepared to function effectively in a problem-based learning instructional environment? As we have noted, students encounter difficulty in making the transition from a traditional to a problem-based learning environment. Medical educators have alluded to these difficulties, and we have observed them as we have worked with aspiring and practicing administrators. If designers properly attend to transitional issues, they can reduce the stress experienced by students and can accelerate their successful adjustment to this instructional approach.

To ease the students' transition to a problem-based learning environment, designers have several options. Besides extensively prestructuring the first few problem-based units, designers can provide students with an orientation to problem-based learning and with some of the foundational skills the process requires. Based on our experience, we have found it helpful to orient students by describing PBL in relation to the following questions:

- What is problem-based learning?
- What is the underlying rationale for PBL?
- How will PBL be incorporated into their training?
- What are the major goals?
- How will the learning groups be constituted?
- How will students be evaluated?

In other words, students need to know how the instructional staff has decided to resolve the various design issues.

The students' transition to PBL can also be facilitated by providing them with training in the kinds of skills they will need to succeed in a problem-based curriculum. For the most part, these skills are the same ones they will need when they become administrators—skills in project and meeting management, problem-solving, conflict resolution, and oral and written communication. Acquisition of these skills is enhanced through their repeated use in the problem-based learning units. Depending on the major goals of the curriculum, students may also need training in locating and evaluating relevant published materials.

Issue Eight. How should faculty be prepared to function effectively in a problem-based learning environment? Even if faculty members favor using a problem-based learning approach, they are likely to encounter difficulty in making the transition. The vast majority of faculty members have been prepared in disciplinary-based programs that rely heavily on two methods—lecture and instructor-led discussions. Having limited or no exposure to the problem-based approach, faculty members understandably will lack some of the basic knowledge and skills needed to design a PBL program and to implement it successfully. Under these conditions, it is important to provide formal training in designing and implementing PBL and to create settings in which instructors can share their difficulties and discuss ways of dealing with them.

PROBLEM-BASED LEARNING: A FUTURE RESEARCH AGENDA

Since problem-based learning is a promising but unproven approach for preparing educational administrators, it represents a potentially fruitful area for investigation. To stimulate interest in studying this instructional approach, we will suggest some directions that research on problem-based learning might take.

Proposed Focus

In our judgment, the educational administration research community should reframe the basic question asked by researchers in medical education. As we indicated earlier, medical educators generally seek to answer some form of the following question: Do problem-based learning programs produce significantly better outcomes for medical students than traditional programs? A more appropriate and potentially more illuminating question is: How effective are the various species of PBL in achieving the different goals of managerial education?

This particular question is more desirable for several reasons. First, this formulation recognizes that there is no agreement among PBL supporters about what problem-based learning means. Second, this formulation acknowledges that we do not currently understand which elements of PBL or combinations of elements are effective in achieving different types of educational goals. This important issue continues to baffle medical educators because of the way in which they have posed their basic research question. Finally, this way of framing the question is less divisive because it does not pit advocates of PBL against the proponents of more established, traditional approaches. As a result, there is likely to be a greater willingness within departments of educational administration to experiment with problem-based learning.

Independent Variables

Program evaluators do not commonly "describe fully, let alone measure, how the programs in 'experimental' and 'control' situations actually differ from one another—or even to certify that they do" (Charters & Jones, 1975, p. 342). We noted this phenomenon in the research on PBL in medical education and pointed out the consequences, namely, the uninterpretability of the results.

In light of what Charters and Jones have noted and what we have observed during our review of research on PBL, we fear that history may repeat itself. To prevent this from happening, PBL researchers in the field of educational administration should specify which species of PBL they are studying. As we have indicated earlier in this chapter, these species can be described in terms of how the faculty chose to resolve each of the eight design issues we highlighted. In addition, researchers should certify that the PBL programs actually operated as they were described. Descriptive studies of how one or more elements (e.g., the small learning groups and the role of the instructor) in the PBL design was implemented would be especially informative.

Dependent Variables

The choice of dependent variables depends primarily on the major goals of the program. PBL programs may, as we have noted, emphasize one or more of the following goals: retrievable/usable knowledge, problem-solving skills, administrative skills, and self-directed learning skills. We will limit our discussion to the two goals that have received the greatest attention by medical researchers, namely, knowledge and problem-solving skills.

In studying the degree to which the knowledge goal has been accomplished, researchers could profitably follow the lead of Bransford et al. (1989). These cognitive psychologists have studied the spontaneous use of knowledge by college students who acquired information under problem-processing and fact-processing instructional formats. Students who learned the information under a problem-processing format were much more likely to use this information spontaneously in developing action plans than were students taught the same information in a fact-processing format. Bransford's work provides a potentially fruitful approach to studying knowledge use and suggests that one or more versions of problem-based learning is likely to be effective in promoting the retrieval and use of knowledge. Alternatively, researchers might examine knowledge retrieval and use in clinical contexts (e.g., internship or on-the-job).

Studying the effects of PBL on administrator problem-solving skills represents a more formidable challenge. "There are no simple tricks to assessing problem-solving skills" (McGuire, 1980, p. 122). The absence of a single yardstick for assessing problem-solving proficiency leads us to propose several approaches to this important but admittedly complex task. What the intellectual yield will be from these various approaches remains a mystery.

Medical educators have tended to assess the effectiveness of problem-solving skills by examining the efficiency of medical students in encoding and chunking information gleaned from simulated patient problems. If this approach were used in the field of educational administration, researchers would ask students to read a case and then to write down all the information they can remember. The efficiency of students in processing the information contained in the case could be gauged by scoring (1) the number of correctly reproduced items of information in the student's recall protocol and (2) the degree to which similar items are grouped together. This approach allows insight into the content and structure of the student's relevant knowledge base, a crucial factor in the ability to solve problems (Claessen & Boshuizen, 1985).

A second approach to studying problem-solving skills is suggested by the work of cognitive psychologists. There is some evidence that knowledge of general mental strategies remains inert, that is, is used only in a restricted set of contexts even though applicable in a wide variety of domains (Bransford et al., 1986). In view of this possibility, researchers may find it fruitful to examine the extent to which graduates of PBL programs spontaneously use the general problem-solving strategies they acquired during their training.

Another approach might focus on the proficiency of those individuals who spontaneously use their newly acquired general problem-solving strategies. Studies of clinical reasoning reveal "that physicians often fail to collect the data they need, to pay attention to the data they do collect, . . . and to incorporate a systematic consideration of alternative risks and values in the actions they take" (McGuire, 1985, p. 594). Administrators are also likely to reveal disquieting defects in their problem-solving processes. Based on our experience, we anticipate that students may bog down as they try to define messy, ill-structured problems and may overlook the need to anticipate the problems and obstacles that arise when they implement a chosen course of action.

The adequacy of an administrator's problem-solving skills can also be assessed by examining the outcomes. A key assumption underlies the emphasis on general problem-solving strategies, namely, that the use of these strategies leads to higher-quality decisions and outcomes. This assumption needs to be tested. One way of testing it is by looking at the degree of postdecisional regret that accompanies major decisions (Janis & Mann, 1977). Presumably, a person who lacks proficiency in using problem-solving strategies when making consequential decisions will experience more postdecisional regret than one who possesses this proficiency.

SUMMARY AND CONCLUSION

According to the critics, current programs for preparing educational administrators are inadequate and should be overhauled. These same critics propose a number of solutions to improve these preparatory programs. One of these proposals calls for increasing the relevance of administrator preparation by making it more problem-based. This proposal, sensible on its face, offers the profession a unique opportunity to build on the work of educators in other fields who are using problem-based learning to train practitioners.

To capitalize on this opportunity, we have reviewed the literature on PBL in medical education. Our review highlights the rationale for this approach and reveals that PBL, compared with traditional programs in medical education, yields superior or equivalent results on a variety of outcome measures. Based on this review and our own personal experiences with PBL, we have identified eight major design issues confronting those who desire to use problem-based learning in preparing educational administrators. We have also proposed a research agenda aimed at increasing the field's understanding of the effectiveness of PBL in educating school administrators.

We hope that our discussion will stimulate others to tackle the intellectual challenges inherent in moving from a traditional to a problem-based learning approach. Those who do rise to confront these challenges are likely to experience the same kind of excitement and renewed fervor for teaching that we and others have experienced.

NOTE

See E. Bridges with assistance of P. Hallinger, *Problem-Based Learning for Administrators* (Eugene, OR: ERIC Clearinghouse for Educational Management, 1992) for numerous examples of how PBL can be incorporated into a curriculum for preparing school administrators.

REFERENCES

Barrows, H. (1984). A specific problem-based, self-directed learning method designed to teach medical problem-solving skills, and enhance knowledge retention. In H. Schmidt & M. deVolder (Eds.), *Tutorials in problem-based learning* (pp. 16–32). Maastricht, The Netherlands: Van Gorcum.

Bok, D. (1989). Needed: A new way to train doctors. In H. Schmidt, M. Lepkin, M. deVries, & J. Greep (Eds.), *New directions for medical education* (pp. 17–38). New York: Springer-Verlag.

Bransford, J., Franks, J., Vye, N., & Sherwood, R. (1989). New approaches to instruction: Because wisdom can't be told. In S. Vosniadou & M. Ortony (Eds.), *Similarity and analogical reasonings* (pp. 470–497). New York: Cambridge University Press.

Bransford, J., Sherwood, R., Vye, N., & Reiser, J. (1986). Teaching thinking and problem-solving. *American Psychologist, 41*(10), 1078–1089.

Charters, W., & Jones, J. (1975). On the neglect of the independent variable in program evaluation. In J. Baldridge & T. Deal (Eds.), *Managing change in educational organizations* (pp. 341–353). Berkeley, CA: McCutchan.

Claessen, H., & Boshuizen, H. (1985). Recall of medical information by students and doctors. *Medical Education, 19,* 61–67.

Coles, C. (1985). Differences between conventional and problem-based curricula in their students' approaches to studying. *Medical Education, 19,* 308–309.

deVolder, M., & deGrave, W. (1989). Approaches to learning in a problem-based medical programme: A developmental study. *Medical Education, 23,* 262–264.

deVries, M., Schmidt, H., & deGraaff, E. (1989). Dutch comparisons: Cognitive and motivational effects of problem-based learning on medical students. In H. Schmidt, M. Lepkin, M. deVries, & J. Greep (Eds.), *New directions for medical education* (pp. 231–238). New York: Springer-Verlag.

Godden, D., & Baddeley, A. (1975). Context-dependent memory in two natural environments: On land and underwater. *British Journal of Psychology, 66,* 325–332.

Griffiths, D., Stout, R., & Forsyth, P. (1988). *Leaders for America's schools.* Berkeley, CA: McCutchan.

Imbos, T., Drukker, J., Van Mameren, H., & Verwijnen, M. (1984). The growth in knowledge of anatomy in a problem-based curriculum. In H. Schmidt & M. deVolder (Eds.), *Tutorials in problem-based learning* (pp. 106–115). Maastricht, The Netherlands: Van Gorcum.

Janis, I., & Mann, L. (1977). *Decision making.* New York: The Free Press.

Jonas, H., Etzel, S., & Barzansky, B. (1989). Undergraduate medical education. *JAMA, 262*(8), 1011–1019.

Jones, J., Bieber, L., Echt, R., Schelfley, V., & Ways, P. (1986). A problem-based curriculum: Ten years of experience. In H. Schmidt & M. deVolder (Eds.), *Tutorials in problem-based learning* (pp. 181–198). Maastricht, The Netherlands: Van Gorcum.

Kaufman, A. (1985). *Implementing problem-based medical education.* New York: Springer.

Kaufman, A., et al. (1989). The New Mexico experiment: Educational innovation and institutional change. *Academic Medicine, 64*(4), 285–294.

McGuire, C. (1980). Assessment of problem-solving skills. *Medical Teacher, 2*(3), 118–122.

McGuire, C. (1985). Medical problem-solving: A critique of the literature. *Journal of Medical Education, 60*(80), 587–595.

Norman, G. (1988). Problem-solving skills, solving problems and problem-based learning. *Medical Education, 22,* 279–286.

Prawat, R. (1989). Promoting access to knowledge, strategies, and disposition in students: A research synthesis. *Review of Educational Research, 59*(1), 1–41.

Schmidt, H. (1983). Problem-based learning: Rationale and description. *Medical Education, 17,* 11–16.

Schmidt, H., & deVolder, M. (1984). *Tutorials in problem-based learning.* Maastricht, The Netherlands: Van Gorcum.

Schmidt, H., Lepkin, M., deVries, M., & Greep, J. (1989). *New directions for medical education.* New York: Springer-Verlag.

Schmidt, H., Dauphinee, W., & Patel, V. (1987). Comparing the effects of problem-based and conventional curricula in an international sample. *Journal of Medical Education, 62,* 305–315.

Slavin, R. (1989). Cooperative learning and student achievement. In R. Slavin (Ed.), *School and classroom organization* (pp. 129–156). Englewood Cliffs, NJ: Prentice-Hall.

Walton, H., & Matthews, M. (1989). Essentials of problem-based learning. *Medical Education, 23,* 542–558.

Conclusion:
The Expertise of Educational Leaders

Kenneth Leithwood, Philip Hallinger, and Joseph Murphy

Our incentive for organizing a conference on cognitive approaches to educational leadership and administration, and for preparing this book as an outgrowth of that conference, can be described simply. Cognitive approaches seem to hold promise as a response to charges of irrelevance and moribundity aimed at the field of leadership and administration, charges of which most in the field are uncomfortably aware. However, few people in the field are actively using cognitive approaches in either their research or their teaching. Many are only vaguely aware of this work and have not had an opportunity to seriously consider its potential contributions.

Chapters in this text illustrate both the promise of cognitive approaches and the limited uses that have been made of them to date in better understanding leadership and in preparing leaders. If the promise is to be realized, there is much work to be done.

Our intent in this chapter is to further that work in two ways. First we summarize the answers to four key questions about expertise in a way we hope will be accessible to those not already steeped in the cognitive sciences. The first two questions: *What is a problem?* and *What is the meaning of expertise?* are critical to a grasp of cognitive approaches and warrant more explicit attention than they were given by our authors. Our answers to the remaining questions—*How do cognitive approaches explain problem-solving?* and *How does problem-solving expertise develop?*—mostly reflect more detailed treatments in other chapters of the text but occasionally go beyond those treatments. The second way we attempt to further the work on cognitive approaches is to briefly set out an agenda for further research.

WHAT IS A PROBLEM?

Cognitive approaches conceptualize educational leaders as problem-finders and problem-solvers with varying levels of expertise. The starting point for clarifying cognitive approaches, then, is with the idea of a problem itself. Standard information-processing frameworks for viewing problems include a current state, a goal state, and operators or solution paths for transforming the current state into the goal state (Baird, 1983; Frederiksen, 1984). These are the components of Newell and Simon's (1972) "problem space." Typically, a problem is said to exist whenever there is a gap between where the solver is (current state) and where she or he wants to be (goal state) and the means for closing the gap is ambiguous (e.g., Gagné, 1985; Hayes, 1981).

This definition of a problem, however, does not accommodate, very well, several critical distinctions in the literature. One distinction is between routine and ill-structured problems. When a leader encounters a situation or a challenge (e.g., setting school goals) that is highly familiar because of past experiences, the response is usually rapid and largely "mindless" or automatic. In such cases the current state, the goal state, and the operators are all known. Other leaders faced with the same challenge, but without the familiarity resulting from past experience, may lack clarity about one, two, or all three elements in the problem space.

It seems confusing to claim that setting school goals is a problem in the second case but not in the first, simply because of variation in leaders' relevant knowledge. And so the distinction between routine and ill-structured problems has arisen, spawning considerable research about differences in processes used to solve each type. In fact, the distinction between experts and nonexperts in knowledge-rich domains (e.g., chemistry) is largely the distinction between those who have acquired sufficient knowledge to respond successfully to challenges considered part of the domain and those lacking such knowledge. For purposes of clarity, it seems useful to define a problem in terms of its objective elements, without reference to the amount of knowledge possessed by the solver regarding those elements. Problems, then, are synonymous with tasks—something to be done, such as setting school goals. Future research aimed at better understanding the task structure of school leadership may prove as useful as have been, for example, Doyle's (1983) efforts to understand the task structure of classrooms.

WHAT IS THE MEANING OF EXPERTISE IN PROBLEM-SOLVING?

Most cognitive science treatments of "expertise" leave the meaning of the concept largely implicit; they jump immediately to such matters as processes associated with expertise, how such processes are developed, and what accounts for them. For example, in a chapter entitled "Expertise in Problem Solving," Chi, Glaser, and Rees (1982) suggest only that "expertise is, by definition, the possession of a large body of knowledge and procedural skill" (p. 8). Posner's (1988) chapter, entitled "What It Is to Be an Expert," dispenses with the concept in an introductory paragraph by referring to exceptional or gifted people, "An adult or child who composes exceptional music, runs extremely fast, or receives particularly high scores on academic or achievement tests" (p. xxix). In this volume, except for Prestine, chapter authors concerned with expertise also bypass serious treatment of expertise as a concept and the consequences of holding different perspectives on the meaning of expertise.

Prestine (this volume), using Kennedy's (1987) categories, points out that there are at least four different conceptions of expertise, no single one of which appears satisfactory. Expertise has been viewed alternatively as "technical skill," "application of theory or general principles," "critical analysis," and "deliberate action." These alternatives differ in the number of components in the problem space they explicitly acknowledge (e.g., technical skills focuses explicitly on operators, giving little or no attention to how current and goal states are defined) and the amount of attention they devote to thought processes alone or both thought and action. The alternatives also vary in their ability to explain the solving of ill-structured (vs. routine) problems.

A further limitation of these alternative views of expertise, even when considered together, is that they do little to distinguish between the terms *expert* and *effective,* at least in the minds of those who are not card-carrying cognitive scientists. Is there a difference between an "effective leader" and an "expert leader"? Common sense uses of the language suggest an answer to this question based on a distinction between action or behavior and the mental processes giving rise to such action. For example, a typical dictionary definition of the term *effective* is "to bring about, accomplish . . . produce" and "producing a decided, decisive or desired outcome." A leader who is effective, in these terms, acts in such a way as to accomplish an outcome that someone values. While this is pretty much the sense in which the term is used in the literature on effective leaders and effective schools, it seems to be the meaning Posner (1988) attributes to expertise. It is also part of Kennedy's (1987) "deliberate action" view of expertise.

In contrast, typical dictionary definitions of an *expert* are more similar to the concept offered by Chi et al. (1982) quoted earlier: "one who has acquired special skill or knowledge of a particular subject." Technical skill, application of principles, and critical analysis views of expertise all conform to this definition. Thus, we might conclude that expertise refers to one's potential for effective action; indeed we will often *infer* expertise, or lack of it, by observing actions and their consequences. But this is an inference and may be in error, since circumstances will sometimes conspire to produce either undesirable or desirable ends incorrectly thought to be caused by the leaders' actions. This is the "attributional bias" associated with leaders, about which so much has been written (e.g., Yukl, 1989).

To this point, then, expertise seems best thought of as the possession of complex skills and knowledge (after Chi et al., 1982) rather than actions or behaviors associated with desirable consequences. But a further refinement appears necessary. Experts are often forgiven for not accomplishing desirable consequences; patients die, defendants end up behind bars, and student achievement scores fall rather than rise. What is unforgiveable is for the expert to engage in actions, no matter how skillfully, intended to accomplish other than generally endorsed goal states. It is also unforgiveable for the expert to demonstrate low levels of skill or knowledge with respect to current states and operators. In addition to simply possessing complex skills and knowledge, expertise includes their use in an effort to accomplish desired goals. It does not include, however, actually accomplishing the desired goals always or even most of the time.

This is a fine point, but one of some consequence. While the expertise of those in most occupations is judged by their accomplishment of desired goals, it is the person's accumulated *record* of accomplishment rather than the person's *individual* accomplishments that is of note. And across occupations, the standards for an acceptable record vary enormously: nothing less than 100 percent in the case of airline personnel (acting as a system) but as low as 20 percent in the case of some baseball batters. The central determinant of these standards appears to be how much control the person has over the outcome, not the consequences of failure to reach the outcome. So baseball batters, teachers, and many types of medical practitioners are judged by relatively low standards of goal accomplishment because pitchers, families, and God are considered to be worthy challengers to their control.

Based on this discussion, then, expertise is defined as (1) the possession of complex knowledge and skill; (2) its reliable application in actions intended to accomplish generally endorsed goal states; and (3) a record of goal accomplishment, as a consequence of those actions, that meets standards appropriate to the occupation or field of practice, as judged by "clients" and other experts in the field. Leaders are *effective* when they accomplish a desired goal state. So experts will sometimes be effective—but not always. And nonexperts will sometimes be effective—but not as often as experts, over the long run.

HOW DO COGNITIVE APPROACHES EXPLAIN THE PROBLEM-SOLVING PROCESS?

Cognitive accounts of problem-solving are embedded in a broader theory of how the mind works. This theory consists of hypothetical structures and relationships explaining why people attend to some aspects of the information available to them in their environments; how their knowledge is stored, retrieved, and further developed; and how it is used (see, for example, Gagné, 1985; Newell, Rosenblum, & Laird, 1990; Rumelhart, 1990). According to this perspective, there are two general categories of processes involved in problem-solving: understanding and solving (Hayes, 1981; VanLehn, 1989; Voss & Post, 1988).

Processes for understanding, an important focus of chapters by Kerchner, Bolman and Deal, Kelsey, and Glidewell (all this volume), serve the purpose of generating a leader's internal representation of the problem—what she or he believes the problem to be. Solving processes aim to reduce the gap between current and desired states—how the leader will transform the current state into the more desirable goal state. Understanding and solving often interact during the course of problem-solving as feedback from initial steps taken toward a solution builds a richer understanding of the problem. Both sets of processes require searching the contents of memory for existing knowledge helpful in either understanding or solving the problem.

Leaders are bombarded with much more information from their environments than they can possibly think about. Furthermore, because this information frequently presents itself as an untidy "mess," rather than a clearly labeled set of possibilities, there may be a host of potential problem formulations. Cognitive approaches, in sum, explain processes primarily involved in understanding problems as follows:

- Understanding involves giving meaning to a situation (or "mess") and evaluating that situation in light of one's expectations or aspirations by comparing it to relevant schemata stored in long-term memory (see Kelsey, Chapter 13; Simon, in press).
- Retrieving stored knowledge to help in understanding is aided by the use of categories. By categorizing the mess, as an instance of a mess with which one has had previous experience, one's search for problem-relevant knowledge is assisted (see Chi, Feltovich, & Glaser, 1981; Kelsey, Chapter 13; and a series of studies by Cowan—1986, 1988, 1990, 1991).
- The search for useful knowledge becomes more precise as one decomposes the problem and sets more precise, manageable goals to be met in solving it. In particular such goals make ill-structured problems more routine by reducing the complexity of comparing goal states with current states as one works toward reducing the gap between these states (see Greeno, 1986; Hayes, 1980; Newell, 1975).

Cognitive approaches explain processes designed primarily for solving problems in these terms:

- Once goals are set for problem-solving, much of problem-solving involves recognizing and dealing with constraints. These may be obstacles (e.g., absence of something needed to continue), errors (e.g., an action that had an unintended effect), or distractions (e.g., another problem requiring attention) (see Reitman, 1965; Shank & Abelson, 1977; Voss & Post, 1988).

- Constraints are dealt with through a series of overt or covert actions or operations. Such operations are guided by procedural schemata located in long-term memory.
- Schemata guiding operations may be well-rehearsed "scripts," in the case of routine problems. In the case of ill-structured problems schemata may be "plans"—novel procedures pieced together from many scripts (see Shank & Abelson, 1977; VanLehn, 1989).
- Even less knowledge-dependent schemata guiding operations are general "heuristics" normally thought to provide weak guidance in solving many types of problems (see Hayes, 1981; Rubinstein, 1985).

Some cognitive processes help equally with understanding and solving problems. Both values and mood appear to serve these functions. Values, in sum:

- Shape one's view of the current and desired goal state and figure prominently in the selection of operators to reduce the perceived gap (see Leithwood & Steinbach, 1992; Raun & Leithwood, Chapter 4).
- Function implicitly in one's problem-solving because they (1) act as "perceptual screens" in the choice of what to think about and (2) are usually embedded tacitly in knowledge structures primarily considered to be about other matters (see Wagner, Chapter 6). When such structures are used as guides to action, the values being expressed may not be evident to the problem-solver (see Hambrick & Brandon, 1988).
- Also may function explicitly in one's problem-solving to the extent that one has developed a value system as an independent knowledge structure; the direct effect of such values on problem-solving is called "behavioral channeling" (see Hambrick & Brandon, 1988).

Intense moods are thought to reduce the flexibility one is able to exercise in both understanding and solving problems (Showers & Cantor, 1985). Such moods restrict one's ability to imagine alternative problem interpretations and solutions.

HOW DOES PROBLEM-SOLVING EXPERTISE DEVELOP?

Seven chapters in this book devote substantial attention to the development of problem-solving expertise. Most address questions concerned with formal instruction. The purpose of Yekovich's chapter (Chapter 9), however, is to

explain those changes in cognitive processes that account for increased expertise, a purpose also addressed directly by Prestine (Chapter 11). Because such
an understanding clarifies the fundamental goals for instruction in problem-
solving expertise, we address this issue first.

Using Anderson's ACT° (adaptive control of thought) theory, Yekovich describes three stages in the development of cognitive skill—the declarative, the
associative, and the autonomous stages. However, these stages serve to simplify
understanding of what is essentially a continuous process of growth: They are
benchmarks in that process. Progression from the declarative to the autonomous stage consists of:

- Acquiring additional domain-specific propositional (or declarative) and procedural knowledge
- Transforming an increasing proportion of propositional knowledge into procedural form. As this occurs, propositional knowledge ceases to be inert and
  becomes a more useful source of guidance in problem-solving
- Increasing the amount of integration and connectedness of the knowledge
  base. This results in more efficient reorganizations of knowledge including its
  being chunked together in ways that allow it to be processed more efficiently
  by working memory; this also increases one's ability to recognize patterns of
  events or cause-effect relationships—a hallmark of expertise
- Greater "conditionalizing" of one's knowledge. This means becoming clearer
  about the circumstances under which certain actions are appropriate, a transformation of more general procedural knowledge into a complex series of "if-
  then" combinations of conditions and actions sometimes referred to as
  domain-specific strategies. Such strategies are much more powerful problem-
  solving tools than are general heuristics.

What can be done in an instructional context to foster such changes in
expertise? Cognitive approaches identify four categories of instructional conditions in response to this question. The first category of conditions is concerned
with the initial development and subsequent refinement of procedural schemata to guide problem-solving. Underlying these conditions are theories about
how information is selectively encoded, integrated, and compared with existing
schemata (Sternberg & Caruso, 1985), the role of practice and feedback in
schema refinement, and the need for careful sequencing of the complexity of
instructional demands on the student (Burton, Brown, & Fischer, 1984). These
theories give rise to specific conditions to be met by an instructional experience.
It should:

- Provide models of expert problem-solving
- Provide practice opportunities across a wide variety of problem types

- Sequence increasingly complex task demands
- Provide performance feedback on individual problem-solving.

Prestine (Chapter 11), Hart (Chapter 12), and Bridges and Hallinger (Chapter 14) elaborate on and exemplify these conditions.

A second set of instructional conditions, identified by cognitive approaches, acknowledges the important role that social interaction plays in learning. The specific conditions in this category arise from theories about the social construction of knowledge (Berger & Luckmann, 1966) and Vygotsky's (1978) concept of a "zone of proximal development." These theories suggest that instructional experiences should:

- Ensure participation in sophisticated group problem-solving processes
- Encourage individual reflection on own and group problem-solving
- Provide performance feedback on contribution of individual to group problem-solving processes.

Evidence concerning the importance of learning in circumstances the same as, or approximating, those circumstances in which knowledge is to be used give rise to a set of two further conditions. Instruction should provide authentic instructional settings and problems and assist in recovering, sharing, and evaluating tacit knowledge. Labeled "situated cognition," theoretical work explaining the importance of authentic instructional settings and tasks as a means of avoiding the acquisition of "inert knowledge" can be found in Brown, Collins, and Duguid (1989) and in Bransford (Chapter 10). Wagner's work (Chapter 6) on tacit knowledge addresses the same problem.

A fifth set of conditions arises from work on the transfer of training. Perkins and Salomon (1988) outline conditions for both "low-road" and "high-road" transfer: The former is relevant to the extension of increasingly automatic responses to a similar array of routine problems; the latter is best suited to fostering highly flexible and deliberate uses of knowledge in response to ill-structured problems. To foster such transfer, instructional settings should assist individuals in decontextualizing and abstracting general features of existing problem-solving practices and provide direct instruction in effective strategies and coaching in their application.

Several chapters in this book describe ways in which leaders can be helped to develop reflective or metacognitive capacities (e.g., Hart, Chapter 12; Bolman & Deal, Chapter 2). Attention to these capacities, similar to what Arygris calls double-loop learning (Arygris, Putnam, & Smith, 1985), has been stimulated considerably by widespread attention to Schön's work (1983, 1987) on the reflective practitioner. At a minimum, to foster reflection, instructional settings should provide cues to stimulate self-questioning and provide reasons for and model metacognition.

NEXT STEPS

Many chapters in this volume comment on possible implications for conducting future research as well as guidelines for future practice. We conclude this chapter with a discussion of three themes that seem important to include in the context of such considerations.

Grounded Descriptions of Expertise

One theme is concerned with the need for a much more extensively grounded conception of the nature of expertise, particularly in educational leadership. While the Yekovich (Chapter 9), Ohde and Murphy (Chapter 5), and Wagner (Chapter 6) chapters all describe elements of expertise, none of these descriptions is based on evidence from educational leaders. The qualities described in these chapters, since they appear to generalize to many other fields, may well prove to be relevant as applied to such leaders. Nevertheless, only the chapters by the Allisons (Chapter 8) and by Leithwood and Steinbach (Chapter 7) provide original empirical data focused specifically on the nature of expertise in educational leaders. The limited amount of data in the text reflects reasonably well the dearth of evidence more generally. Beyond other studies also reported by the Allisons and their colleagues and by Leithwood and his colleagues, there is little original research about educational leaders' expertise, as we have defined it in this chapter.

There is some evidence about the problem-solving processes of school administrators with unknown levels of expertise. Bolman and Deal (Chapter 2) describe the processes of problem-framing used by principals in three different settings. Raun and Leithwood (Chapter 4) describe the nature and uses of values among CEOs. However, without more specific information about *expert* practice, one of the main claims for the benefits of cognitive approaches to educational leadership and administration will be frustrated. As Prestine notes: "Cognitive learning precepts argue for teaching the processes experts use to handle complex tasks by externalizing the cognitive and metacognitive processes usually carried out internally" (Chapter 11).

Grounded Definitions of the Knowledge Domain

A second theme in need of much more attention concerns definition of the knowledge domain relevant for educational leaders. Such definition requires a

fresh look at the world of educational leaders in order to discover what knowledge is actually useful to them in expertly solving the problems they face. As Bransford argues in Chapter 10, variations in expertise can be explained, in significant measure, by the possession of quite specific problem-related knowledge. Defining the problem-relevant knowledge required by educational leaders would involve (1) identifying the stream of problems or challenges with which they are faced over the course of a large cycle of their work; (2) searching for ways of classifying these streams of problems so as to reflect the underlying procedural and propositional knowledge required to solve them expertly; (3) enquiring about the nature of the knowledge used by experts in solving each of these categories of problems; and (4) reconstructing at least parts of the curriculum for the preparation of educational leaders in order to provide such knowledge. This is work, begun by Silver (1987) before her untimely death, that needs to be revitalized. Much of the knowledge provided by current curricula has marginal, instrumental value in solving the problems of educational leaders (Murphy, 1992).

Grounded Strategies for Stimulating Development Expertise

A third theme for future consideration is the forms of experience, including instruction, that best foster the development of leadership expertise. More than half the chapters in this book have explored strategies believed to be consistent with cognitive approaches to instruction. In Chapter 14, Bridges and Hallinger provided a general model for such instruction—problem-based learning. Nevertheless, evidence about the impact of the strategies encompassed by this model on the development of leadership expertise remains thin. As Bridges and Hallinger note, it is difficult to be confident about the impact of problem-based learning on medical students (the focus of the literature they reviewed) because of the minimal effort that has been devoted to the systematic study of such impact. Furthermore, problem-based learning strategies discussed in other chapters have been extrapolated from research with children in school contexts, for the most part. So taking up the issues and the agenda spelled out in the Bridges and Hallinger chapter provides a way of pushing forward with the important job of determining suitable instructional strategies to foster educational expertise in particular. We cannot simply rely on extrapolations from often weak evidence, collected outside our own field, for instructional guidelines. Such a strategy will provide limited leverage for bringing about meaningful change and lasting impact on school leaders. Studies by Kelsey (Chapter 13), Hart (Chapter 12), and Leithwood and Steinbach (1992) illustrate the type of work that needs to be expanded.

Not addressed by any of the chapters in this text, however, are stimulants to the development of expertise that lie outside formal instruction. There is a small but growing body of evidence generally concerned with the socialization of leaders and administrators in education (Hart, 1991; Leithwood, Steinbach, & Begley, 1992; Miklos, 1985). This evidence suggests that such informal experiences as on-the-job leadership opportunities, under particular circumstances, can stimulate the development of expertise; indeed, they may be more powerful stimulants than traditional forms of instruction. The implication for both research and practice from such evidence is to learn more about socialization variables and to begin to redesign the work context of administrators so as to contribute to growth in expertise; McPherson's (1988) exploration of how superintendents might delegate their work is an intriguing illustration. This is consistent with redesigning a school district in ways that foster organizational learning, as Senge (1991) has suggested.

The Challenge

This agenda for future work might be viewed as intimidating in its scope. It is clearly challenging. Yet the subtext of this agenda portrays the field of leadership study and development as open-ended, as full of new possibilities and yet-to-be-discussed insights. This is hardly the moribund picture painted by critics of the field. Cognitive approaches to educational leadership and administration can be revitalizing. We encourage more of our colleagues to join with us in carrying the agenda forward.

REFERENCES

Arygris, C., Putnam, R., & Smith, D. (1985). *Action science*. San Francisco: Jossey-Bass.

Baird, L. L. (1983). *Review of problem solving skills* (Research rep.). Princeton, NJ: Educational Testing Service.

Berger, P., & Luckmann, T. (1966). *The social construction of reality*. Garden City, NJ: Doubleday.

Brown, J. S., Collins, A., & Duguid, P. (1989). Situated cognition and the culture of learning. *Educational Researcher, 18*(1), 32–42.

Burton, R. R., Brown, J. S., & Fischer, G. (1984). Skiing as a model of instruction. In B. Rogoff & J. Lave (Eds.), *Everyday cognition: Its development in social context* (pp. 139–150). Cambridge: Harvard University Press.

Chi, M. T. H., Feltovich, P. J., & Glaser, R. (1981). Categorization and representation of physics problems by experts and novices. *Cognitive Science, 5*(2), 121–152.

Chi, M. T. H., Glaser, R., & Rees, E. (1982). Expertise in problem solving. In R. A. Sternberg (Ed.), *Advances in the psychology of human intelligence* (pp. 7–75). Hillsdale, NJ: Lawrence Erlbaum Associates.

Cowan, D. A. (1986). Developing a process model of problem recognition. *Academy of Management Review, 11*(4), 763–776.

Cowan, D. A. (1988). Executives' knowledge of organizational problem types: Applying a contingency perspective. *Journal of Management, 14*(4), 513–527.

Cowan, D. A. (1990). Developing a classification structure of organizational problems: An empirical investigation. *Academy of Management Journal, 33*(2), 366–390.

Cowan, D. A. (1991). The effect of decision-making styles and contextual experience on executives' descriptions of organizational problem formulation. *Journal of Management Studies, 28*(5), 465–483.

Doyle, W. (1983). Classroom organization and management. In M. Wittrock (Ed.), *Handbook of research on teaching* (pp. 392–431). New York: Macmillan.

Frederiksen, N. (1984). Implications of cognitive theory for instruction in problem solving. *Review of Educational Research, 54*(3), 363–407.

Gagné, E. D. (1985). *The cognitive psychology of school learning.* Boston: Little, Brown & Co.

Greeno, J. G. (1986). A study of problem solving. In R. Glaser (Ed.), *Advances in instructional psychology* (pp. 47–69). Hillsdale, NJ: Lawrence Erlbaum Associates.

Hambrick, D. C., & Brandon, G. L. (1988). Executive values. In D. C. Hambrick (Ed.), *The executive effect: Concepts and methods for studying top managers* (pp. 3–34). London: JAI Press.

Hart, A. W. (1991). Leader succession and socialization. *Educational Administration Quarterly, 61*(4), 451–474.

Hayes, J. R. (1980). Teaching problem-solving mechanisms. In D. Tuma & R. Feif (Eds.), *Problem solving and education* (pp. 141–150). New York: John Wiley & Sons.

Hayes, J. R. (1981). *The complete problem solver.* Philadelphia: The Franklin Institute Press.

Kennedy, M. (1987). Inexact sciences: Professional education and the development of expertise. *Review of Research in Education, 14,* 133–168.

Leithwood, K. A., & Steinbach, R. (1992, April). *Cognitive processes used by chief education officers to solve problems in groups.* Paper presented at the annual meeting of the American Educational Research Association, San Francisco.

Leithwood, K. A., Steinbach, R., & Begley, P. (1992). Socialization experiences: Becoming a principal in Canada. In F. Parkay & G. Hall (Eds.), *Becoming a principal* (pp. 284–307). Boston: Allyn & Bacon.

McPherson, R. B. (1988). Superintendents and the problem of delegation. *Peabody Journal of Education, 65*(4), 113–130.

Miklos, E. (1985). Administrator selection, career patterns, succession and socialization. In N. J. Boyan (Ed.), *Handbook of research in educational administration* (pp. 53–76). New York: Longman.

Murphy, J. (1992). *The landscape of leadership preparation: Reframing the education of school administrators.* Newbury Park, CA: Corwin Press.

Newell, A. (1975). Discussion of papers by Robert M. Gagné and John R. Hayes. In B. Kleinmuntz (Ed.), *Problem solving: Research, method and theory* (pp. 171–182). Huntington, NY: Robert E. Kreiger.

Newell, A., Rosenblum, P., & Laird, J. (1990). Symbolic architectures for cognition. In M. Posner (Ed.), *Foundations of cognitive science* (2nd ed.) (pp. 93–132). Cambridge: The MIT Press.

Newell, A., & Simon, H. (1972). *Human problem solving*. Englewood Cliffs, NJ: Prentice-Hall.

Perkins, D. N., & Salomon, G. (1988). Teaching for transfer. *Educational Leadership, 46*(1), 22–32.

Posner, M. I. (1988). What is it to be an expert? In M. Chi, R. Glaser, & M. Farr (Eds.), *The nature of expertise* (pp. xxix–xxxvi). Hillsdale, NJ: Lawrence Erlbaum Associates.

Reitman, W. (1965). *Cognition and thought*. New York: John Wiley & Sons.

Rubenstein, M. F. (1985). *Patterns of problem solving*. Englewood Cliffs, NJ: Prentice-Hall.

Rumelhart, D. E. (1990). The architecture of mind: A connectionist approach. In M. Posner (Ed.), *Foundations of cognitive science* (2nd ed.) (pp. 133–160). Cambridge: The MIT Press.

Schön, D. (1983). *The reflective practitioner*. New York: Basic Books.

Schön, D. (1987). *Educating the reflective practitioner*. San Francisco: Jossey-Bass.

Senge, P. (1991). *The fifth discipline*. New York: Doubleday.

Shank, R., & Abelson, R. (1977). *Scripts, plans, goals and understanding*. Hillsdale, NJ: Lawrence Erlbaum Associates.

Showers, C., & Cantor, N. (1985). Social cognition: A look at motivated strategies. *Annual Review of Psychology, 36*, 275–305.

Silver, P. (1987). The center for advancing principalship excellence (APEX): An approach to professionalizing educational administration. In J. Murphy & P. Hallinger (Eds.), *Approaches to administrative training in education*. Albany: SUNY Press.

Simon, H. A. (in press). Decision making: Rational, nonrational and irrational. *Educational Administration Quarterly, 29*(3).

Sternberg, R. J., & Caruso, O. R. (1985). Practical modes of knowing. In E. Eisner (Ed.), *Learning and teaching the ways of knowing* (pp. 133–158). National Society for Studies of Education Yearbook, Chicago: University of Chicago Press.

VanLehn, K. (1989). Problem solving and cognitive skill acquisition. In M. Posner (Ed.), *Foundations of cognitive science* (pp. 527–580). Cambridge: The MIT Press.

Voss, J. F., & Post, T. A. (1988). On the solving of ill-structured problems. In M. Chi, R. Glaser, & M. Farr (Eds.), *The nature of expertise* (pp. 261–286). Hillsdale, NJ: Lawrence Erlbaum Associates.

Vygotsky, L. S. (1978). *Mind in society*. Cambridge: Harvard University Press.

Yukl, G. (1989). *Leadership in organizations* (2nd ed.). Englewood Cliffs, NJ: Prentice-Hall.

Index

About the Contributors

Derek J. Allison is currently an Associate Professor in the Division of Educational Policy Studies at the University of Western Ontario in London, Ontario. His current research interests revolve around the nature of administrative work in schools and school systems with special reference to problem-solving, values, and organizational characteristics.

Patricia A. Allison has served as a Senior Research Officer on a variety of projects at the Ontario Institute for Studies in Education and the Faculty of Education at the University of Western Ontario. She is currently involved in developing and delivering training programs for principals with a number of related research projects, particularly the ongoing Western Ontario study of principal problem-solving.

Lee G. Bolman is Lecturer on Education, Director of the National Center for Educational Leadership, and Co-Director of the Harvard School Leadership Academy at the Harvard Graduate School of Education. He is a specialist in leadership and organizational behavior.

John D. Bransford is Centennial Professor of Psychology at Vanderbilt University. He is a Co-Director of the Learning Technology Center in Peabody College. His current work focuses on how instructional technologies can be used to foster the development of student thinking and problem-solving.

Edwin M. Bridges is Professor of Education and Director of the Prospective Principals Program at Stanford University. His recent research focuses on problem-based learning and its promise for administrative training.

Larry Cuban is Professor of Education in the School of Education at Stanford University. He specializes in school reform and the history of curriculum, instruction, and educational administration.

Terrence E. Deal is Professor of Educational Leadership, Peabody College of Vanderbilt University. He is also the Co-Director of the National Center for Educational Leadership. Terry is a specialist in the area of organizational culture. Recent work focuses on leadership issues in organizations.

John C. Glidewell is Emeritus Professor of Psychology at Peabody College of Vanderbilt University. He is a Diplomate, American Board of Professional Psychology.

Philip Hallinger is Associate Professor of Education in Peabody College of Vanderbilt University. He also serves as a Senior Researcher in the National Center for Educational Leadership and as Director of the Center for the Advanced Study of Educational Leadership.

Ann Weaver Hart is Associate Dean of the Graduate School of Education and Associate Professor of Educational Administration at the University of Utah. Her research focuses on the relationships among social, organizational, and personal factors in schools affecting attitudes and performance.

J. G. T. Kelsey is Associate Professor in Educational Administration at the University of British Columbia, Canada. His interest is in the processes of teaching and learning creative problem formulation.

Charles T. Kerchner is Professor of Education and Public Policy at the Claremont Graduate School. His research interests include the study of problem-solving.

Kenneth Leithwood is Professor of Educational Administration at the Ontario Institute for Studies in Education in Toronto. He serves as Director of the Centre for Leadership Development, where he has been engaged in the study of administrative problem-solving.

Joseph Murphy is Professor and Chair, the Department of Educational Leadership, Peabody College of Vanderbilt University. He is also a Senior Research Fellow with the National Center for Educational Leadership. His work focuses on the issue of school improvement.

Kathleen L. Ohde is a Research Fellow with the National Center for Educational Leadership. She is a specialist in the study of expertise.

Nona A. Prestine is Assistant Professor of Educational Administration at the University of Illinois at Urbana-Champaign. Her research interests include applications of cognitive learning theory to the redesign of administrator preparation programs and investigation of the organizational change processes involved in school restructuring and reform efforts.

Tiiu Raun is a Ph. D. student working with Dr. Kenneth Leithwood in the Department of Educational Administration, Ontario Institute for Studies in Education, Toronto.

Rosanne Steinbach is a Senior Research Officer with the Centre for Leadership Development at the Ontario Institute for Studies in Education. Her current research interests include the study of administrative expertise and how it develops.

Richard K. Wagner is a Professor of Psychology at Florida State University. His research focuses on the study of expertise.

Frank R. Yekovich is currently Professor and Chair of the Department of Education at the Catholic University of America. His research interests revolve around cognitive theories of learning and memory, and the application of those theories to school environments.